COMPENSATING YOUR EMPLOYEES FAIRLY

A GUIDE TO INTERNAL PAY EQUITY

Stephanie R. Thomas

Apress·

President and Publisher: Paul Manning
Acquisitions Editor: Robert Hutchinson
Editorial Board: Steve Anglin, Mark Beckner, Ewan Buckingham, Gary Cornell,
    Louise Corrigan, Morgan Ertel, Jonathan Gennick, Jonathan Hassell,
    Robert Hutchinson, Michelle Lowman, James Markham, Matthew Moodie,
    Jeff Olson, Jeffrey Pepper, Douglas Pundick, Ben Renow-Clarke,
    Dominic Shakeshaft, Gwenan Spearing, Matt Wade, Tom Welsh
Coordinating Editor: Rita Fernando
Copy Editor: Laura Poole
Compositor: SPi Global
Indexer: SPi Global
Cover Designer: Anna Ishchenko

Distributed to the book trade worldwide by Springer Science+Business Media New York, 233 Spring Street, 6th Floor, New York, NY 10013. Phone 1-800-SPRINGER, fax (201) 348-4505, e-mail orders-ny@springer-sbm.com, or visit www.springeronline.com. Apress Media, LLC is a California LLC and the sole member (owner) is Springer Science + Business Media Finance Inc (SSBM Finance Inc). SSBM Finance Inc is a Delaware corporation.

For information on translations, please e-mail rights@apress.com, or visit www.apress.com.

Apress and friends of ED books may be purchased in bulk for academic, corporate, or promotional use. eBook versions and licenses are also available for most titles. For more information, reference our Special Bulk Sales–eBook Licensing web page at www.apress.com/bulk-sales.

Any source code or other supplementary materials referenced by the author in this text is available to readers at www.apress.com. For detailed information about how to locate your book's source code, go to www.apress.com/source-code/.

Apress Business: The Unbiased Source of Business Information

Apress business books provide essential information and practical advice, each written for practitioners by recognized experts. Busy managers and professionals in all areas of the business world—and at all levels of technical sophistication—look to our books for the actionable ideas and tools they need to solve problems, update and enhance their professional skills, make their work lives easier, and capitalize on opportunity.

Whatever the topic on the business spectrum—entrepreneurship, finance, sales, marketing, management, regulation, information technology, among others—Apress has been praised for providing the objective information and unbiased advice you need to excel in your daily work life. Our authors have no axes to grind; they understand they have one job only—to deliver up-to-date, accurate information simply, concisely, and with deep insight that addresses the real needs of our readers.

It is increasingly hard to find information—whether in the news media, on the Internet, and now all too often in books—that is even-handed and has your best interests at heart. We therefore hope that you enjoy this book, which has been carefully crafted to meet our standards of quality and unbiased coverage.

We are always interested in your feedback or ideas for new titles. Perhaps you'd even like to write a book yourself. Whatever the case, reach out to us at editorial@apress.com and an editor will respond swiftly. Incidentally, at the back of this book, you will find a list of useful related titles. Please visit us at www.apress.com to sign up for newsletters and discounts on future purchases.

The Apress Business Team

For Marty

The higher, the fewer.

Contents

About the Author

Stephanie R. Thomas is the CEO of Thomas Econometrics Inc., a consulting service specializing in compensation gender equity, equal employment opportunity issues, and the quantitative examination of employment practices in the workplace. Her clients include Fortune 500 companies, small businesses, major law firms, and federal and state governments and agencies such as the Department of Justice and the FBI.

Formerly a New York University faculty member, Dr. Thomas speaks to legal groups, industry organizations, and the media on equal employment opportunity and affirmative action compliance issues, internal equity in compensation, and employment discrimination litigation avoidance. She is the author of *Statistical Analysis of Adverse Impact*. Her articles on compensation gender equity have been featured in many professional periodicals, including *Bloomberg Law Reports, Corporate Counselor,* and *Journal of Compensation and Benefits*. She was an expert commentator on National Public Radio discussing the gender wage gap and the Paycheck Fairness Act, and she is the host of *The Proactive Employer* radio show, the leading weekly broadcast dedicated to equal employment opportunity issues.

Dr. Thomas earned her PhD and MA in Economics from the New School for Social Research and her BA magna cum laude from Elmira College.

Acknowledgments

In many ways, this book is the culmination of 14 years of fieldwork on the topic of pay equity. During this time, I have had the opportunity to learn from colleagues, practitioners, and legal professionals too numerous for individual recognition. I have benefited greatly from our exchanges, whether friendly or adversarial, and I thank you.

I am grateful to my fellow Compensation Café contributors for continually challenging my thinking on compensation: Ann Bares, E. James (Jim) Brennan, Chuck Czismar, Derek Irvine, Margaret O'Hanlon, Laura Schroeder, Dan Walter, and Jacque Vilet.

Thank you to my editors, Robert Hutchinson and Rita Fernando, for their invaluable guidance at every turn. Your capable hands made the publishing process not only efficient but enjoyable.

I am forever grateful for the support of my family. Special thanks are due to Gabrielle, equally gifted with the red pen and words of encouragement, for her judicious use of both.

Why Equity in Compensation Matters

Do you compensate your employees fairly?

Answering that question is not as simple as you might think. There are a variety of ways it could be interpreted. The question could pertain to the policies and procedures used to make compensation decisions. It could be asking about the actual compensation outcomes. Or it could relate to how each employee feels about the compensation decision-making process, his or her actual compensation outcome, what information was communicated about the decision-making process and compensation outcome, and how that information was communicated.

One way to approach the concept of fairness is from an organizational justice perspective. Organizational justice theorists argue that fairness, at its core, has four dimensions:

1. Distributive justice.

2. Procedural justice.

3. Interactional justice.

4. Informational justice.

Distributive justice is the perceived fairness of the actual outcome. When we talk about equity and fairness of bonus payments, merit increases in base salary, or the size of promotional increases, we are talking about distributive justice. Distributive justice answers the question, "Did I receive what I should have received?" When we talk about *intentional discrimination* in pay, we are typically discussing distributive justice: whether the money was distributed among the employees equitably, given the compensation policies and practices.[1]

Procedural justice is the perceived fairness of the policies and procedures used to arrive at the actual outcomes. Procedural justice includes the criteria used to determine bonus payments, how merit increases in base salary are determined, and the guidelines governing the size of promotional increases. Procedural justice answers the question, "Was what I received determined fairly?" When we talk about *unintentional discrimination* in pay, we're typically discussing procedural justice: whether the rules we use to distribute money affect different groups of employees differently.[2]

Interactional justice is the perceived fairness of the treatment received in the application of the actual outcome. It refers to the "warm fuzzy" or "cold prickly" feeling we get based on the way the outcome is presented to us. Interactional justice answers the question, "Was I treated with politeness, dignity, and respect?"

Informational justice is the perceived fairness or adequacy of the information provided regarding the actual outcome. In the realm of compensation, this idea is frequently referred to as *transparency*. Without informational justice, there can be no overall fairness. An organization's compensation decisions could be internally equitable, based on objective and well-defined factors, and communicated with the utmost courtesy and respect. However, if the only communication is "your bonus is $X" or "your merit increase is Y%" and no supporting information is provided, the decision may be interpreted as unfair.

Even if employees disagree with the actual outcome and/or the policies and procedures used to arrive at it, they are more likely to perceive decisions as fair if they understand how those decisions were made.

---

[1] Intentional discrimination is referred to in the legal lexicon as *disparate treatment*, which is discussed in Chapter 2.
[2] Unintentional discrimination is referred to in the legal lexicon as *disparate impact*, which is discussed in Chapter 2.

Fairness is both science and art. Within the context of this book, we focus on the scientific aspects of fairness. Specifically, we address statistical testing of compensation outcomes for disparate treatment and statistical testing of compensation policies and practices for disparate impact. Broadly speaking, we focus on distributional justice and procedural justice. Issues of interactional justice and informational justice are outside of the scope of this book.

Before discussing the statistical examination of compensation for discrimination, it is important to put the issue of internal pay equity into context. This can best be accomplished by reviewing federal equal pay laws and regulations in recent history.

Federal Equal Pay Laws and Regulatory Climate of the Twentieth Century

Figure 1-1 provides an overview of the equal pay laws of the twentieth century. As can be seen, the first equal pay policy was implemented in 1918 by the War Labor Board. World War I saw the entrance of women into the manufacturing workforce to take the place of male employees serving in the military. Under an equal pay policy implemented by the War Labor Board, manufacturers were obligated to pay female employees the same wages paid to their male counterparts.[3]

---

[3] "National War Labor Board: Its Establishment and Historical Setting," in *War Labor Reports*, vol. 1, Bureau of National Affairs, 1942.

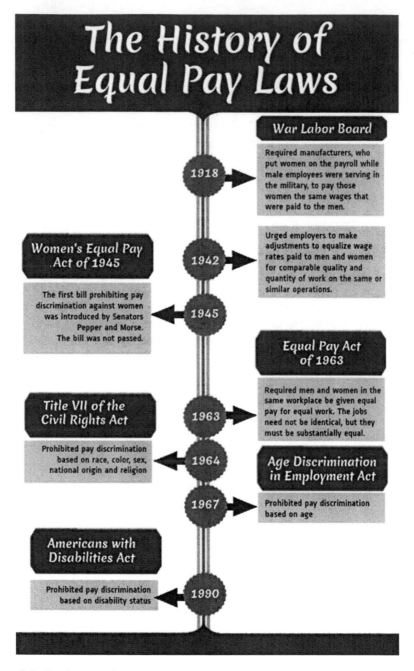

Figure 1-1. The history of U.S. equal pay laws

With the arrival of World War II in the 1940s, an even greater number of women entered the workforce. The majority of these women were hired into positions within war industries, and for many it was the first time they were employed outside of the home.

Nearly a quarter of a century after the War Labor Board enacted the first equal pay policy, it encouraged employers to make "adjustments which [would] equalize wage or salary rates paid to females with the rates paid to males for comparable quality and quantity of work on the same or similar operations."[4] Around this same time, the "Women's Equal Pay Act of 1945" was introduced to the U.S. Senate. Neither this bill nor similar bills introduced in the 1950s were passed. The 1960s ushered in major reforms to civil rights in the United States, and pay equity was part of this sea of change. The Equal Pay Act was signed into law by John F. Kennedy on June 10, 1963. Under this act, it became illegal to pay employees lower wages than their counterparts on the basis of sex:

> No employer having employees subject to any provisions of this section shall discriminate, within any establishment in which such employees are employed, between employees on the basis of sex by paying wages to employees in such establishments at a rate less than the rate at which he pays wages to employees of the opposite sex in such establishments for equal work on jobs the performance of which requires equal skill, effort, and responsibility, and which are performed under similar working conditions, except where such payment is made pursuant to (i) a seniority system, (ii) a merit system, (iii) a system which measures earnings by quantity or quality of production, or (iv) a differential based on any other factor other than sex: provided, that an employer who is paying a wage rate differential in violation of this subsection shall not, in order to comply with the provisions of this subsection, reduce the wage rate of any employee.

The following year, the Civil Rights Act of 1964 was signed into law. Title VII spoke specifically to employment practices. Under Title VII, the following are unlawful employment practices:

1. *To fail or refuse to hire or to discharge any individual, or otherwise discriminate against any individual with respect to his compensation, terms, conditions, or privileges of employment, because of such individual's race, color, religion, sex or national origin.*

2. *To limit, segregate, or classify employees or applicants for employment in any way which would deprive or tend to deprive any individual of employment opportunities or otherwise adversely affect his status as an employee, because of such individual's race, color, religion, sex, or national origin.*

---

[4]*War Labor Reports*, National War Labor Board, 1945.

With the passage of the Age Discrimination in Employment Act of 1967, age became a protected characteristic as well. The act made it unlawful for an employer:

1. *To fail or refuse to hire or to discharge any individual or otherwise discriminate against any individual with respect to his compensation, terms, conditions, or privileges of employment because of such individual's age.*

2. *To limit, segregate, or classify employees in any way which would deprive or tend to deprive any individual of employment opportunities or otherwise adversely affect his status as an employee because of such individual's age.*

3. *To reduce the wage rate of any employee in order to comply with this chapter.*

The issue of discrimination against individuals on the basis of disability status came to the forefront in the early 1970s. It wasn't until 1988, however, that the first Americans with Disabilities Act was introduced in Congress. On July 26, 1990, President George H. W. Bush signed the bill in to law. The Americans with Disabilities Act made it unlawful for an employer to discriminate on the basis of disability status. Specifically, the Americans with Disabilities Act states that no covered entity shall discriminate against a qualified individual on the basis of disability in regard to job application procedures; the hiring, advancement, or discharge of employees; employee compensation; job training; and other terms, conditions, and privileges of employment.

Equal Pay Laws and Regulations in the Twenty-first Century

Among the equal pay laws and regulations of the twenty-first century, the Lilly Ledbetter Fair Pay Act of 2009 is probably the most recognized. Other regulatory changes have been championed by the National Equal Pay Enforcement Task Force, a little-known federal body that is dramatically altering the regulatory climate with respect to equal pay and pay discrimination.

The Ledbetter Fair Pay Act

The issue of pay discrimination again rose to a position of prominence in 2007 when the U.S. Supreme Court issued its decision in *Ledbetter v. Goodyear Tire and Rubber Co.* The case began in 1998 when Lilly Ledbetter, a production supervisor at a Goodyear tire plant in Alabama, filed an equal pay claim under Title VII of the Civil Rights Act of 1964 alleging pay discrimination. After years in the lower courts, the case finally appeared before the Supreme Court.

Interestingly, the question addressed by the Supreme Court was not whether Goodyear had discriminated against Ledbetter; instead, the court addressed a technical issue in the case. Specifically, the court considered whether Ledbetter's complaint was time-barred because the discriminatory compensation decisions had been made more than 180 days prior to the filing of her charge of discrimination.

On May 29, 2007, the Supreme Court ruled by a 5–4 vote that Ledbetter's claim was in fact time-barred. Justice Samuel Alito delivered the opinion of the court:

> *Ledbetter's arguments here—that the paychecks that she received during the charging period and the 1998 raise denial each violated Title VII and triggered a new EEOC charging period—cannot be reconciled with Evans, Ricks, Lorance, and Morgan. Ledbetter, as noted, makes no claim that intentionally discriminatory conduct occurred during the charging period or that discriminatory decisions that occurred prior to that period were not communicated to her. Instead, she argues simply that Goodyear's conduct during the charging period gave present effect to discriminatory conduct outside of that period. . . . But current effects alone cannot breathe life into prior, uncharged discrimination; as we held in Evans, such effects in themselves have "no present legal consequences." 431 U.S., at 558. Ledbetter should have filed an EEOC charge within 180 days after each allegedly discriminatory pay decision was made and communicated to her. She did not do so, and the paychecks that were issued to her during the 180 days prior to the filing of her EEOC charge do not provide a basis for overcoming that prior failure.[5]*

In the dissenting opinion, Justice Ruth Bader Ginsburg stated:

> *The Court's insistence on immediate contest overlooks common characteristics of any discrimination. Pay disparities often occur, as they did in Ledbetter's case, in small increments; cause to suspect that discrimination is at work develops only over time. . . . Small initial discrepancies may not be seen as meet for a federal case, particularly when the employee, trying to succeed in a nontraditional environment, is averse to making waves.*

> *Pay disparities are thus significantly different from adverse actions "such as termination, failure to promote, . . . or refusal to hire," all involving fully communicated discrete acts, "easy to identify" as discriminatory. . . . It is only when the disparity becomes apparent and sizable, e.g., through future raises calculated as a percentage of current salaries, than an employee in Ledbetter's situation is likely to comprehend her plight and, therefore, to complain. Her initial readiness to give her employer the benefit of the doubt should not preclude her from later challenging the then current and continuing payment of a wage depressed on account of her sex.[6]*

---

[5]*Ledbetter v. Goodyear Tire & Rubber Co.* (No. 05-1074), 421 F.3d 1169.
[6]Ibid.

Ginsburg concluded the dissenting opinion with the following statement:

> *This is not the first time the Court has order a cramped interpretation of Title VII, incompatible with the statute's broad remedial purpose. . . . Once again, the ball is in Congress's court. As in 1991, the Legislature may act to correct this Court's parsimonious reading of Title VII.*[7]

Approximately two weeks after the ruling, House Majority Leader Steny Hoyer and Education and Labor Committee Chairman George Miller announced their intent to introduce legislation that would "make it clear" that discrimination occurs not only when the discriminatory decision is made but also when an individual becomes subject to that discriminatory decision, and when an individual is affected by the discriminatory decision, including each time they are issued a discriminatory paycheck.

The bill was originally defeated in 2008 and was reintroduced in January 2009. It passed in both the Senate and the House of Representatives, and was signed in to law on January 29, 2009, by President Barack Obama.

The Lilly Ledbetter Fair Pay Act amended Title VII of the Civil Rights Act of 1964 and the Age Discrimination in Employment Act of 1967, and modified the Americans with Disabilities Act of 1990 and the Rehabilitation Act of 1973. The amendments clarify that a discriminatory compensation decision or other practice that is unlawful under such acts occurs each time compensation is paid pursuant to the discriminatory compensation decision or other practice.[8]

National Equal Pay Enforcement Task Force

In his January 27, 2010, State of the Union address, President Obama stated: "We're going to crack down on violations of equal pay laws—so that women get equal pay for an equal day's work."[9] As a result of this renewed commitment to equal pay, the National Equal Pay Enforcement Task Force was created.[10] The interagency task force consists of members from four different agencies: the Department of Labor, the Office of Personnel Management, the U.S. Department of Justice, and the U.S. Equal Employment Opportunity Commission (EEOC).

---

[7]Ibid.

[8]The implications for employers of the Ledbetter Fair Pay Act of 2009 are discussed in detail in Chapter 8.

[9]Remarks by President Barack Obama, State of the Union Address, January 27, 2010.

[10]At the time of its creation, the interagency group was known as the National Equal Pay Enforcement Task Force. In 2012, however, the group referred to itself as the Equal Pay Task Force. See, for example, "Equal Pay Task Force Accomplishments," White House, April 2012, www.whitehouse.gov/sites/default/files/equal_pay_task_force.pdf.

The task force has been instrumental in changing the ways regulatory agencies such as the EEOC and the Office of Federal Contract Compliance Programs (OFCCP) initiate investigations of pay discrimination, the compensation data and information employers are required to provide to the regulatory agencies, and the analysis methods the regulatory agencies use in making a determination of whether pay discrimination occurred.

For example, at the urging of the task force, the EEOC has begun its Equal Pay Act Directed Investigation Pilot Program. Under this program, the EEOC is exercising its authority to initiate investigations of compensation discrimination at its discretion, rather than only in response to a claim of compensation discrimination.[11] The OFCCP is planning on rescinding the *Interpretive Standards for Systemic Compensation Discrimination*, which outlined the methodology the agency would use in examining contractor compensation data for pay discrimination. The *Standards* will be replaced by ad hoc analysis methods that are "consistent with broad Title VII principles."[12] In addition to complete discretion in the selection of analysis tools and methodology, OFCCP is also proposing to dramatically increase the types and amounts of contractor compensation data it collects.[13]

As a result of task force recommendations and proposed legislation, employers are facing increased scrutiny of their compensation policies and practices, while simultaneously receiving little guidance about how their practices will be examined and how to avoid potential violations of evolving regulations.

Proposed Legislation

As of this writing, there are two pieces of proposed legislation regarding pay equity under consideration. Although both bills are aimed at improving pay equity and eliminating compensation discrimination, they approach the problem differently. The Fair Pay Act of 2011 focuses on remedying occupational segregation. The hope is that with less segregation of women and racial minorities into lower-wage occupations, wage differentials by gender and race will be lessened or even eliminated.

The second piece of legislation—the Paycheck Fairness Act—is concerned with the gender pay gap. The act centers around modifying employer defenses to claims of gender discrimination in compensation and enhancing the legal remedies available to victims of pay discrimination, namely, compensatory and punitive damages.

---

[11]The pilot program is discussed in detail in Chapter 8.

[12]*Interpretive Standards for Systemic Compensation Discrimination and Voluntary Guidelines for Self-Evaluation of Compensation Practices under Executive Order 11246; Notice of Proposed Rescission,* 76 Federal Register, January 3, 2011.

[13]The rescission of the *Guidelines* and the proposed compensation data collection are discussed in detail in Chapter 8.

The Fair Pay Act of 2011

On April 12, 2011, the Fair Pay Act of 2011 was introduced into the Senate by Tom Harkin and into the House of Representatives by Eleanor Holmes Norton. The act seeks to amend the Fair Labor Standards Act of 1938 to prohibit discrimination in the payment of wages on the basis of sex, race, or national origin.

The impetus for the act is occupational segregation.[14] The bill references the existence of wage rate differentials between equivalent jobs segregated by sex, race, and national origin and proposes to remedy the situation as follows.[15]

> *(A) Except as provided in subparagraph (B), no employer having employees subject to any provisions of this section shall discriminate, within any establishment in which such employees are employed, between employees on the basis of sex, race or national origin by paying wages to employees in such establishment in a job that is dominated by employees of a particular sex, race or national origin at a rate less than the rate at which the employer pays wages to employees in such establishment in another job that is dominated by employees of the opposite sex or of a different race or national origin, respectively, for work on equivalent jobs.*

> *(B) Nothing in subparagraph (A) shall prohibit the payment of different wage rates to employees where such payment is made pursuant to (i) a seniority system, (ii) a merit system, (iii) a system that measures earnings by quantity or quality of production, or (iv) a differential based on a bona fide factor other than sex, race or national origin, such as education, training, or experience, except that this clause shall apply only if the employer demonstrates that (aa) such factor is job-related with respect to the position in question or (bb) furthers a legitimate business purpose....*

> *(C) The Equal Employment Opportunity Commission shall issue guidelines specifying criteria for determining whether a job is dominated by employees of a particular sex, race or national origin....*

> *(D) An employer who is paying a wage rate differential in violation of subparagraph (A) shall not, in order to comply with the provisions of such paragraph, reduce the wage rate of any employee.*

The act was referred to the Senate Committee on Health Education, Labor and Pensions on April 12, 2011, and was referred to the House Subcommittee on Workforce Protections on May 20, 2011.

---

[14]Occupational segregation, particularly by gender, is discussed in detail in Chapter 9.
[15]S. 788: Fair Pay Act of 2011, H.R. 1493: Fair Pay Act of 2011.

On January 29, 2013 the act was reintroduced in the Senate as the Fair Pay Act of 2013.[16] The future of the Fair Pay Act remains to be seen, and it is unclear whether any further action will be taken on it. This particular piece of proposed legislation has taken a back seat to the bill that has become the centerpiece of equal pay in recent times: the Paycheck Fairness Act.

The Paycheck Fairness Act

The Paycheck Fairness Act was first introduced into the House of Representatives by Rosa DeLauro on January 6, 2009, and into the Senate by Hillary Clinton on January 8, 2009. It was later reintroduced into the Senate by Harry Reid on September 13, 2010, and by Barbara Mikulski on April 12, 2011.

According to the text of the bill, the act seeks to amend the Fair Labor Standards Act of 1938 to provide more effective remedies to victims of discrimination in the payment of wages on the basis of sex and for other purposes.

Specifically, the act would replace the "any factor other than sex" provision of the Fair Labor Standards Act with "a bona fide factor other than sex, such as education, training or experience," and would add the following:

> *The bona fide factor defense . . . shall apply only if the employer demonstrates that such factor is (i) not based upon or derived from a sex-based differential in compensation; (ii) is job-related with respect to the position in question; and (iii) is consistent with business necessity. Such defense shall not apply where the employee demonstrates that an alternative employment practice exists that would serve the same business purpose without producing such differential and that the employer has refused to adopt such alternative practice.[17]*

The Nonretaliation Provision of the Fair Labor Standards Act would also be amended as follows:

> *(a)(3)(A) has made a charge or filed any complaint or instituted or caused to be instituted any investigation, proceeding, hearing, or action under or related to this Act, including ay investigation conducted by the employer, or has testified or is planning to testify or has assisted or participated in any manner in any such investigation, proceeding, hearing, or action, or has served or is planning to serve on an industry committee; or*

> *(a)(3)(B) has inquired about, discussed, or disclosed the wages of the employee or another employee; and*

---

[16]S. 168: Fair Pay Act of 2013
[17]S. 168: The Paycheck Fairness Act, H.R. 438: The Paycheck Fairness Act.

(a)(3)(C) Subsection (a)(3)(B) shall not apply to instances in which an employee who has access to the wage information of other employees as a part of such employee's essential job functions discloses the wages of such other employees to an individual who does not otherwise have access to such information, unless such disclosure is in response to a charge or complaint or in furtherance of an investigation, proceeding, hearing, or action under section 6(d), including an investigation conducted by the employer. Nothing in this subsection shall be construed to limit the rights of an employee provided under any other provision of law.[18]

Additionally, the Paycheck Fairness Act would modify legal remedies available to victims of discrimination (i.e., compensatory and punitive damages); provide grants for negotiation skills training for girls and women; authorize research, education, and outreach aimed at eliminating gender pay disparities; authorize the collection of pay information by the EEOC; and reinstate pay equity programs by OFCCP and pay equity data collection by the Bureau of Labor Statistics.

The Paycheck Fairness Act died in the Senate on June 5, 2012, when it failed to garner the sixty votes necessary to override a filibuster and be opened for debate on the Senate floor.

Given the priority status of gender pay equity and the Obama administration's belief that the Paycheck Fairness Act is a "commonsense" piece of legislation with the power to end the gender pay gap and gender pay discrimination, it is very likely that it will be reintroduced to Congress in the near future.

The Business Case for Internal Pay Equity

Why should businesses care about internal pay equity? The simple answer is, because regulatory agencies and your employees care about internal pay equity.

The general argument for internal pay equity is a logical one: people who have similar responsibility levels within the organization and who are performing similar work requiring similar skills and abilities should be paid similarly.

From a risk management perspective, the argument for internal pay equity centers on litigation avoidance: if employees are paid equitably, the likelihood of a pay discrimination claim being filed against the organization is reduced. This, in turn, reduces the financial exposure of the company to damages stemming from claims of pay discrimination. Additionally, if no claims of pay discrimination are filed, the company does not have to expend resources on legal services defending itself.[19]

---

[18]Ibid.

[19]Studies indicate that the average cost to a company of defending an employment practices claim in litigation is approximately $250,000. This estimate is exclusive of any damages, fines, or penalties assessed in the event the company is found liable.

There is also a socioeconomic argument to be made for internal pay equity. In her 2012 Equal Pay Day address, Secretary of Labor Hilda Solis made the following statement:

> Women now make up nearly half of the nation's workforce, and 60 percent of all women work full time. In almost two-thirds of families led by single mothers or two parents, mothers are either the primary or co-breadwinner. Pay equity is not simply a question of fairness; it is an economic imperative with serious implications not just for women, but for their families, their communities and our nation.[20]

In short, addressing the pay gap affects the earnings of women and minorities, their well-being, the well-being of their families, and the economy.

The arguments for internal pay equity from the logical, the risk management, and the socioeconomic perspectives are very straightforward. The business case for internal pay equity, however, is more complex. It involves business strategy, employee retention and engagement, productivity, and competitive advantage:

> The company that helps give women control over their own lives . . . will see more women stay. It's not a compliance issue; it's not a diversity issue, and it's not a social responsibility issue. Yes, it's the right thing to do, but it's also the strategic thing to do.[21]

Many have argued that internal pay equity provides businesses with competitive advantages in attracting and retaining top talent in tight labor markets. Improving pay practices and ensuring internal pay equity allows companies to offer their employees and potential job candidates a compensation package based on objective and measurable criteria that can be explained in clear terms. This leads to higher rates of employee retention. High rates of employee retention, in turn, lead to lower costs associated with turnover.

Additionally, internal pay equity can also lead to reductions in employee absenteeism, increases in employee performance and productivity, and improved motivation and employee engagement, as well as enhanced organizational innovation.

In fact, employers were cognizant of these benefits as early as 1951. In case studies conducted by the U.S. Department of Labor, management indicated

---

[20]Statement by Secretary of Labor Hilda L. Solis on Equal Pay Day, April 17, 2012, available at www.dol.gov/opa/media/press/opa/OPA20120751.htm.

[21]David Morgan, Westpac CEO, quoted in "Fulfilling the Promise: Closing the Pay Gap for Women and Minorities in Colorado," Colorado Pay Equity Commission, March 2008 (www.coworkforce.com/PayEquityReport.pdf).

that internal pay equity improved employee morale, such that women's attitudes toward their work improved, their efficiency increased, and turnover was decreased.[22]

Although these kinds of arguments are frequently made, there is little analytical literature discussing the costs and benefits of internal pay equity. As noted by Marie-Thérèse Chicha, the empirical evaluation of pay equity policies has not received as much attention as the empirical evaluation of diversity management policies.[23] The small amount of empirical literature that does exist is not specific enough and not deep enough to gain a clear understanding of the effectiveness—and usefulness—of pay equity policies. This literature is unsystematic and purely descriptive, offering no insight into the dynamics of pay equity policies.

This lack of empirical literature can be explained by two factors. First, to conduct a meaningful analysis, it is necessary to collect company information before and after the introduction of an internal pay equity policy and track these data over a number of years. It is difficult to obtain company-specific data, largely because companies are extremely reluctant to grant full access to their data. This reluctance is magnified where antidiscrimination policies are concerned. As noted by Chicha, "secrecy prevails and it is difficult to obtain the data required to make an assessment."[24]

Second, even with full access to company data, it is very difficult to quantitatively define the precise linkages between internal pay equity and measures such as productivity, employee performance and motivation, and employee retention. There is no direct line of sight, for example, between internal pay equity and the quality of work produced by employees. Productivity, performance, engagement, and retention are complex issues that are affected by a variety of social and psychological factors.

For example, one study found that work-role fit was the best predictor of employee engagement.[25] Other studies have found that the establishment of clear goals, presence of effective leadership, and opportunities for training and development enhance employee engagement. By their very nature, these kinds of qualitative variables are difficult to quantify and vary from person to person. Employee A may view company-sponsored attendance at an annual

---

[22]"Case Studies in Equal Pay for Women," U.S. Department of Labor, Women's Bureau, D-16, September 1951.

[23]Marie-Thérèse Chicha, "A Comparative Analysis of Promoting Pay Equity: Models and Impacts," working paper, International Labour Organization, 2006.

[24]Ibid.

[25]Sebastiaan Rothmann and Sebastiaan Rothmann Jr., "Factors Associated with Employee Engagement in South Africa," *South African Journal of Industrial Psychology* 36(2) (2010); doi: 10.4102/sajip.v36i2.925.

professional conference as a satisfactory level of training and development opportunities, whereas Employee B may think this is inadequate.

We have a qualitative understanding of the linkages between internal pay equity and performance measures like productivity, employee retention, and overall company profits. To date, these relationships have not been quantified in such a way that one can definitively say that a 1% improvement in internal pay equity leads to an X% increase in productivity, a Y% increase in employee engagement, or a Z% reduction in employee turnover.[26]

Even though empirical literature is limited, there is a wealth of qualitative literature indicating that internal pay equity does provide businesses with a competitive advantage in terms of attraction and retention of top talent, improved employee absenteeism rates, increased efficiency, employee performance, employee engagement, and enhanced organizational innovation.

Gender Equity versus Overall Equity

Most of the current public discussion of internal pay equity focuses on the gender pay gap and the frequently cited "77 cents" statistic: women earn, on average, 77 cents for every $1 earned by their male counterparts.[27] Although race is sometimes mentioned in the current discussion, gender takes priority.[28]

Gender pay equity is an important part of internal pay equity. To fully leverage the competitive advantages provided, organizations must ensure that *all* employees are paid fairly, irrespective of sex, race, ethnicity, age, or other protected characteristic.

Why Gender Equity Is the Focus

Gender pay equity has become the centerpiece of the internal pay equity discussion for a variety of reasons. First, the entrance of women into the

---

[26]This is a potential area for future research. It is likely, however, that the magnitude of these relationships will be sensitive to a variety of external factors (e.g., individual firm performance, the overall economic climate).

[27]As discussed in Chapter 9, the 77 cents statistic is a misleading comparison of average rates of pay by gender, because it does not consider differences by gender in factors such as occupation, industry, hours worked, compensation expectations and willingness to negotiate, and the role of personal choices.

[28]Differences in average pay rates by race are typically mentioned as a footnote to differences in average pay rates by gender (e.g., "women earn, on average, 77 cents for every dollar earned by their male counterparts, and the difference is even larger for women of color").

labor force is one of the most significant socioeconomic changes in the past century. As noted by John Podesta:

> The Center for American Progress decided to closely examine the consequences of what we thought was a major tipping point in our nation's social and economic history: the emergence of working women as primary breadwinners for millions of families at the same time that their presence on America's payrolls grew to comprise fully half the nation's workforce. . . . When we look back over the 20th century and try to understand what's happened to workers and their families and the challenges they now face, the movement of women out of the home and into paid employment stands out as a unique and powerful transformation.[29]

In light of this, it should come as no surprise that gender has emerged as the centerpiece of the internal pay equity debate.

Additionally, the internal pay equity discussion focuses on gender because it is an argument that easily gains public support. Most (if not all) Americans would say that they support equal pay for women. Although we may disagree on how to achieve this—as well as how far away we are from achieving it—the goal itself garners nearly universal support.[30] We embrace this goal because it appeals to our sense of distributional justice, and we are easily able to image how we would feel if our mother, our sister, or our daughter were paid less than her male counterpart simply because she is a woman. The argument for gender pay equity quickly resonates with our sense of fairness.

Furthermore, the vast majority of public discourse on internal pay equity has focused on gender. A substantial body of scholarly and governmental research exists regarding women's earnings, the gender pay gap, and barriers faced by women in the workplace with respect to compensation and career advancement. Education and outreach programs by federal and state governments and regulatory agencies have historically framed internal pay equity in terms of the gender pay gap, and overall internal pay equity—that is, pay equity for all employees irrespective of gender, race, or other protected characteristic—has not been discussed.

Because the public discourse has focused on gender pay equity, we have been conditioned to think of internal pay equity as a gender issue. We, as a culture,

---

[29]John D. Podesta, "Preface," in *The Shriver Report: A Woman's Nation Changes Everything— A Study by Maria Shriver and the Center for American Progress*, ed. Heather Boushey and Ann O'Leary, October 2009, pp. i–iii; available at www.americanprogress.org/issues/women/ report/2009/10/16/6789/the-shriver-report/.

[30]When discussing this point in past lectures and presentations, I have often used the following analogy: "stating that you oppose equal pay for women is like saying you hate kids with cancer—it's not a popular position to take."

automatically link internal pay equity to gender as the key characteristic and don't really think about internal pay equity in broader terms.

Why You Should Be Concerned About General Equity

Though there may be specific circumstances necessitating a review of internal pay equity with respect to women, racial minorities, and other common protected groups, as in the case of litigation and regulatory investigation, the strategic benefits and competitive advantages afforded by internal pay equity can only be realized through an examination of general pay equity. This means placing as much concern on the equity of white males as on women and racial minorities.[31]

There is no reason to expect that male employees or white employees are less sensitive to issues of distributive, procedural, interactional, or informational justice. The relationships between internal pay equity and performance, productivity, and engagement exist for male employees and white employees just as they do for female employees and nonwhite employees.

Failure to address internal pay equity issues with respect to male employees and white employees can create the same problems with respect to attracting and retaining top talent, turnover, and absenteeism.

The goal of this book is to provide readers with an understanding of how to examine internal pay equity with respect to all employees, irrespective of protected characteristics, so that the strategic and competitive advantages of compensating your employees fairly can be realized by all employers.

---

[31] It should be noted that white males are also protected by equal pay laws. The laws are written to prevent discrimination on the basis of gender or race and ethnicity and do not state that only women or racial minorities are covered under the laws. For example, if a man is paid less than a woman solely because he is a man, the employer could be found liable for gender discrimination. Similarly, if an employee is paid less because he is white, the employer could be found liable for race discrimination.

Types of Discrimination in Compensation

Under U.S. law, two main theories of discrimination are recognized by the courts. According to Ramona Paetzhold and Steven Willborn, these theories "reflect the two different conceptions of the behaviors and processes that produce discriminatory results."[1] One theory focuses on the intent of the decision maker; discrimination occurs when a decision maker acts with discriminatory intent, known as *disparate treatment*. The other theory focuses on the policies and procedures used by the decision maker; discrimination occurs when a given policy or procedure has disproportionate effects on members of different groups, called *disparate impact*.

Disparate Treatment

Disparate treatment is what we typically think of when we think about discrimination. It occurs when a decision maker intentionally treats members of one group differently than those of another group. As defined by the U.S. Supreme Court, *disparate treatment* is discrimination in which "the employer

---

[1]Ramona Paetzhold and Steven Willborn, *The Statistics of Discrimination: Using Statistical Evidence in Discrimination Cases*, 2011–2012 edition (West Publishing, 2011), 2.

simply treats some people less favorably than others because of their race, color, religion, sex or national origin."[2]

Note Disparate treatment is a question of motivation. The intent of the decision maker is the central issue. An employer will be found liable for disparate treatment if it is determined that some employees were treated less favorably because of protected characteristics.

Within the compensation context, examples of disparate treatment include setting the pay rates for women lower than those for men simply because of gender, granting larger pay increases to whites and smaller pay increases to nonwhites because of race, or paying larger discretionary bonuses to younger individuals and smaller ones to older individuals because of age.

The Theory of Disparate Treatment

The key feature of a disparate treatment claim is the existence of discriminatory intent.[3] The definition of what constitutes discriminatory intent, however, has varying interpretations. As noted by Paetzhold and Willborn:

> Although the precise content of the "intent" requirement is problematic, it is clear that a plaintiff need not prove actual, subjective animus against a protected group to present a successful disparate treatment case. Differential treatment designed to shield a protected group from harm, based on a rational assessment of true differences between groups, or caused by stereotypical or even subconscious attitudes may well lead to liability.[4]

The demonstration of discriminatory intent varies depending on the decisions being challenged, the law(s) under which the lawsuit is filed, and the facts specific to each claim.[5]

Disparate treatment claims can be broken down into two basic variants: individual claims and systemic claims. Individual disparate treatment occurs when an employer treats a person differently because of that person's race, color, religion, sex, national origin, or age. Common examples of individual claims of

---

[2]International Brotherhood of Teamsters v. US, 431 U.S., 431 324 (1977). Race, color, religion, sex, and national origin are characteristics used to define protected groups. A protected group is a group of people who qualify for special protection by a law or policy. For example, the Equal Pay Act of 1963 affords protection based on sex.

[3]As discussed later in this chapter, claims under the Equal Pay Act do not require the demonstration of discriminatory intent.

[4]Paetzhold and Willborn, *The Statistics of Discrimination*, 3.

[5]Demonstration of intent is discussed in a subsequent subsection.

disparate treatment include intentionally denying an employee over the age of forty a promotional opportunity because of his age, failing to consider a job applicant because of the candidate's religious beliefs, or terminating a person because of her race.

Individual claims of disparate treatment center on the employer's treatment of an individual employee and are the most common type of claim advanced in employment discrimination claims. Individual claims of disparate treatment may seem straightforward; however, proving such a claim can be very difficult, because the intent of the employer can easily be disguised.

Systemic claims of disparate treatment center on the employer's treatment of a group of individuals as a whole, rather than a specific individual. Common examples of systemic disparate treatment include denying promotional opportunities to all employees over the age of forty because of their age, failing to consider job applicants who hold a given religious belief, or paying women less than their male counterparts because of their gender.[6]

Stages of a Disparate Treatment Claim

Generally speaking, all claims of individual and systemic disparate treatment share three stages:[7]

1. The plaintiff has the burden for establishing a prima facie case raising an inference of discrimination;[8]

2. The burden then shifts to the defendant to articulate a legitimate and nondiscriminatory reason for its action;

3. The plaintiff must then prove that the employer's articulated legitimate and nondiscriminatory reason is a pretext for discrimination.[9]

These three phases are illustrated using the Equal Pay Act, Title VII, the Age Discrimination in Employment Act, and the Americans with Disabilities Act: the four federal laws under which pay discrimination claims can be brought.

---

[6] These claims are sometimes referred to as pattern or practice claims.

[7] This model was created by the U.S. Supreme Court and is typically referred to as the McDonnell Douglas Burden Shifting Formula named after the case in which it was first articulated: McDonnell Douglas Corp. v. Green, 411 U.S. 792 (1973).

[8] *Prima facie* is literally translated as "on its face." A plaintiff makes a prima facie case by presenting enough evidence to support a claim of discrimination unless contradictory evidence is presented.

[9] *Pretext* generally refers to a reason for an employment action that is false and offered to hide the true motives for the action.

The Prima Facie Case

The purpose of the prima facie case is to "eliminate the most obvious, lawful reasons for the defendant's action."[10] In cases of compensation discrimination, the way(s) the plaintiff makes a prima facie case differ depending on the law(s) under which the claims are brought. The elements of prima facie cases under the Equal Pay Act are substantially different from those under Title VII of the Civil Rights Act (Title VII), the Age Discrimination in Employment Act (ADEA), and the Americans with Disabilities Act (ADA).

First, under the Equal Pay Act, the plaintiff is *not* required to demonstrate discriminatory intent. The plaintiff can recover damages simply by proving that she received lower pay for substantially equal work; no demonstration of discriminatory intent is required. In contrast, the demonstration of discriminatory intent on the part of the employer is required until Title VII, the ADEA, and the ADA for recovery of damages by the plaintiff.[11]

Note The Equal Pay Act creates a type of strict liability in that no intent to discriminate needs to be shown for the plaintiff to prevail on a claim of pay discrimination.

Second, under the Equal Pay Act, the plaintiff is required to prove the requirements of "substantially equal" work and "similar working conditions." Claims of pay discrimination filed under Title VII, the ADEA, or the ADA do not require jobs to be "substantially equal."[12]

The Prima Facie Case under the Equal Pay Act

As articulated in *Corning Glass Works v. Brennan* (417 U.S., 94 S. Ct. 2223, 1974), "to state a claim for relief under the Equal Pay Act, plaintiff must establish a prima facie case of wage discrimination by showing that the employer pays different wages to employees of the opposite sex for substantially equal work."

The first step is to establish that the employer did in fact pay different wages to employees of the opposite sex. Here, *wages* include all types of compensation, including but not limited to regular and overtime pay, bonuses, expense accounts, vacation and paid leave, holiday pay, shift differentials, premium pay for weekends and/or holidays, gasoline allowances, and so on.

---

[10]Pivirotto v. Innovative Systems, Inc., 191 F.3d, 344 352 (1999).

[11]Harold Lewis Jr. and Elizabeth Norman, *Employment Discrimination Law and Practice*, 2nd ed. (Thomson West, 2001), § 7.15.

[12]Ibid.

After establishing differences in compensation by gender, it must be shown that these differences relate to "substantially equal" work. Identical work is not required under the Equal Pay Act (EPA). In determining whether work is "substantially equal" job content—not job title—is examined. Specifically, the following characteristics of the job are examined:[13]

- Skill: *measured by factors such as ability, education, training and experience required to perform the job. The issue is what skills are required for the job, not what skills individual employees have. For example, two bookkeeping jobs could be considered equal under the EPA even if one of the job holders has a master's degree in physics since that degree would not be required for the job.*

- Effort: *the amount of physical or mental exertion required to perform the job. For example, suppose that men and women work side by side on a line assembling machine parts. The person at the end of the line must also lift the assembled product as he or she completes the work and place it on a board. That job requires more effort than the other assembly line jobs if the extra effort of lifting the assembled product off the line is substantial and is a regular part of the job. As a result, it would not be a violation to pay that person more, regardless of whether the job is held by a man or a woman.*

- Responsibility: *the degree of accountability required to perform the job. For example, a salesperson who is delegated the duty of determining whether to accept customers' personal checks has more responsibility than other salespeople. On the other hand, a minor difference in responsibility, such as turning out the lights at the end of the day, would not justify a pay differential.*

- Working conditions: *the physical surroundings, such as temperatures, fumes and ventilation, and hazards.*

- Establishment: *an establishment is a distinct physical place of business, not an entire business or enterprise consisting of several places of business. In some circumstances, physically separate places of business may be treated as one establishment. For example, if a central administrative unit hires employees, sets their compensation, and assigns them to separate work locations, the separate work sites can be considered part of one establishment.*

---

[13]"Facts About Equal Pay and Compensation Discrimination," U.S. Equal Employment Opportunity Commission, www.eeoc.gov/eeoc/publications/fs-epa.cfm.

Once the plaintiff has established a prima facie case, the burden shifts to the defendant. There are a variety of "affirmative defenses" permitted under the Equal Pay Act, discussed in a subsequent section.

The Prima Facie Case under Title VII, ADEA, and ADA

Title VII, the ADEA, and the ADA all prohibit compensation discrimination on the basis of race, color, religion, sex, national origin, age, or disability. The requirements for establishing a prima facie case of compensation discrimination under these laws are less stringent than those under the Equal Pay Act. However, there is no requirement that the claimant's job must be substantially equal to that of a higher-paid person outside of the claimant's protected class. Furthermore, these laws do not require the claimant to work in the same establishment as a comparator.

Generally speaking, to establish a prima facie case under Title VII, the ADEA, or the ADA, the plaintiff must show that he or she is a member of a protected class, the job he or she occupied was similar to higher-paying jobs occupied by members of the nonprotected class, and the employer acted with discriminatory intent.[14]

There are several ways the plaintiff can demonstrate the employer acted with discriminatory intent. One way is through the introduction of direct evidence, which is evidence of discrimination that is so clear that no one would have to infer or imply any meaning. Examples of direct evidence include statements or documents from the employer that clearly demonstrate it has illegally considered protected class status in its decision making.

Direct evidence is rarely available; in most cases, plaintiffs produce circumstantial evidence, from which discrimination can be inferred indirectly. Examples of indirect evidence include patterns of conduct, derogatory or discriminatory comments, or other evidence of differential treatment based on protected class status. Frequently, statistical analysis is introduced as indirect evidence of discrimination.

Affirmative Defenses

Once the plaintiff has established a prima facie case of pay discrimination, the burden shifts to the defendant employer to articulate a legitimate and non-discriminatory reason for its action. These reasons are often referred to as

---

[14]The nonprotected class is defined based on the plaintiff's protected class. For example, if the plaintiff is alleging gender discrimination and is female, the nonprotected class is defined as males. If the plaintiff is alleging race discrimination and is African American, the nonprotected class will (in most cases) be defined as whites.

"affirmative defenses." There are a variety of affirmative defenses under the relevant laws.

The Equal Pay Act outlines four affirmative defenses available to employers:

> *No employer having employees subject to any provisions of this section shall discriminate, within any establishment in which such employees are employed, between employees on the basis of sex by paying wages to employees in such establishments at a rate less than the rate at which he pays wages to employees of the opposite sex in such establishments for equal work on jobs the performance of which requires equal skill, effort, and responsibility, and which are performed under similar working conditions,* **except where such payment is made pursuant to (i) a seniority system, (ii) a merit system, (iii) a system which measures earnings by quantity or quality of production, or (iv) a differential based on any other factor other than sex:** *provided, that an employer who is paying a wage rate differential in violation of this subsection shall not, in order to comply with the provisions of this subsection, reduce the wage rate of any employee. (emphasis added)*

The first defense argues that the difference in pay between the plaintiff and her male comparators is the result of a bona fide seniority system. To establish this, the employer must show that it uses a system that gives employees certain rights and benefits that improve or increase the longer they are employed by the employer. In general terms, bona fide seniority systems have rules that:

- define when the seniority clock begins;
- specify when and under what circumstances an employee's seniority may be halted or lost;
- define which time will count toward the accrual of seniority and which time will not;
- specify the types of employment conditions that will be governed by seniority and those that will not.

For the employer to successfully demonstrate a bona fide seniority system, it must regularly consider seniority (rather than doing so randomly or on a case-by-case basis), and the seniority system must be applied uniformly in the decision-making process.

The second affirmative defense argues that the difference in pay between the plaintiff and her male comparators is the result of a bona fide merit system. To establish that a merit system exists, the employer must show an organized and structured procedure for systematically evaluating employees according to established standards designed to determine their relative merits. The criteria on which employees are systematically evaluated must be predetermined.[15] In addition, there must be an organized means of advancement or reward for merit.[16] For the merit system to be valid, the employer must inform employees of its existence (either in writing or some other manner) and the merit system must not be based on gender.

The third affirmative defense argues that the difference in pay between the plaintiff and her male comparators is the result of a bona fide system measuring quantity or quality of production. The employer must show that such a system is in place and has been applied to compensation decisions regularly and consistently. For a system of this type of be valid, the employee's earnings must be measured by the quantity or quality of production.

The quantity test refers to equal dollar per unit compensation rates. The employer is not liable for pay discrimination if it has implemented a system in which two employees receive the same pay rate, but one receives more total compensation because he or she produces more.

The quality test refers to increased compensation for higher-quality products. The employer is not liable for pay discrimination if it regularly rewards male and female employees equally for producing higher-quality products through compensation incentives.

The fourth and final affirmative defense argues that the difference in pay between the plaintiff and her male comparators is the result of any factor other than sex. Factors other than sex can include things like education, experience, licenses and certifications, and even market forces.[17]

---

[15]Ryduchowski v. Port Authority, 203 F.3d 135, 26 142-43 2nd Cir., 2000.

[16]EEOC v. Sears, Roebuck & Co., 839 F.2d 302, 345-46 7th Cir., 1988.

[17]Some courts have held that market forces are not a "factor other than sex." For example, in Corning Glass Works v. Brennan, the employer created a night shift inspector position at a time when New York and Pennsylvania prohibited female employees from working at night. To recruit and retain male employees for this position, the employer paid male night shift inspectors more than female day shift inspectors. The employer argued that the pay differential was not based on sex but on the company's need to recruit and retain male night shift inspectors. The Supreme Court rejected this argument and found that the employer's decision to pay women less for the same work men performed exploited market forces. The Court held that market forces cannot be—in this case—a "factor other than sex," because sex is precisely the factor on which those market forces have been based. Other courts, however, have held that employers can consider market forces when determining the salaries of employees. The Seventh Circuit issued just such an opinion in Merillat v. Metal Spinners, Inc. (470 F.3d 685, 7th Cir. 2006) (although the Court did caution against employers taking advantage of market forces to justify discrimination).

The four affirmative defenses articulated in the Equal Pay Act are incorporated into Title VII through the Bennett Amendment.[18] The purposes of the amendment were to "resolve any potential conflicts between Title VII and the Equal Pay Act" and to clarify that "the standards of the Equal Pay Act would govern even those wage discrimination cases where only Title VII would otherwise apply."[19] In *County of Washington v. Gunther*, the Supreme Court interpreted the Bennett Amendment to not incorporate the Equal Pay Act's "equal work" requirement in Title VII sex-based pay claims, but to subject such claims to the four affirmative defenses of the Equal Pay Act.[20]

Generally, the four affirmative defenses of the Equal Pay Act are also incorporated into the ADEA. As noted by Mack Player:

> The ADEA has its legislative roots near those of Title VII of the Civil Rights Act of 1964. Much of the operative, substantive language of the ADEA was drawn from that previously found in Title VII. Because of this similarity the courts have indicated that as a general proposition Title VII and ADEA litigation should follow a parallel course.[21]

It should be noted that under the ADEA, differentiation on the basis of age pursuant to bona fide benefit plans such as retirement, pension, or insurance is permitted.

Pretext

Once the defendant has articulated a legitimate and nondiscriminatory reason for its action, the burden shifts to the plaintiff to prove that the employer's articulated legitimate and nondiscriminatory reason is a pretext for discrimination.

The pretext stage of employment discrimination cases is "pivotal."[22] The plaintiff's prima facie case has been established, and the defendant has offered legitimate, nondiscriminatory reasons for its actions. During the pretext stage, the plaintiff must demonstrate that the reasons offered by the defendant are a pretext, not the true reasons for the alleged discriminatory acts, and that the employer engaged in intentional discrimination. The finder of fact then makes

---

[18]The Bennett Amendment is a provision in §703(h) of Title VII that incorporates the affirmative defenses under the Equal Pay Act.

[19]County of Washington v. Gunther, 452 U.S. 161 (1981).

[20]Ibid.

[21]Mack A. Player, "Proof of Disparate Treatment Under the Age Discrimination in Employment Act: Variations on a Title VII Theme," *Georgia Law Review* 17, no. 3 (1983), 623.

[22]Paetzhold and Willborn, *The Statistics of Discrimination*, 83.

a decision as to the employer's true motive(s) for the alleged discriminatory acts.[23]

It should be noted that even if the plaintiff successfully proves that the employer's defense is pretextual, a finding of unlawful discrimination is not mandatory. In *St. Mary's Honor Center v. Hicks*, the Supreme Court held that in an employment discrimination case, the plaintiff is not automatically entitled to prevail even if he establishes a prima facie case of discrimination and demonstrates that all of the reasons advanced by the employer for the alleged discriminatory action are false. The finder of fact may still conclude that the employer's action is not discriminatory.[24]

Use of Statistics in Disparate Treatment Claims

Statistical analysis is frequently used in claims of disparate treatment because of its relevance in creating an inference of discrimination. As noted by the Ninth Circuit in *Lowe v. City of Monrovia*:

> *Statistical data is relevant because it can be used to establish a general discriminatory pattern...Such a discriminatory pattern is probative of motive and can therefore create an inference of discriminatory intent.*[25]

Statistical analysis can be used to establish the claim of a pattern or practice of discrimination or to bolster circumstantial evidence of discrimination. Courts have held that statistical evidence demonstrating a pattern can substantiate the employer's motive and can therefore create an inference of discriminatory intent.[26]

Plaintiffs routinely offer statistical analysis as indirect evidence of discrimination when making a prima facie case. As early as 1977, the Supreme Court held that gross statistical disparities can provide prima facie proof of discrimination.[27] As noted by the Supreme Court in its decision in *City of Richmond v. J.A. Croson Company*:

> *There is no doubt that where gross statistical disparities can be shown, they alone in a proper case may constitute prima facie proof of a pattern or practice of discrimination under Title VII.*[28]

---

[23]The "finder of fact" can be either the jury, in the case of a jury trial, or the judge, in the case of a bench trial.

[24]St. Mary's Honor Center v. Hicks, 509 U.S. 502, 1993.

[25]Lowe v. City of Monrovia, 775 F.2d 998, 1008, 9th Cir., 1986.

[26]See, for example, Cooper v. Southern Co., 260 F. Supp. 2d 1258 (2003).

[27]International Brotherhood of Teamsters v. United States, 431 U.S. 324, 339–340, 1977.

[28]City of Richmond v. J.A. Croson Company, 488 U.S. 469, 501, 1989.

Within the context of compensation discrimination, plaintiffs typically offer statistical analysis in the form of a multiple regression to demonstrate the employer's pattern or practice of discrimination and establish a prima facie case.

The use of statistical analysis as evidence of pretext was first recognized by the Supreme Court in 1978.[29] Lower courts have followed suit in cases of individual and systemic disparate treatment. In *Sweat v. Miller Brewing Company*, the U.S. Court of Appeals for the Eleventh Circuit held:

> *Statistical information concerning an employer's general policy and practice concerning minority employment may be relevant to a showing of pretext, even in a case alleging an individual instance of discrimination rather than a "pattern or practice" of discrimination.*[30]

Defendant employers also frequently use statistical analysis to demonstrate affirmative defenses. It is not uncommon for defendants to present their own statistical analysis, often modifying the plaintiffs' analyses to incorporate legitimate, nondiscriminatory factors that have been omitted.

Identifying and Preventing Disparate Treatment

A statistical analysis of internal pay equity is the most effective way of identifying disparate treatment in compensation. Reviewing compensation for internal equity with quantitative tools not only identifies potential problem areas but also provides the employer with an opportunity to correct them before formal charges of discrimination are filed and litigation commences. The specific form of statistical analysis chosen will depend on the type(s) of compensation under examination and the nature of the question(s) being addressed. Various types of statistical analyses, including multiple regression analysis, are discussed in detail in later chapters.

The possibility of disparate treatment in compensation cannot be completely eliminated. There are some actions that employers can take to minimize the likelihood of disparate treatment manifesting in compensation decisions.

First and foremost, it is important to have a specific set of criteria for making compensation decisions. They should be based on a set of consistent and well-articulated factors. It should be clear to anyone reviewing the policy what factors and metrics are used when making compensation decisions. If these factors and metrics cannot easily be identified, the policy itself should be revisited. Compensation decisions should be based on tangible, measurable criteria; decisions should not be arbitrary or completely discretionary.

---

[29]Furnco Construction Corporation v. Waters, 438 U.S. 567, 579–580, 1978.
[30]Sweat v. Miller Brewing Company, 708 F.2d 655, 11th Cir., 1983.

Managers and supervisors should be trained on compensation policies and how to use them in making compensation decisions. Employers should develop and implement audit procedures for ensuring that managers and supervisors comply with the policies when making pay decisions.

Specific attention should be paid to initial pay settings for newly hired employees. Those hired for positions with similar functions and responsibility levels, which require similar skills and qualifications, should be compensated similarly. Any disparities created by initial pay setting can compound over time, potentially leading to larger disparities in the future. A small differential in initial pay may seem innocuous, but it can develop into a substantial problem years down the road.

Disparate Impact

The second theory of discrimination, disparate impact, focuses on the criteria used by decision makers. Unlike disparate treatment, the intent of the decision maker is irrelevant. In some respects, disparate impact is purely a statistical question. It occurs when a facially neutral policy or practice has a disproportionate effect on members of different groups of employees. Even if the employer is not motivated by discriminatory intent, disparate impact may still occur.

▓ **Note** Disparate impact is a statistical question. The intent of the decision maker is irrelevant. Disparate impact claims boil down to a mathematical comparison of employment outcomes by protected group status. An employer can be found liable for disparate impact even if the decisions were not motivated by discriminatory intent.

Disparate impact is often used interchangeably with the term *adverse impact*. Formally, disparate impact is a legal theory of liability under Title VII. Adverse impact is one element of that theory; it measures the effect of an employment policy or practice on a class protected by Title VII.[31]

---

[31] It should be noted that disparate impact can exist in contexts other than employment decisions. For example, disparate impact may exist in lending if the criteria used in a loan-making process (e.g., mortgage) affect different groups differently. Common examples of the occurrence of disparate impact outside the employment context include jury selection, credit scores, housing, education, and political processes. The term *adverse impact* refers to disparate impact specifically within the employment context.

The Theory of Disparate Impact

The central issue in the disparate impact model is the challenged employ-ment policy or practice. In general, a policy or practice will be found to have a disparate impact if that policy or practice (1) disproportionately screens out members of a protected group from employment opportunities or benefits, and (2) does not advance the employer's legitimate business interests.

A use of a facially neutral policy or practice having a disparate impact on members of a protected group is not automatically prohibited. Title VII of the Civil Rights Act prohibits such policies and practices if they have an *unjustified* disparate impact. If an employer can demonstrate that the policy or practice is job-related and consistent with business necessity, then that policy or practice is permitted under Title VII.

For example, in *Zamlen v. City of Cleveland*, a group of women challenged a pre-employment test for firefighters as having a disparate impact by gender. According to the complaint, the test required the following:

> *While wearing a custom-tailored self-contained breathing apparatus, candidates must drag two lengths of standard 2 ½" hose 180 feet (90 feet one way, drop the coupling, run to the other end of the hose, pick up and return 90 feet, drop coupling in designated area), run 75 feet to pumper, remove a one-person ladder (approximately 35 pounds) from the side of the pumper, carry the ladder to the fire tower, place it against the back rail of the first landing and continue up the inside stairwell to the fifth floor where a monitor observes the candidate's arrival. Then candidates return to the first landing, retrieve the ladder and place it on the pumper.*[32]

None of the female candidates successfully completed this test. Despite the fact that it had a disparate impact on candidates by gender, the test was found to be lawful based on its direct relationship to firefighting.

Note Disparate impact is not always illegal. If an employment policy or practice has an adverse impact, its use is not prohibited if the employer can establish its job-relatedness and business necessity.

It should be noted that an employer can be found liable for discrimination when any part of its selection process has a disparate impact, even if the final

---

[32]Zamlen v. City of Cleveland, 906 F. 2d 209 53 Fair Empl. Prac. Cas. 70, 53 Empl. Prac. Dec. P 40, 004 (1989).

result of the process is balanced with respect to protected group status. In *Connecticut v. Teal*, the Supreme Court rejected the "bottom-line defense":

> *Despite petitioner's nondiscriminatory "bottom line," respondents' claim of disparate impact from the examination, a pass-fail barrier to employment opportunity, states a prima facie case of employment discrimination under 703(a)(2) of Title VII, which makes it an unlawful employment practice for an employer to "limit, segregate or classify his employees" in any way which would deprive "any individual of employment opportunities" because of race, color, religion, sex or national origin. To measure disparate impact only at the "bottom line" ignores the fact that Title VII guarantees these individual black respondents the opportunity to compete equally with white workers on the basis of job-related criteria. Respondents' rights under 703(a)(2) have been violated unless petitioners can demonstrate that the examination in question was not an artificial, arbitrary or unnecessary barrier but measured skills related to effective performance as a supervisor.*[33]

Because of this, it is important to examine each step of a selection process for disparate impact. Employers should not assume that a nondiscriminatory bottom line result insulates them from claims of disparate impact.

Stages of a Disparate Impact Claim

Generally speaking, there are four stages of a disparate impact claim.

1. The plaintiff must isolate and identify the particular employment policy or practice creating the alleged disparate impact.

2. The plaintiff must demonstrate that the identified employment policy or practice has a disparate impact on a protected group.

3. Assuming that the plaintiff successfully demonstrates disparate impact, the defendant bears the responsibility of demonstrating that the challenged policy or practice is job-related for the position in question and is consistent with business necessity.

4. Assuming that the defendant is able to demonstrate the job-relatedness and business necessity of the challenged employment policy or practice, the plaintiff must then show that there exists an alternative policy or practice that meets the defendant's business interests but has a lesser impact on the protected group.

---

[33]Connecticut v. Teal, 457 U.S. 440, 1982.

To illustrate these four phases, we consider the seminal disparate impact case, *Griggs v. Duke Power Company*. In *Griggs*, Duke Power required employees to have a high school diploma to be eligible for transfer to desirable departments. The plaintiffs claimed that the educational requirement had an unjustified adverse impact on African American employees. Therefore, in the first phase of the claim, the plaintiffs identified the high school diploma requirement as the challenged employment practice.

The plaintiffs presented evidence that approximately 34% of white males in the geographic area where the plant was located had high school diplomas. In contrast, approximately 12% of black males in this same area had high school diplomas. Because of this difference, the plaintiffs were able to demonstrate that the high school diploma requirement had a disparate impact on blacks.

The employer was then required to demonstrate that the diploma requirement was job-related and consistent with business necessity, but was unable to demonstrate this. The requirement of a high school diploma was adopted without a meaningful study of the relationship between the educational requirement and job duties. Additionally, there were employees without high school diplomas who were working in the desirable departments and performing successfully.

In its decision, the Supreme Court stated:

> The [Civil Rights] Act proscribes not only overt discrimination, but also practices that are fair in form, but discriminatory in operation. The touchstone is business necessity. If an employment practice which operates to exclude Negroes cannot be shown to be related to job performance, the practice is prohibited. On the record before us, neither the high school completion requirement nor the general intelligence test is shown to bear a demonstrable relationship to successful performance of the jobs for which it was used. . . .
>
> Congress directed the thrust of the Act to the consequences of employment practices, not simply the motivation. More than that, Congress has placed on the employer the burden of showing that any given requirement must have a manifest relationship to the employment in question. The facts of this case demonstrate the inadequacy of broad and general testing devices, as well as the infirmity of using diplomas or degrees as fixed measures of capability. . . .
>
> Diplomas and tests are useful servants, but Congress has mandated the common sense proposition that they are not to become the masters of reality.[34]

Had the employer been able to demonstrate the job-relatedness and business necessity of the high school diploma requirement, the case would have moved into the fourth stage. The plaintiffs would have been required to demonstrate that there was an alternate process that met the employer's requirement but with a lesser impact on the protected group. Few disparate impact cases reach the fourth and final stage.

---

[34]Griggs v. Duke Power Company, 401 U.S. 424 (1971).

Use of Statistics in Disparate Impact Claims

Statistical analysis is central to demonstrating the presence or absence of disparate impact. In its decision in *Hazelwood School District v. United States*, the Supreme Court held that a plaintiff can establish a prima facie case of class hiring discrimination by presenting statistical evidence comparing the racial composition of an employer's workforce with that of the relevant labor market.[35]

The central assumption of the statistical model of disparate impact is as follows. If the challenged employment policy or practice is neutral with respect to protected status, then the selection rates for the protected group and the nonprotected group should be equal. For example, if 20% of the nonprotected group is selected, we would expect that under a neutral selection process, 20% of the protected group would be selected as well.

Another way of expressing this is with respect to the composition of the overall study population. For example, assume that we are interested in examining a prerequisite in the employer's hiring process. Also assume that 30% of the candidates are protected and 70% of the candidates are nonprotected. If the prerequisite has no disparate impact, we would expect that 30% of the candidates satisfying the prerequisite would be protected and 70% would be nonprotected. That is, we would expect the percentage of protected candidates satisfying the prerequisite to mirror the percentage of protected candidates in the study population.

As can be seen from these two examples, the presence or absence of disparate impact is demonstrated using evidence relating to the protected group as a whole. Statistical analysis typically serves as this evidence. Statistical models and techniques for assessing the presence or absence of disparate impact are discussed in Chapter 6.

Disparate Impact in Compensation

Disparate impact is typically associated with policies and practices related to employee selection (e.g., candidate screening, hiring, promotion, termination). There are situations, however, where claims of disparate impact present themselves in the content of compensation decisions. One common presentation is in the context of a formula-based compensation system.[36]

---

[35]Hazelwood School District v. United States, 433 U.S. 299, 1977.

[36]Formula-based compensation is a system in which compensation is mathematically calculated using a predetermined formula and various inputs, such as measures of employee production.

Typically, formula-based compensation systems are protected under Section 703(h) of Title VII:

> *It shall not be an unlawful employment practice for an employer to apply different standards of compensation or different terms, conditions, or privileges of employment pursuant to a bona fide seniority or merit system, or a system which measures earnings by quantity or quality of production or to employees who work in different locations, provided that such differences are not the result of an intention to discriminate because of race, color, religion, sex, or national origin.*

Under this provision of Title VII, disparate impact alone is not enough to invalidate a bona fide merit, seniority, or production-based compensation system.[37] Unless a plaintiff can prove that the compensation system was adopted with actual discriminatory purpose, it is immunized from violation of Title VII.[38]

There have been cases, however, in which plaintiffs have argued that a bonus program or other formulaic element of compensation was not protected under Title VII. *Goodman v. Merrill Lynch & Co., Inc.* is one such case.

Goodman involved a transition "stay bonus" program that Merrill Lynch adopted in connection with a merger with the Bank of America. The program provided stay bonus payments only to Merrill Lynch's most productive financial advisors. The amounts of the bonus payments were directly tied to advisors' production.

The plaintiff made the following arguments:[39]

- Protections in Title VII for production and merit-based programs do not apply if production is infected with discrimination (e.g., client leads that generate production are given to men but not to women).

- Under the language of the statute, protections do not apply if the compensation program is adopted with "intent to discriminate" and such intent on the part of the employer can be inferred if that employer adopts a

---

[37]A bona fide compensation system has the following characteristics: (1) the system was adopted without discriminatory intent; (2) the system is an established system based on predetermined criteria for measuring seniority, merit, or productivity; (3) the system has been communicated to employees; and (4) the system has been consistently applied to all employees, irrespective of gender, race, national origin, and so on.

[38]Discriminatory purpose means more that "intent as volition or intent of awareness of consequences." To violate Title VII, the compensation system must be selected or reaffirmed "at least in part 'because of,' not merely 'in spite of,'" its adverse impact on the protected class. See Accord Day v. Patabsco & Back Rivers R.R. Co., 504 F. Supp. 1301, 1310, D. Md., 1981.

[39]Complaint and Amended Complaint, Goodman v. Merrill Lynch & Co., Inc., 716 F. Supp. 2d (2010).

> program knowing there is underlying discrimination that infects the production on which the program is based.

In its decision, a court in the Southern District of New York held that:

> *A merit, seniority, or production-based compensation system is "bona fide" if it applies equally to all employees in the same way. Even if the compensation system perpetuates the effect of other acts of discrimination that clearly violate Title VII, as long as the compensation system itself was adopted without discriminatory intent, it is immunized under Section 703(h). To the extent that other acts of discrimination in violation of Title VII affects the "inputs" into a bona fide merit, seniority, or other production-based compensation system, a plaintiff's remedy lies in challenging those other violations directly.*[40]

The court also rejected plaintiff's second argument, stating that "knowledge of past and even present discrimination alone does not make it plausible that defendants actually adopted the [stay bonus program] with discriminatory intent."[41]

Identifying and Preventing Disparate Impact

The concept of disparate impact has been around for approximately fifty years. Even though the idea is widely understood, employers are faced with hundreds of disparate impact lawsuits every year. A potential root cause of this is that employers take the wrong approach to managing the risk of disparate impact.

Employers have traditionally approached discrimination prevention with training. Recent estimates indicate that companies in the United States spend nearly $300 million annually on diversity training programs. Employees, managers, and supervisors spend countless hours in seminars and training events every year discussing conflict resolution, communication skills, and the importance of having a diverse and inclusive workplace.

The time and money spent on conventional training does not address disparate impact and is not effective at preventing this type of discrimination. Interpersonal skills and techniques addressed in conventional training are, in many respects, irrelevant to the issue of disparate impact. Disparate impact does not happen through personal interaction; it resides in the policies and practices of the organization. Nearly every decision an employer makes—in recruiting and hiring, compensation, promotion, discipline, and termination— can be affected by disparate impact.

---

[40]Opinion and Order, U.S. District Judge Shira A. Scheindlin, Goodman v. Merrill Lynch & Co., Inc.,716 F. Supp. 2d (2010).
[41]Ibid.

Disparate impact is less obvious than other forms of discrimination, and it does not manifest in the clear ways that intentional discrimination does. The only way to successfully manage the risk of disparate impact is with proactive examination of policies and practices with quantitative tools. If employers are not examining their policies and practices for disparate impact, they may be unaware that one of their policies or practices is creating disparate impact until they are faced with a lawsuit.[42]

Note Disparate impact frequently hides in the employment policies and practices of an organization. Employers may not be aware that one of their policies or practices has a disparate impact until it's too late and they are faced with litigation. The risk of disparate impact litigation can be minimized by conducting some basic statistical analyses with respect to equity.

Documentation also plays an important role in preventing and detecting disparate impact. With respect to formula-based compensation systems, documentation is critical for establishing that the system is bona fide. The criteria used in the compensation system (e.g., the basis for measuring seniority, merit, or productivity) and eligibility criteria for participation should be thoroughly documented. In addition, the business reasons for adopting the program should be clearly delineated in writing. The compensation program should be clearly and transparently communicated to employees in writing. Most important, once the formula-based system is in place, it should be applied consistently to all eligible employees without exception.

---

[42]For a discussion of how employment policies and practices can be examined for adverse impact using quantitative tools, see Stephanie Thomas, *Statistical Analysis of Adverse Impact: A Practitioner's Guide* (Authorhouse, 2011).

Multiple Regression Analysis

How do we examine compensation data for the presence or absence of discrimination?

The first thought that may come to mind is to look at average pay rates for different groups. Averages are easy to calculate and interpret, and most people have a basic intuitive understanding of what an average is and what it represents.

A comparison of simple average rates of pay, however, does not—and in fact cannot—account for legitimate, nondiscriminatory factors that employers consider when setting hourly rates of pay. Because of this, a simple comparison of average compensation, in most cases, cannot provide an appropriate assessment of the presence or absence of discrimination. To see this, consider the following example.

Assume that we are interested in examining hourly rates of pay for the presence or absence of gender discrimination among a group of employees. Further assume that an employee's hourly rate of pay at the time of hire is set to $10, irrespective of gender, and that the initial hourly rate of pay has been fixed at $10 per hour for the past five years. Employees are given a $1 per hour annual increase for every year of seniority with the company. Finally, assume that Table 3-1 represents pay, seniority, and gender data for the group of employees we are examining.

Table 3-1. Hypothetical Pay Rates, Seniority, and Gender

Employee ID	Sex	Seniority (in years)	Pay Rate ($)
100001	M	5	15
100002	M	5	15
100003	M	5	15
100004	M	4	14
100005	M	3	13
100006	F	3	13
100007	F	2	12
100008	F	1	11
100009	F	1	11
100010	F	0	10

The average hourly rate of pay for men is $14.40,[1] and the average hourly rate of pay for women is $11.40.[2] A comparison of the average hourly rates of pay for men and women reveals a $3 per hour difference.[3]

Based solely on this comparison of average pay rates by gender, one may be tempted to infer that gender discrimination exists: women are paid, on average, $3 per hour less than their male counterparts. With no further information, one may infer that the reason for this difference is discrimination.

This analysis, however, fails to consider the role of seniority in an employee's hourly rate of pay. We know that (1) an employee's hourly rate of pay at the time of hire is set to $10, (2) the initial hourly rate of pay has been fixed at $10 per hour for the past five years, and (3) employees are given a $1 per hour annual increase for every year of seniority with the company.

A simple comparison of the average hourly rates of pay for men and women does not consider how seniority influences pay. In fact, by definition, a simple comparison of average hourly rates of pay for men and women *cannot* consider any information other than hourly pay rate and gender.

When we consider information regarding how hourly rates of pay are determined, we see that the $3 per hour difference in average hourly rates of pay by gender is completely explained by differences in average seniority by gender. The average

---

[1]($15.00 + $15.00 + $15.00 + $14.00 + $13.00) / 5 = $14.40.
[2]($13.00 + $12.00 + $11.00 + $11.00 + $10.00) / 5 = $11.40.
[3]$14.40 − $11.40 = $3.00.

seniority among male employees is 4.4 years,[4] whereas the average seniority among female employees is 1.4 years.[5] A comparison of the average years of seniority for men and women reveals a three-year difference in seniority.[6]

This three-year difference in seniority by gender explains the $3 difference in hourly pay rates. Based on the information regarding how hourly rates of pay are determined, along with data on seniority and hourly pay rates for this group of employees, we would expect a $3 per hour difference in pay between men and women if there was a three-year difference in seniority between men and women.

When we account for differences in seniority by gender in our examination of average hourly pay rates by gender, we see that the difference is perfectly explained by differences in seniority. We therefore would not conclude that pay discrimination exists.[7]

In this example, one way seniority would be accounted for or incorporated into the analysis of compensation is through the use of multiple regression analysis.

Correlation and Causality

In simple terms, multiple regression analysis is a statistical tool through which the relationship between a variable of interest and other variables that provide information about the variable of interest can be explored. In terms of the example given in Table 3-1, multiple regression analysis could be used to explore the relationship between the hourly pay rate (the variable of interest) and seniority and gender (the other variables that provide information about the variable of interest).[8]

---

[4] $(5 + 5 + 5 + 4 + 3) / 5 = 4.4$ years.

[5] $(3 + 2 + 1 + 1 + 0) / 5 = 1.4$ years.

[6] $4.4 - 1.4 = 3$ years.

[7] Note that based on this analysis, there is no evidence of *pay* discrimination. The difference in average seniority by gender may be based on legitimate, nondiscriminatory factors, or it may be based on discrimination. For example, it may be the case that no qualified female applicants applied for employment with this employer until three years ago. This would be a legitimate, nondiscriminatory reason for the difference in average seniority by gender. It may also be the case that the employer refused to hire qualified female applicants before three years ago based on the gender of the applicant. This would be a discriminatory reason for differences in seniority. Although this may support a claim of hiring discrimination, this is a separate issue unrelated to the claim of compensation discrimination.

[8] For simplicity in explanation, I focus on a two-variable model. The discussion will be expanded to a multivariable model later in this chapter.

Correlation

Multiple regression analysis is based on the concept of correlation. In simplest terms, *correlation* refers to whether—and how strongly—two variables are related. For example, there is a positive correlation between education and income; people with more years of education tend to have higher income levels. As the number of years of education increases, income levels increase. A positive correlation is a relationship in which both variables move in the same direction (i.e., increases in one lead to increases in the other).

On the other hand, a negative correlation is a relationship in which the variables move in opposite directions. As one variable increases, the other decreases. An example of a negative correlation is the relationship between education and time spent in prison. As years of education increase, the number of years a person spends in jail decreases.

Examples of positive and negative correlations are shown graphically in Figures 3-1A and 3-1B.

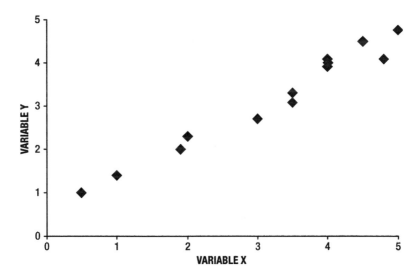

Figure 3-1A. Positive correlation

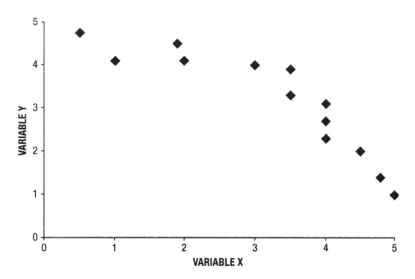

Figure 3-1B. Negative correlation

Correlation is typically measured using the Pearson's correlation coefficient:

$$\rho(X,Y) = \frac{Cov(X,Y)}{\sigma_X \sigma_Y} \qquad (3.1)$$

where

$$Cov(X,Y) = \text{covariance of } X \text{ and } Y$$

$$\sigma_X = \text{standard deviation of } X$$

$$\sigma_Y = \text{standard deviation of } Y$$

Covariance is a measure of the linear relationship between two variables. The *correlation coefficient* is a scaled version of covariance and ranges from −1.0 to +1.0. A value of +1.0 indicates that the two variables are perfectly positively linearly related. A value of −1.0 indicates that the two variables are perfectly negatively linearly related. A value of 0.0 indicates that there is no linear relationship between the variables.

Correlation has two main shortcomings. First, it is limited to examining the relationship between two variables. In most cases related to compensation discrimination, it will be important to examine the interrelationships between more than just two variables. For example, correlation could not be used to examine the interrelationships between hourly pay rates, seniority, and gender described earlier.

Second, correlation can only identify whether a linear relationship exists between two variables, and if so, how strong the relationship is. It cannot tell us, for example, how much the hourly pay rate increases as a result of a one-year increase in seniority. To examine the magnitudes of the interrelationships between multiple variables, a different technique is required.

Causality

It is important to note that although correlation implies a relationship between two variables, it does *not* imply causation. As noted by Ramona Paetzhold and Steven Willborn:

> *It would be inappropriate to interpret a large correlation between work experience and salary level as meaning that work experience leads to (i.e., causes) increased salary. Causation may work in the opposite direction, for example; large salaries may cause individuals to continue employment in the same profession or career longer, thereby producing greater work experience. Or, there may be no apparent causal relationship at all.*[9]

One popular example of inappropriately inferring causality where only a correlative relationship exists is the folk tale that babies are delivered by storks. When the number of breeding pairs of white storks is compared to the number of human births, there is a positive correlation between the two. Robert Matthews performed such an empirical study, and found a correlation of $\rho = 0.62$.[10] He calculated that if there really was no relationship between stork populations and human birthrates, the likelihood of seeing this relationship as a result of chance was 1 out of 125.[11] He notes:

> *This does not imply that the probability that mere fluke really is the correct explanation is just 1 in 125; still less does it imply a 124/125 = 99.2% probability that storks really do deliver babies.*[12]

If causality was attributed to this correlative relationship, we would infer that storks deliver babies. This would be an incorrect inference (and at odds with basic biology). In this example, the relationship between storks and babies can

---

[9]Ramona Paetzhold and Steven Willborn, *The Statistics of Discrimination: Using Statistical Evidence in Discrimination Cases* (Thompson/West, 2006), 263.

[10]Robert Matthews, "Storks Deliver Babies (p = 0.008)?," *Teaching Statistics* 22, no. 2 (Summer 2000), 36–38.

[11]One out of 125 is equivalent to a probability value of 0.008, or approximately 2.4 units of standard deviation. As discussed in a subsequent section, this result is statistically significant.

[12]Matthews, "Storks Deliver Babies," 38; emphasis in original.

be explained by the fact that the stork population and the human birthrate are both correlated with a third variable: weather patterns nine months prior to the observations.

Returning to the previous example of hourly rates of pay, seniority, and gender in Table 3-1, we can think of hourly pay rates as the human birthrate and gender as the stork population. There is a correlative relationship between gender and hourly rates of pay—women are paid, on average, $3 per hour less than their male counterparts.

In this example, inferring that being female *causes* lower hourly rates of pay (i.e., gender discrimination) is incorrect; a relationship exists between gender and hourly rates of pay because both are correlated with seniority. In this example, seniority is the determinant of hourly wage rates.

The distinction between correlation and causality is critical when interpreting the results of a multiple regression analysis and making inferences regarding the presence or absence of discrimination. I return to this point later in the chapter.

The Basics of Regression Analysis

Regression analysis is a tool for statistically describing the relationships between a variable of interest—typically referred to as the "dependent variable"—and other variables that provide information about the variable of interest, typically referred to as "independent variables" or "explanatory variables."[13] In general terms, regression analysis seeks to quantify the relationship between variations in the independent variables and variation in the dependent variable.

To demonstrate how regression analysis describes the relationships between dependent and independent variables, we return to the previous example of hourly pay rates, seniority, and gender. For ease of explanation, I initially will limit the discussion to a two-variable regression analysis, focusing only on the hourly rate of pay and seniority. The discussion will later be expanded to a three-variable analysis that examines the relationship between the hourly rate of pay, seniority, and gender.

---

[13]Paetzhold and Willborn argue that the phrase "independent variable" is misleading, because the explanatory variables are not independent of the dependent variable, and it is the relationship between the dependent and explanatory variables that is being examined (*The Statistics of Discrimination*, p. 267). However, the dependent variable/ independent variable nomenclature is commonly used in statistics and social sciences and is therefore presented herein.

Two-Variable Analysis

To statistically describe the relationship between the hourly rate of pay and seniority, we need a data set that contains a number of observations *i* for each variable. Returning to Table 3-1, we see that this data set contains hourly pay rates and seniority for ten employees (i.e., ten observations). Therefore, we can use this data set as the basis for our analysis.

We also need a hypothesis that sets forth the mathematical relationship between the hourly pay rate and seniority. We can take as our initial hypothesis the relationship between hourly rates of pay and seniority articulated by the employer in this example: an employee's hourly rate of pay at the time of hire is set to $10, irrespective of gender, and employees are given a $1 per hour annual increase for every year of seniority with the company.

We can graph the data set given in Table 3-1 using a scatter plot to visually examine the relationship between the hourly rate of pay and seniority. This scatter plot is shown in Figure 3-2.

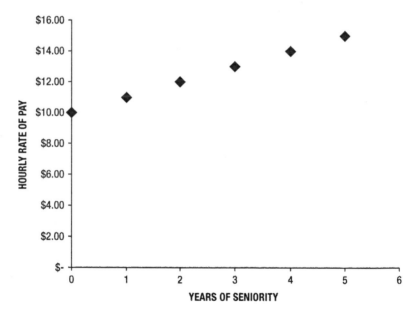

Figure 3-2. Hourly pay rate and seniority

As can be seen from Figure 3-2, there is a perfectly positively correlated linear relationship between the hourly rate of pay and seniority: as years of seniority increase, the hourly rate of pay increases. This is consistent with the relationship between hourly pay rates and seniority articulated by the employer.

Assuming a linear relationship between the hourly rate of pay and seniority, we can express this relationship mathematically as follows:[14]

$$pay = \beta_0 + (\beta_1 * seniority) \qquad (3.2)$$

where

β_0 = intercept

β_1 = change in pay as a result of a one unit change in seniority

When we fit a line to the data points shown in Figure 3-2, we see that the equation takes the following form.[15]

$$pay = \$10 + (1 * seniority) \qquad (3.3)$$

The intercept of the equation (where the regression line crosses the vertical axis) is $10. In other words, the hourly pay rate for a newly hired employee with 0 years of seniority is $10. This coincides with the company's stated starting pay rate of $10 per hour.

The slope of the line is 1: a one-unit change in years of seniority is associated with a one-unit change in pay. This also coincides with the company's stated $1 per hour annual increase for every additional year of seniority with the company. This mathematical relationship between hourly pay rates and seniority is expressed graphically as a straight line in Figure 3-3.[16]

---

[14]It is possible, and under some circumstances likely, that a nonlinear relationship exists between variables. Nonlinear relationships between variables are discussed in a subsequent section of this chapter. The estimation of nonlinear models is beyond the scope of the current discussion.

[15]Readers familiar with the mathematical formula for a straight line ($y = mX + \beta$) will recognize the similarity between this equation and the one describing the relationship between hourly rates of pay and seniority.

[16]A linear relationship between two or more variables will be expressed as a straight line. Nonlinear relationships can take various curvilinear forms and are beyond the scope of the current discussion.

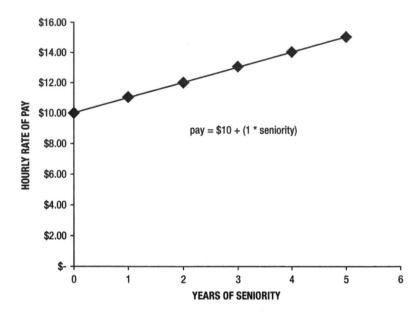

Figure 3-3. Hourly pay rate and seniority with regression line

As can be seen from Figure 3-3, the line describing the relationship between hourly rates of pay and years of seniority given in Equation 3.3 fits the data points perfectly; the line passes through the center of each data point. This is attributable to the fact that the correlation coefficient for hourly rates of pay and seniority is 1.0; there is perfect correlation.

Rarely in real life do we see such a perfect relationship between two variables. More often than not, it will not be possible to draw a straight line through a set of data points that perfectly connects all points. In these cases, the task at hand is to find a line that *best* describes the data points.

For example, assume that we are interested in exploring the relationship between the annual salary and time in job data given in Table 3-2.

Table 3-2. Hypothetical Annual Salary and Time in Job

Employee ID	Time in Job (years)	Annual Salary ($)
422	4.0	42,000
461	3.0	30,000
463	3.5	30,000
464	2.0	24,000
479	3.0	27,000
491	3.5	36,000
507	2.5	25,000
510	2.5	30,000

The data given in Table 3-2 are expressed graphically in Figure 3-4.

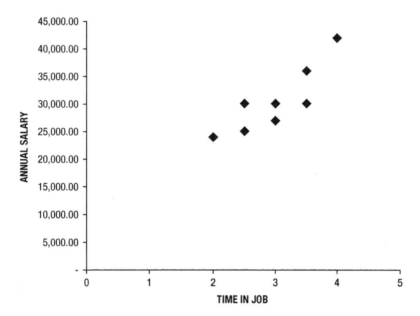

Figure 3-4. Annual salary and time in job

Based on a review of the information in Table 3-2 and Figure 3-4, we see that there is a positive, although not perfect, correlation between annual salary and time in job. Generally speaking, higher annual salaries are associated with more time in job. The calculated correlation coefficient for annual salary and time in job is **0.862.**

Unlike the previous example, where all of the observations of hourly rate of pay and seniority fell on a straight line, we cannot draw a straight line through the centers of all of the data points for annual salary and time in job because the correlation is not perfect (i.e., it is not equal to 1.0).

In cases of less than perfect correlation, the task then becomes finding a line that *best describes* the relationship between annual salary and time in job. There are hundreds of different lines that could be drawn through these data points.

As shown in Figure 3-5, one option would be to draw a line through the highest and lowest combinations of annual salary and time in job (Employees 422 and 464, respectively).

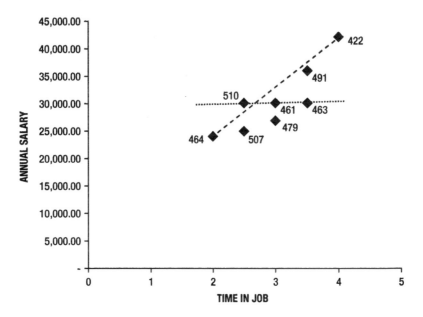

Figure 3-5. Annual salary and time in job with employee ID numbers

Alternatively, we could draw a line through those data points with an annual salary of $30,000 (Employees 510, 461, and 463), as shown in Figure 3-5.

Unfortunately, neither of these lines shown in Figure 3-5 best describe the data set. Drawing a line through the highest and lowest combinations of annual salary and time in job (Employees 422 and 464, respectively) ignores the majority of data points, which would fall below this line.

Similarly, drawing a line through those data points with an annual salary of $30,000 (Employees 510, 461, and 463) ignores the trend line of the data (a positive correlation demonstrated by the clustering of data points from lower left to upper right).

Finding the line that best describes the data can be found using a calculation known as ordinary least squares (OLS) regression analysis. OLS is a mathematical calculation that finds the "line of best fit" that "minimizes the sum of the squared deviations from the points on the graph to the points of the straight line (with distances measured vertically)."[17] This least squares criterion can be expressed mathematically as follows:

$$\text{Minimize} \sum_{i=1}^{N}(Y_i - \hat{Y}_i)^2 \tag{3.4}$$

where

Y_i = the actual value of Y for observation i

N = the number of observations

$\hat{Y}_i$ = the fitted or predicted value of Y_i

The OLS calculation finds the slope and intercept of the line that satisfies the least squares criterion using the following solutions:

$$\beta_1 = \frac{N \sum x_i Y_i - \sum x_i \sum Y_i}{N \sum x_i^2 - \left(\sum x_i\right)^2} \tag{3.5}$$

$$\beta_0 = \frac{\sum Y_i}{N} - \beta_1 \frac{\sum x_i}{N} \tag{3.6}$$

where

Y_i = the actual value of Y for observation i

X_i = the actual value of X for observation i

The line of best fit using the slope and intercept calculated from the OLS solution is shown in Figure 3-6.

---

[17]Robert Pindyck and Daniel Rubinfeld, *Econometric Models and Economic Forecasts*, 4th ed. (Irwin/McGraw-Hill, 1998), 5.

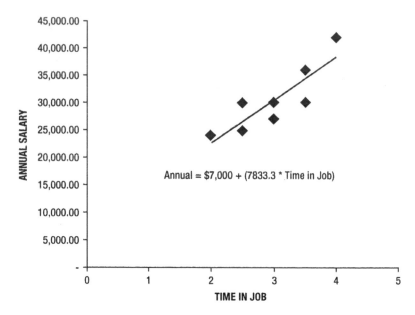

Figure 3-6. Annual salary and time in job with regression line

Mathematically, the line of best fit can be described as follows:

$$annual\ salary = \$7,000 + (7,833.30 * time\ in\ job) \tag{3.7}$$

This equation can be interpreted as follows. The intercept of the equation is $7,000, meaning that annual salary for an individual with 0 years of time in job is $7,000. The slope of the line is 7,833.30, meaning that an additional one year of time in job leads to a $7,833.30 increase in annual salary.

Three-Variable Analysis

Although the two-variable analysis is useful for illustrative purposes, it is insufficient for describing the way in which real-world compensation decisions are typically made. Rarely, if ever, is compensation determined by only one factor. In most cases, a variety of factors are considered. These factors may include measures of seniority or time in job, employee performance ratings, education, prior relevant labor market experience, and so forth.

To statistically describe the relationship between compensation and the various factors that determine it, it is necessary to construct a model that represents as closely as possible the actual decision-making process used by the employer.[18] Because multiple factors are typically considered when making compensation decisions, the two-variable analysis is insufficient; the analysis must be extended to the multivariate framework.

To see how the two-variable analysis extends to the multivariate framework, we begin with a three-variable analysis. Assume that we are interested in examining the relationship between annual salary, time in job, and gender. Further assume a data set containing this information for eight employees, as shown in Table 3-3.

Table 3-3. Hypothetical Annual Salary, Time in Job, and Gender

Employee ID	Time in Job (years)	Annual Salary ($)	Gender
422	4.0	42,000	M
491	3.5	36,000	M
461	3.0	30,000	F
463	3.5	30,000	F
510	2.5	30,000	M
479	3.0	27,000	M
507	2.5	25,000	F
464	2.0	24,000	F

Graphically, this data can be represented as a three-dimensional scatter plot, as shown in Figure 3-7: time in job is shown along the x-axis, annual salary is shown along the y-axis, and gender is shown along the z-axis.

---

[18]This point is fully discussed in Chapter 4.

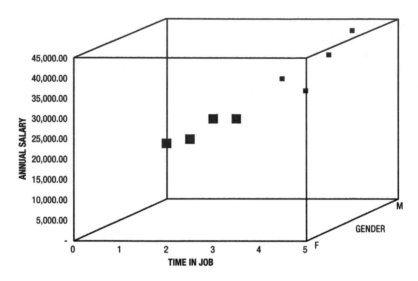

Figure 3-7. Scatter plot of annual salary, time in job, and gender

Assuming a linear relationship between annual salary, time in job, and gender, we can express this relationship mathematically as follows:[19]

$$salary = \beta_0 + (\beta_1 * time\ in\ job + \beta_2 * gender) \qquad (3.8)$$

In the three-variable analysis, the OLS calculation finds the slope and intercept of the line that satisfies the least squares criterion using the following solutions:

$$\hat{\beta}_1 = \frac{\left(\sum x_{1i}Y_i\right)\left(\sum x_{2i}^2\right) - \left(\sum x_{2i}Y_i\right)\left(\sum x_{1i}x_{2i}\right)}{\left(\sum x_{1i}^2\right)\left(\sum x_{2i}^2\right) - \left(\sum x_{1i}x_{2i}\right)^2} \qquad (3.9)$$

$$\hat{\beta}_2 = \frac{\left(\sum x_{2i}Y_i\right)\left(\sum x_{1i}^2\right) - \left(\sum x_{1i}Y_i\right)\left(\sum x_{1i}x_{2i}\right)}{\left(\sum x_{1i}^2\right)\left(\sum x_{2i}^2\right) - \left(\sum x_{1i}x_{2i}\right)^2} \qquad (3.10)$$

$$\hat{\beta}_0 = \overline{Y} - \hat{\beta}_1\overline{X}_1 - \hat{\beta}_2\overline{X}_2 \qquad (3.11)$$

---

[19]In this equation, gender would be represented by a dummy variable that would take on a value of 0 for men and a value of 1 for women. Dummy variables are discussed in detail in Chapter 4.

where

$$\bar{X}_1 = \text{average of } X_1 = \frac{\sum X_{1i}}{N}$$

$$\bar{X}_2 = \text{average of } X_2 = \frac{\sum X_{2i}}{N}$$

Y_i = the actual value of Y for observation i

X_{1i} = the actual value of X_1 for observation i

X_{2i} = the actual value of X_2 for observation i

Note that in Equations 3.9 through 3.11, the estimated slope and intercept coefficients (also known as parameters) are denoted by $\hat{\beta}_1$, $\hat{\beta}_2$, and $\hat{\beta}_0$, respectively.[20]

In Equations 3.9 and 3.10, the subscripts refer to the variable and observation number. For example, X_{1i} refers to the ith observation of X_1, where i refers to the observation number. Referring back to Table 3-3, we can relabel the data using the notation of Equations 3.9 and 3.10, as shown in Table 3-4.

Table 3-4. Hypothetical Annual Salary, Time in Job, and Gender

Employee ID	Time in Job (years)	Annual Salary ($) (X_{1i})	Gender (X_{2i})
422	4.0	42,000 (X_{11})	M (X_{21})
491	3.5	36,000 (X_{12})	M (X_{22})
461	3.0	30,000 (X_{13})	F (X_{23})
463	3.5	30,000 (X_{14})	F (X_{24})
510	2.5	30,000 (X_{15})	M (X_{25})
479	3.0	27,000 (X_{16})	M (X_{26})
507	2.5	25,000 (X_{17})	F (X_{27})
464	2.0	24,000 (X_{18})	F (X_{28})

---

[20] In statistical language, these coefficients are referred to as "beta one hat," "beta two hat," and "alpha hat." The "hat"—or accent mark over the coefficient—is used to indicate that the coefficient is estimated, and not necessarily the true parameter of the study population. The true parameters are expressed without the hat.

Applying these solutions to the data set shown in Table 3-3, the line of best fit can be described as follows:

$$Salary = \$11,650 + (6,800 * time\ in\ job) + (-3,100 * female) \qquad (3.12)$$

The interpretation of the three-variable model is similar to that of the two-variable model, with the exception of an important caveat regarding the slope coefficients. The estimated slope coefficient $\hat{\beta}_1$ expresses the change in salary as a result of a one-unit change in time in job, all other things held constant.[21] The estimated slope coefficient $\hat{\beta}_2$ expresses the change in salary as a result of being female (as opposed to being male), all other things held constant. From a gender pay equity perspective, this result would imply that among males and females with identical time in job, women earn \$3,100 less than their male counterparts.[22]

The three-variable analysis is a special form of the classical linear regression model in that it limits the analysis to only three variables: one dependent variable and two independent variables. The general form of the classical linear regression model can include four or more variables: one dependent variable and three or more independent variables.

The Classical Linear Regression Model

The general form of the classical linear regression model expresses the relationship between the dependent variable (Y) and k independent variables (X's) is as follows:

$$Y_i = \beta_0 + \beta_1 X_{1i} + \beta_2 X_{2i} + \cdots + \beta_k X_{ki} + \varepsilon_i \qquad (3.13)$$

where

k = number of independent variables

β_k = kth coefficient

X_{ki} = ith observation of the kth independent variable

ε_i = error term

---

[21]"All other things held constant" is frequently expressed in its Latin equivalent, ceteris paribus.

[22]Note that this difference refers only to the size of the estimated coefficient and does not consider whether the difference is statistically significant or "meaningful" from a statistical perspective. Interpretation of regression results are discussed in detail in a subsequent section.

Because we are dealing with four or more dimensions, it is often useful to represent the model in matrix form.[23]

$$Y = X\beta + \varepsilon \qquad (3.14)$$

where

$$
Y = \begin{bmatrix} Y_1 \\ Y_2 \\ \cdots \\ Y_N \end{bmatrix}
\quad
X = \begin{bmatrix} 1 & X_{21} & \cdots & X_{k1} \\ 1 & X_{22} & \cdots & X_{k2} \\ \cdots & \cdots & & \cdots \\ 1 & X_{2N} & \cdots & X_{kN} \end{bmatrix}
\quad
\beta = \begin{bmatrix} \beta_1 \\ \beta_2 \\ \cdots \\ \beta_N \end{bmatrix}
\quad
\varepsilon = \begin{bmatrix} \varepsilon_1 \\ \varepsilon_2 \\ \cdots \\ \varepsilon_N \end{bmatrix}
$$

This least squares criterion can be expressed in matrix form as follows:

$$\text{Minimize} \sum_{i=1}^{N} (Y - \hat{Y})^2 \qquad (3.15)$$

or alternatively:

$$\text{Minimize } \hat{\varepsilon}'\hat{\varepsilon} \qquad (3.16)$$

The OLS calculation finds the vector of parameters $\hat{\beta}$ that satisfies the least squares criterion using the following solution:

$$\hat{\beta} = (X'X)^{-1}X'Y \qquad (3.17)$$

Note that a detailed understanding of the mathematical notation and the calculations involved in multiple regression analysis is not required for nonexpert readers. A general understanding of the concept of regression analysis and a basic grasp of what the analysis is calculating is sufficient for the nontechnical audience.

Assumptions of the Classical Linear Regression Model

The classical linear regression model given by Equation 3.13 is based on a set of five assumptions regarding the dependent variable, the independent variables, and the error term of the model. These assumptions are given in Table 3-5.

---

[23]Note that matrix form is printed in bold to distinguish it from non-matrix form.

Table 3-5. Assumptions of the Classical Linear Regression Model

1.	The dependent variable can be calculated as a linear function of a specific set of independent variables and an error term, as given in Equation 3.13.
2.	The error term has zero expected value for all observations.
3.	Errors have constant variance for all observations and are not correlated.
4.	No exact linear relationship exists between two or more independent variables.
5.	The independent variables are nonstochastic (i.e., can be considered fixed in repeated sampling).

As will be discussed, violations of any of these assumptions can result in serious problems ranging from errors in estimated coefficient values and incorrect inferences regarding the relationships among variables, to simply not being able to execute the mathematical calculations required to perform the multiple regression analysis.

Violating Assumption 1: Misspecification

The first assumption of the classical linear regression model is that the dependent variable can be calculated as a linear function of the independent variables and an error term, given by Equation 3.13. This assumption can be violated in one of three ways:

1. The specified set of independent variables omits relevant variables or includes irrelevant variables.

2. The parameters associated with the independent variables do not remain constant.

3. The relationship between the dependent variable and independent variables is nonlinear.

Collectively, these three violations of assumption 1 are referred to as *misspecification*.

Omitted and/or Irrelevant Variables

In constructing a model of compensation, the goal is to build a model that approximates the actual compensation decision-making process as closely as possible. The model should include all factors considered by the decision maker when arriving at an employee's specific compensation amount.[24] Furthermore, the model should be limited to only those factors that enter into the decision-making process; it should not contain irrelevant variables.

Omitted Variables

To see how omitting variables can impact the results of the regression analysis, consider the following example. Assume that for a given group of employees, compensation is determined based on a combination of factors as shown in Table 3-6.

Table 3-6. Hypothetical Determinants of Compensation

Skill: 50%

- Education
- Degree of technical skills

Responsibility: 30%

- Scope of control

Effort: 20%

- Degree of problem solving

The relationship between compensation and education, technical skills, scope of control, and degree of problem solving can be mathematically expressed as follows:

$$Y = \beta_0 + \beta_1 X_1 + \beta_2 X_2 + \beta_3 X_3 + \beta_4 X_4 \tag{3.18}$$

where

$$X_1 = \text{educational attainment}$$

$$X_2 = \text{degree of technical skill}$$

$$X_3 = \text{scope of control}$$

$$X_4 = \text{degree of problem solving}$$

Assume, however, that educational attainment is omitted from the model and we estimate the relationship between the rest of the variables.

---

[24]It should be noted that the law does not require all relevant explanatory variables to be included in the model. Rather, as stated in *Bazemore v. Friday:* "failure to include variables will affect the analysis' probativeness, not its admissibility" (*Bazemore v. Friday*, 478 U.S. 385, 106 S. Ct. 3000, 92 L. Ed. 2d 315, 32 Ed. Law Rep. 1223, 41 Fair Empl. Prac. Cas. [BNA] 92, 40 Empl. Prac. Dec. [CCH] ¶ 36199, 4 Fed. R. Serv. 3d 1259 [1986]).

Because an important explanatory variable (educational attainment) has been omitted, the results of the estimation suffer from omitted variable bias.[25] Simply put, the model will compensate for the missing explanatory variable by under- or overestimating one of the other factors. Omitted variable bias creates bias in the estimated parameters.[26] In other words, the estimated parameter values differ from the *true* parameter values because of this bias.

For example, it could be the case that the relationship between compensation and degree of problem solving is overestimated, meaning that our estimate of β_4 is measuring not only the relationship between compensation and degree of problem solving but also the relationship between compensation and educational attainment. This distorts the picture of the true relationship between compensation and degree of problem solving and can lead to incorrect inferences about the direction, magnitude, and strength of the relationship between compensation and degree of problem solving.

There are two sources of omitted variable bias: (1) choosing the wrong model; and (2) the required variable is not measurable or is not contained in the data set. To avoid omitted variable bias stemming from choosing the wrong model, it is imperative to consider how the compensation decisions are made. As previously noted, the model should approximate the actual compensation decision-making process as closely as possible.

The model should include all factors considered by the decision maker when arriving at an employee's specific compensation amount. Furthermore, the model should be limited to only those factors that enter into the decision-making process; it should not contain irrelevant variables. Building a model that incorporates all of the factors considered in the decision-making process reduces the risk of parameter estimates being infected by omitted variable bias.

Dealing with omitted variable bias attributable to a required variable's inability to be measured or failure to be included in the data set will be discussed in detail in Chapter 4.

Inclusion of Irrelevant Variables

Because of omitted variable bias, one may be tempted to include as many variables as possible in the model.[27] However, inclusion of irrelevant variables poses its own set of problems for multiple regression analysis.

---

[25]Omitted variable bias has been described by some as "the biggest problem in econometrics." See, for example, Charlie Gibbons, Lecture on "Omitted Variable Bias," University of Berkeley, October 18, 2009.

[26]There are different kinds of bias. Omitted variable bias is just one kind.

[27]This is sometimes referred to as the "kitchen sink" approach, because everything possible—including the kitchen sink—is included in the model.

Returning to the previous example given in Table 3-6, assume that we include educational attainment, degree of technical skill, scope of control, and degree of problem solving as independent variables in our model. Further assume that we include the number of times during the year the employee wore a blue shirt to work, even though it has no relation to how compensation decisions are made. I refer to this as the "blue shirt" model.

Unlike omitted variables, the inclusion of an irrelevant variable does not cause bias in the estimated parameters. Instead, the inclusion of an irrelevant variable causes the estimated parameters to have a greater variance than they would in the "appropriate" model (i.e., the model that does not include the irrelevant variables).

This becomes particularly important when evaluating the statistical significance of the estimated parameters. In the blue shirt model, the estimates of the relationships between educational attainment, degree of technical skill, scope of control, degree of problem solving, and compensation will have greater variance. In simple terms, this greater variance causes us to be less sure—from a statistical perspective—about these relationships. This greater uncertainty may cause us to infer, based on the results of our analysis, that the relationship between educational attainment, for example, and compensation is not meaningful from a statistical perspective. Inclusion of irrelevant variables leads to greater uncertainty and less statistical power, which can lead to inferences that are at odds with the *true* relationship between the dependent and independent variables.

Structural Change

The previous discussion has focused on examples in which the effects of the independent variables on the dependent variable are the same, irrespective of the particular values of the variables. There are cases, however, where the effects of the independent variables are different for different values of the variables.

For example, assume that an employee's hourly rate of pay at the time of hire is set to $10. Further assume that employees are given a $1 per hour increase for every year of seniority with the company for the first five years, and a $2 per hour increase for every year of seniority after five years. Finally, assume that Table 3-7 represents hourly pay rate and seniority data for the group of employees we are examining.

Table 3-7. Hypothetical Pay Rates and Seniority

Employee ID	Seniority (in years)	Pay Rate ($ per hour)
116	0	10
115	1	11
114	1	11
113	2	12
112	3	13
111	3	13
110	4	14
109	5	15
108	5	15
107	5	15
106	6	17
105	7	19
104	8	21
103	9	23
102	10	25
101	12	29

In this example, the impact of seniority on an employee's hourly rate of pay depends on that person's seniority. Longer-tenured employees receive a larger hourly increase than shorter-tenured employees. The impact of seniority on hourly pay rates is not constant across all values of seniority.

This can clearly be seen in Figure 3-8; when hourly pay rates and years of seniority are plotted against one another, we can graphically see that the slope of the dotted line connecting the data points changes at five years of seniority.

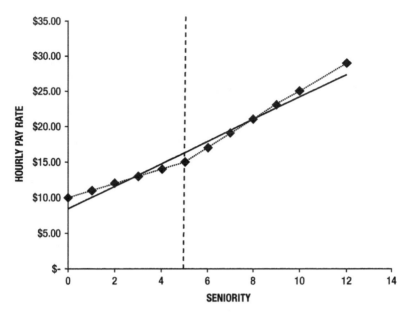

Figure 3-8. Structural change

If the model of compensation ignored the fact that the company granted $1 per hour increases for employees with five years of seniority or less and $2 per hour increases for employees with six or more years of seniority, the regression estimate would be given by the solid line in Figure 3-8. In this example, the intercept (i.e., the hourly pay rate for new hires) is underestimated, and hourly rates of pay are both under- and overestimated, depending on the number of years of seniority. This presents a significant problem when using regression analysis to examine internal pay equity.[28]

A model that incorporated information about the differentiation between "five years or less of seniority" and "six or more years of seniority" would do a better job of describing the actual compensation process. There are various ways to incorporate this information into the model; these techniques are discussed in subsequent chapters.

---

[28] This problem becomes even more pronounced when regression analysis is used to develop "predicted" pay rates and internal equity is assessed on the basis of the difference between "predicted" and actual rates of pay. This is discussed in detail in Chapter 5.

Nonlinear Models

The previous examples have all assumed that the relationship between the dependent variable and the independent variables can be expressed as a linear function (i.e., models that take the form of Equation 3.13). There are many examples, however, of nonlinear relationships between a dependent variable and independent variables. In some cases, a nonlinear relationship can be transformed into a linear relationship.[29] In other cases, it is not possible to transform the relationship from a nonlinear form into a linear form. These cases are said to be *inherently nonlinear*. Equation 3.19 is an example of an inherently nonlinear relationship between a dependent variable and k independent variables:

$$Y_i = \beta_0 + \beta_1 X_{1i}^{\alpha_1} + \beta_2 X_{2i}^{\alpha_2} + \cdots + \beta_k X_{ki}^{\alpha_k} + \varepsilon_i \tag{3.19}$$

Within the compensation realm, inherently nonlinear relationships are rare. If a nonlinear relationship exists, it is likely that it can be transformed into a linear relationship. For example, consider the nonlinear relationship between the dependent variable Y and an independent variable X shown in Figure 3-9. One can clearly see that when the two variables are plotted against each other, the data points take on the shape of a curve.

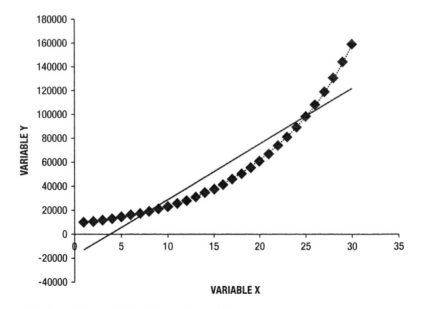

Figure 3-9. A nonlinear relationship with trend line

---

[29] A variety of transformations exist; common ones include logarithmic and power transformations.

If the relationship between X and Y was estimated using linear multiple regression analysis, we would be forcing that relationship to take the following form:

$$Y = \beta_0 + \beta_1 X \qquad (3.20)$$

The result of this estimation would be the straight line shown in Figure 3-9.

Clearly, this line does a poor job of describing the relationship between X and Y. If, however, a logarithmic transformation is applied to the independent variable Y, we can express the relationship as follows:

$$\log(Y) = \beta_0 + \beta_1 X \qquad (3.21)$$

This relationship is graphically depicted in Figure 3-10.

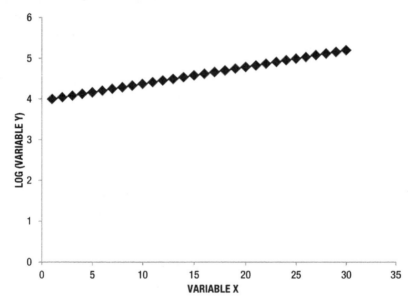

Figure 3-10. Logarithmic transformation of nonlinear relationship

The relationship between X and Y has been transformed from nonlinear to linear by taking the logarithm of Y, and can now be estimated using linear regression analysis.

As with other specification errors, using linear regression analysis to estimate a nonlinear relationship can lead to incorrect inferences regarding the relationships between the dependent variable and the independent variables.

Violating Assumption 2: Nonzero Error

The second assumption of the classical linear regression model is that the error term has zero expected value for all observations. In simple terms, this assumption means that all of the variables in the regression model have been measured accurately and without error.[30] In practice, however, measurement errors do occur. These errors can occur in either the measurement of the dependent variable or in the measurement of the independent variables.

Errors in Measurement of Dependent Variable

Within the context of compensation analysis, the dependent variable will be some measure of compensation: hourly pay rates, annual salary amounts, overtime earnings, incentive pay, etc. If the dependent variable is measured with error, it is still possible to estimate the relationships between the dependent and independent variables. The estimated parameters associated with the independent variables will be unaffected as long as the measurement error in the dependent variable is unrelated to the independent variables. In the unlikely event that the measurement error in the dependent variable is correlated with one or more of the independent variables, the estimated parameters will be affected, which could lead to incorrect inferences about the *true* relationships being investigated.

Errors in Measurement of Independent Variables

Errors in the measurement of independent variables are more common than errors in the measurement of the dependent variable and, unfortunately, are less benign.[31] If an independent variable suffers from measurement error, the estimated parameters in the model will be biased and will not reflect the *true* parameter values.

To see why this occurs, consider Equation 3.13. The classical linear regression model expresses the dependent variable as a function of a series of independent variables and an error term (denoted by ε). If one of the independent variables is measured with error, that error is "mixed" with the error term of the original model. This creates a compound error term. The problem is that this compound error term is correlated with the independent variable that

---

[30]It should be noted that measurement error differs from data error. Measurement error is systemic in that all observations of a given variable are impacted. A simple example of measurement error is weighing a group of individuals using a scale that is incorrectly calibrated. The measurement of each person's weight is impacted by the incorrect calibration of the scale. Data errors, on the other hand, are not systemic; they are random in the sense that they affect some observations but don't affect others.

[31]Potential sources of measurement error in independent variables are discussed in detail in Chapter 4.

was measured with error. Because of this correlation, the estimated parameters are biased and do not reflect the true relationships between the dependent and independent variables. This can lead to incorrect inferences about the relationships being examined.

There are some statistical techniques for dealing with measurement error in an independent variable. The most commonly used technique is instrumental variables estimation. In simple terms, this technique substitutes a different variable Z for the independent variable X that was measured with error. This different variable Z should be highly correlated with the independent variable it is replacing, should not be measured with error, and should be uncorrelated with the error term of the original model.

It should be noted that it may be difficult or perhaps impossible to find a new variable Z that satisfies the required conditions just outlined. Furthermore, even if a new variable Z is found and the instrumental variables estimation technique is used, it is possible that the estimation process will generate biased parameter estimates.

Violating Assumption 3: Nonspherical Disturbances

The third assumption of the classical linear regression model is that the errors have constant variance for all observations and are not correlated. Violation of this assumption can occur in two ways: nonconstant variance across observations (referred to as *heteroscedasticity*) and correlated errors (referred to as *serial correlation*). As with other violations of the assumptions of the general linear model, the presence of heteroscedasticity or serial correlation poses problems for estimation and the interpretation of results.

Heteroscedasticity

If a data set has unequal variance across observations, it is said to be heteroscedastic.[32] To see what is meant by unequal variance across observations, consider the following example. Imagine we are interested in examining the relationship between family income and expenditures.[33] We would expect low-income families to have steady expenditure rates. Because income is limited, these families are likely to budget their money carefully and spend the same amount each month on rent, utilities, food, entertainment, and so on. On the other hand, we would expect high-income families to have more variability in their expenditure

---

[32] A data set is said to be homoscedastic if it has constant variance across all observations.
[33] This example was studied in detail by S. Prais and H. Houthkker, *The Analysis of Family Budgets* (Cambridge: Cambridge University Press, 1955).

rates. Because these families have more discretionary income (i.e., they have more money left over after purchasing essentials like food and shelter) their total expenditures are likely to vary from month to month. Some months this discretionary income may be saved, some months a portion may be saved and a portion spent, and in other months it may be spent completely.

If we were to build a model of expenditures as a function of family income, we would see that error variances of high-income families are greater than the error variances of low-income families. Because of the greater variability in expenditures of high-income families relative to low-income families, our model would suffer from heteroscedasticity.

There are various formal statistical tests for heteroscedasticity.[34] Often differences in error variances across observations can be seen visually. Figures 3-11A and 3-11B show homoscedastic and heteroscedastic data sets, respectively. As can be seen in Figure 3-11A, if we were to draw a straight line through the data points, they would be basically clustered around that line. The differences between the straight line and the data points would generally be the same size across all observations of X.

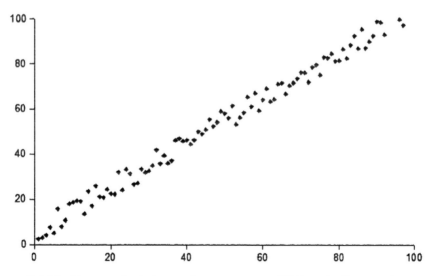

Figure 3-11A. Homoscedastic data set (image courtesy of Wikimedia Commons)

---

[34]The Goldfield-Quandt test (S. Goldfield and R. Quandt, "Some Tests for Homoscedasticity," *Journal of the American Statistical Society* 60, [1965], 539–47) and the Breusch-Pagan test (T. Breusch and A. Pagan, "A Simple Test for Heteroscedasticity and Random Coefficient Variation," *Econometrica* 47 [1979], 1287–94) are two of the commonly used tests.

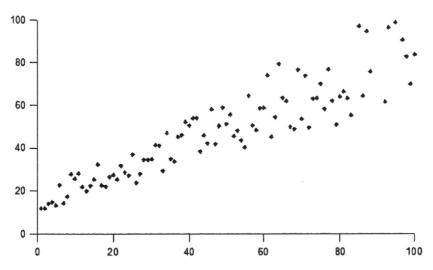

Figure 3-11B. Heteroscedastic data set (image courtesy of Wikimedia Commons)

On the other hand, Figure 3-11B illustrates a heteroscedastic data set. If we were to draw a straight line through the data points, they would be relatively close to that line for small values of X and would spread out farther away from the line for larger values of X. The data points essentially form a "cone" shape around the straight line.

Note that the data shown in Figure 3-11B make up only one example of a heteroscedastic data set. It is also possible for smaller values of X to have larger variances and larger values of X to have smaller variances. In this case, the cone shape observed in Figure 3-11B would be upside-down.

Heteroscedasticity is more common in cross-sectional data sets than in time-series data sets.[35] Within the context of reviewing compensation for internal pay equity, the presence of heteroscedasticity may present itself depending on the type of pay structure (e.g., broadband structures), the type of compensation being examined (e.g., incentive pay), and the way in which similarly situated employee groupings have been defined.[36]

---

[35]A cross-sectional data set contains observations at a given point in time across a sample of things. An example of a cross-section data set would be hourly pay rates as of December 31, 2013, for all employees in a specific job title. A time-series data set is one that contains observations across time for a given thing. An example of a time-series data set would be John Smith's annual earnings for the years 1999 to 2013.

[36]Similarly situated employee groupings are discussed in detail in Chapter 4.

If heteroscedasticity is present, the regression estimation procedure places more weight on observations with large error variances than on those with small error variances. This weighting occurs because the estimation procedure is minimizing the sum of squared errors (see Equation 3.4), and the sum of squared errors for large error variances is likely to be substantially larger than those of small error variances. Minimizing the sum of squared errors can best be accomplished by ensuring a very good fit in the large variance portion of the data.

Left uncorrected, heteroscedasticity creates greater variance in the estimated parameters. This increased variance causes greater uncertainty and less statistical power, which can lead to inferences that are at odds with the true relationship between the dependent and independent variables.

Autocorrelation

Autocorrelation[37] occurs when the error term of one observation is correlated with the error terms for other observations. To see how autocorrelation presents itself, consider the following example. Imagine that we are forecasting the growth of stock dividends over time. An overestimate of growth in one time period is likely to lead to overestimates of growth in later time periods. Similarly, an underestimate of growth in one time period is likely to lead to underestimates of growth in later time periods. This is an example of positive autocorrelation. The "direction" of the error (either over- or underestimation) carries forward into future time periods.

Although less common, negative autocorrelation can also occur. Negative autocorrelation occurs when an underestimate in one period leads to overestimates in future periods, or when an overestimate in one period leads to underestimates in future periods. The direction of the error (over- or underestimation) changes in future time periods.

Examples of positive and negative autocorrelation are given in Figures 3-12A and 3-12B.

---

[37]Autocorrelation is sometimes referred to as serial correlation.

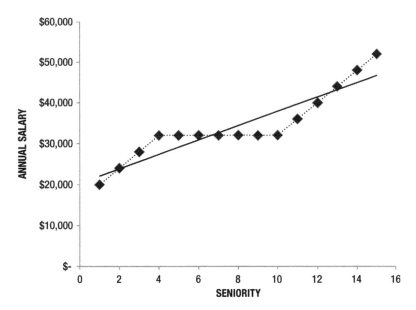

Figure 3-12A. Positive autocorrelation

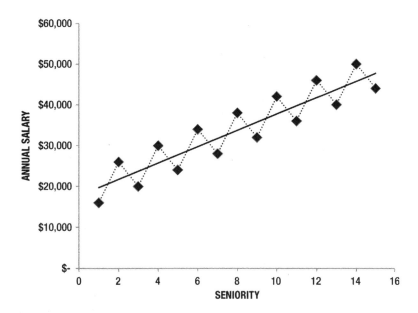

Figure 3-12B. Negative autocorrelation

Autocorrelation is more common in time-series data sets than in cross-sectional data sets.[38] There are a variety of statistical tests to detect the presence of auto-correlation; the Durbin-Watson test is the most commonly used test.[39]

If left uncorrected, autocorrelation can create errors in estimation. To visually see how this happens, consider Figures 3-13A and 3-13B, which depict positive autocorrelation.

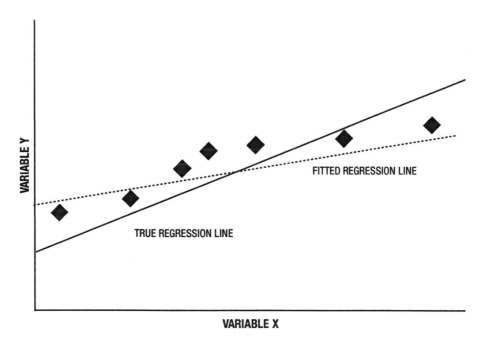

Figure 3-13A. Example of positive autocorrelation with initial positive error

[38]As noted by Pindyk and Rubinfeld, "positive serial correlation frequently occurs in time series studies either because of correlation in the measurement error component of the error term or, more likely, because of the high degree of correlation over time that is present in the cumulative effects of omitted variables." Pindyck and Rubinfeld, *Econometric Models and Economic Forecasts*, 159.

[39]J. Durbin and G. S. Watson, "Testing for Serial Correlation in Least-Squares Regression," *Biometrioka* 38 (1951), 159–77.

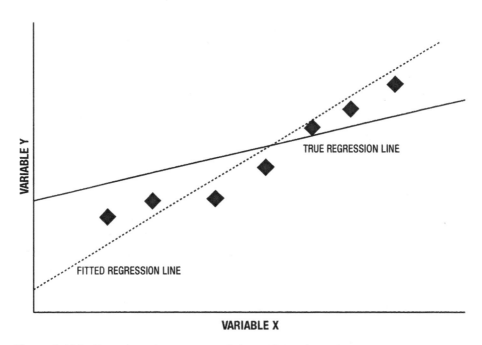

Figure 3-13B. Example positive autocorrelation with initial negative error

In Figure 3-13A, the solid line represents the true relationship between X and Y, and the dotted line represents the estimated relationship between X and Y. The error term of the first observation is positive. Because of autocorrelation, this leads to a series of correlated error terms; the first five are positive and the last two are negative. As can be seen, the intercept of the estimated regression line is greater than the true intercept, and the slope of the estimated regression line is less than the true slope.

In Figure 3-13B, again the solid line represents the true relationship between X and Y, and the dotted line represents the estimated relationship between X and Y. The error term of the first observation is negative. Because of autocorrelation, this leads to a series of correlated error terms; the first four are negative and the last three are positive. As can be seen, the intercept of the estimated regression line is smaller than the true intercept, and the slope of the estimated regression line is greater than the true slope.

In Figures 3-13A and 3-13B, the estimated regression line fits the data points better than the true regression line. This leads to the conclusion that the parameter estimates are more precise than they really are. This, in turn, can lead to incorrect inferences about the true relationships between the dependent and independent variables. We are more likely to conclude that a strong relationship exists, when in fact that may not be the case.

Violating Assumption 4: Multicollinearity

The fourth assumption of the classical linear regression model is that no exact linear relationship exists between two or more independent variables. If there is a perfectly linear relationship between two or more independent variables, this assumption is violated.[40]

If there is a *perfectly* linear relationship between two or more independent variables, it is mathematically impossible to calculate the parameter estimates. The ordinary least squares solutions cannot be calculated. As noted by Peter Kennedy, "the estimating procedure simply breaks down for mathematical reasons, just as if someone tried to divide by zero."[41]

Rarely does a perfectly linear relationship between independent variables exist; usually it only occurs in data sets that have been artificially constructed. It is common, however, to have an *approximate* linear relationship between independent variables (or combinations of independent variables). The existence of this type of approximate linear relationship is referred to *multicollinearity*.

Multicollinearity can make it difficult to know the true values of the coefficients being estimated. When two or more independent variables are correlated (even if not perfectly), they move together. Thus, any variation in one of the independent variables is mirrored by variation in the correlated independent variable(s). Because of this, there is very little variation that is unique to any of the correlated independent variables.

Remember that the parameters generated by regression express how changes in one independent variable affect the dependent variable while all other independent variables are held constant. In the case of multicollinearity, it is difficult to hold all other independent variables constant because some are correlated with the independent variable under investigation. This makes it difficult to determine which of the independent variables "deserves the credit" for the jointly explained variation in the dependent variable.

Essentially, multicollinearity causes coefficients to be estimated using less information. Basing coefficient estimates on less information means that we are less certain of their true value, causing those parameter estimates to have a higher variance. This increased variance causes greater uncertainty and less statistical power, which can lead to inferences that are at odds with the true relationship between the dependent and independent variables.

---

[40]A perfectly linear relationship between X_1 and X_2 would exist if, for example, X_2 could be calculated according to the following: $X_2 = \alpha X_1$.
[41]Peter Kennedy, *A Guide to Econometrics*, 3rd ed. (MIT Press, 1992), 176.

Violating Assumption 5: Simultaneous Equations

The fifth assumption of the classical linear regression model is that the independent variables can be considered fixed in repeated sampling. In simple terms, this means that the independent variables are not determined simultaneously. Simultaneous equations frequently appear in applied business and economic modeling. The classic example of this in economics is the model of supply and demand. In this model, the price of the good or service is simultaneously determined by the interaction of buyers and sellers in the marketplace. The price has to be agreed on by both: the buyer has to agree to pay the price for the good or service, and the seller has to agree to accept the price as payment.

Within the context of examining compensation for internal equity, simultaneous equations rarely (if ever) present themselves. Typically, we are examining compensation data that have already occurred; employees have already been paid an hourly wage or annual salary, have received an incentive payment, and so on. Because we examine events that have already occurred, their values are known with certainty and do not change.[42]

Theoretically, it is possible to have compensation determined as a set of simultaneous equations. For our purposes, it is extremely rare and thus will not be discussed at length.[43]

Interpretation of Regression Results

Assuming that the model has been properly specified and any issues with violations of the assumptions of the general linear regression model have been dealt with, the model is estimated. Estimation of the regression model involves the use of statistical software to calculate the estimated parameters as given in Equation 3.17.[44]

To illustrate the interpretation of regression results, assume that we are interested in examining the relationship between annual salary, time in job, having a particular certification, and gender. We can mathematically express this relationship as follows:

$$SALARY = \beta_0 + \beta_1 TIJ + \beta_2 CERT + \beta_3 F \qquad (3.22)$$

---

[42]We know, for example, that John Smith and Bob Jones received bonus payments in 2012 of \$105,000 and \$112,000, respectively. It does not matter whether we measure these bonus payments today, tomorrow, or one month from now; the amounts will not change. They are fixed because they have already occurred.

[43]Readers who are interested in the estimation of simultaneous equations are referred to standard econometrics textbooks.

[44]Available statistical software packages are briefly discussed at the end of this chapter.

where

$$SALARY = \text{annual salary}$$

$$TIJ = \text{time in job}$$

$$CERT = \text{dummy variable for having certification}$$

$$F = \text{dummy variable for female}$$

Depending on the software, the output generated will vary in appearance, but will contain standard information that allows for basic evaluation of the results. Figure 3-14 provides an example of what the regression output may look like when Equation 3.22 is estimated.

```
Dependent Variable              |   SALARY
N                               |   78
Adjusted Squared Multiple R     |   0.924
Standard Error of Estimate      |   698.851
```

Regression Coefficients B = (X′X)⁻¹X′Y

Effect	Coefficient	t	p-Value
CONSTANT	24041.667	2.387	0.025
TIJ	1241.448	6.208	0.001
CERT	728.00	0.985	0.336
FEMALE	-7158.333	2.391	0.026

Figure 3-14. Example regression output

From a practical perspective, there are five key aspects to consider when evaluating the results of a multiple regression analysis: the values of the estimated coefficients, the statistical significance and practical significance of the estimated coefficients, the size of the sample, and the overall explanatory power of the model.

Coefficients

As can be seen from Figure 3-14, the regression output shows the estimated values of all of the parameters. The estimate of the intercept term, β_0 (labeled as CONSTANT in the regression output) is \$24,041.67. As noted previously, the intercept term is where the estimated regression line crosses the vertical axis.

The estimate of β_1, the coefficient associated with time in job, is \$1,241.45. As already mentioned, an estimated coefficient expresses the effect of a one-unit change in the independent variable on the dependent variable, all other factors held constant. The estimated value of β_1 expresses the additional amount of annual salary we would expect an employee to receive as a result of an additional year of time in job, ceteris paribus. In other words, if we have two employees of the same sex who both possess (or both do not possess) the particular certification, and one of those employees has one more year of time in job than the other employee, we would expect the annual compensation of the employee with the additional year of time in job to be \$1,241.45 greater than that of the other employee.

The estimate of β_2, the coefficient associated with possession of the particular certification, is \$728.00. The estimated value of β_2 expresses the additional amount of annual salary we would expect an employee to receive as a result of having the particular certification, ceteris paribus. In other words, if we have two employees of the same gender with identical time in job, and one has the certification and the other does not, we would expect the annual compensation of the employee with the certification to be \$728.00 greater than that of the other employee.

Our estimates of β_0, β_1, and β_2 all have positive signs, meaning that the effect of having more years of time in job or possessing the particular certification has a positive effect on compensation (e.g., more time in job leads to higher salary, possessing the certification leads to higher salary).

However, the estimate of β_3 has a negative sign; the estimated coefficient is *negative* \$7,158.33 (–\$7,158.33). The estimated value of β_3 expresses the additional amount of annual salary we would expect an employee to receive as a result of being female, ceteris paribus. In other words, if we have two employees with identical time in job who both possess (or both do not possess) the particular certification, and one of those employees is male and the other employee is female, we would expect the annual compensation of the female to be \$7,158.33 *less* than the male employee.[45]

---

[45]Note that in this example, our dummy variable for gender takes on a value of 1 for female and 0 for male. If this were reversed, and the dummy variable took on a value of 1 for male and 0 for female, the sign of the estimated coefficient would be positive, indicating the amount of additional annual salary an employee is expected to receive for being male, ceteris paribus. I return to this point in Chapter 4.

The sign of the estimated coefficient (positive or negative) indicates the direction of the relationship. In terms of examining internal pay equity with respect to gender, race and ethnicity, or other protected characteristic, the sign of the coefficient indicates whether there is an "advantage" or "penalty" (in terms of compensation) for being a particular gender, race or ethnicity, or other protected characteristic.

The magnitude of the estimated coefficient (e.g., $1,241.45) expresses the size of the effect. The magnitude of the estimated coefficients plays an important role in assessing regression results for practical significance, which is discussed in a subsequent subsection.

Statistical Significance

Though examination of the sign and magnitude of the estimated coefficients is important, the coefficients alone cannot tell us whether the observed relationship is meaningful from a statistical perspective. The estimated coefficients must also be examined for statistical significance.

In simple terms, statistical significance addresses the question of whether an observed outcome is "sufficiently rare" such that it is unlikely to occur due to chance variation.[46]

Formally, when we evaluate the estimated coefficients for statistical significance, we conduct the following hypothesis test:

$$null\ hypothesis: H_0 : \beta_i = 0 \qquad\qquad (3.23)$$

$$alternate\ hypothesis: H_A : \beta_i \neq 0$$

The null hypothesis states that the *true* value of the estimated coefficient is equal to 0, meaning that there is no relationship between the independent variable and the dependent variable. If the null hypothesis is true, then any observed relationship between the independent and dependent variables is not because of a true underlying relationship but is attributable to random chance variation.

The alternate hypothesis states that the true value of the estimated coefficient is not equal to 0, meaning that there is a relationship between the independent variable and the dependent variable. Thus, the observed relationship between the independent and dependent variables is not attributable to chance variation.

---

[46]Readers who are unfamiliar with the basic concept of statistical significance are referred to the Appendix.

Within the regression analysis context, the formal statistical test for rejecting null hypotheses associated with estimated coefficients is typically based on the t-distribution.[47] The test statistic is calculated as:

$$t = \frac{\hat{\beta}_i}{se(\hat{\beta}_i)} \qquad (3.24)$$

If the calculated t-statistic is greater than the critical value (t_c), we reject the null hypothesis; if the calculated t-statistic is less than the critical value, we cannot reject the null hypothesis. As noted by Pindyck and Rubinfeld:

> Since t_c = 1.96 for large samples and a 5 percent significance level, a frequent rule of thumb is that a t value with a magnitude of 2 or larger allows us to reject the null hypothesis.[48]

Returning to the example regression output shown in Figure 3-14, the calculated t-statistics associated with each of the independent variables are shown in the column labeled "t." For example, the calculated t-statistic associated with the estimated coefficient for time in job is equal to 6.208. Because this value is greater in magnitude than the critical value of 2, we would reject the null hypothesis and infer that a nonzero relationship exists between annual salary and time in job. Because we have rejected the null hypothesis, we would conclude that this result is "statistically significant."

The calculated t-statistic associated with the estimated coefficient for possession of a particular certification is equal to 0.985. Because this value is not greater in magnitude than the critical value of 2, we cannot reject the null hypothesis that there is no relationship between annual salary and possession of a particular certification. We have not rejected the null hypothesis, so we would conclude that this result is "statistically insignificant" or "not statistically significant."

In addition to the t-statistic, most statistical software also provides additional information in the form of a p-value. In Figure 3-14, p-values are given in the last column. The p-value shows the exact level of significance associated with an estimated coefficient. For example, the p-value associated with the estimated coefficient for time in job is equal to 0.001. This means that the observed result is statistically significant at the 0.1% significance level.

---

[47]The t-distribution is relevant because a sample estimate of the error variance, rather than the true error variance, is used for this statistical test. Pindyck and Rubinfeld, *Econometric Models and Economic Forecasts*, 67.
[48]Ibid., 68.

The level of significance is best understood in the context of what errors are possible when performing hypothesis tests. There are two kinds of errors one can make when performing hypothesis tests:

- Type I error: incorrectly rejecting a true null hypothesis
- Type II error: incorrectly accepting a false null hypothesis

The level of significance refers to the probability of making a Type I error. There is always a trade-off between Type I and Type II errors. The probability of making a Type I error cannot be reduced without increasing the probability of making a Type II error and vice versa. The generally accepted level of significance within the statistical and social sciences communities is 5% ($p = 0.05$). This definition has also been adopted by the courts.[49]

There is one critical point to keep in mind regarding statistical significance when reviewing regression results. If an estimated coefficient is not statistically significant, it is not statistically different from 0. In Figure 3-14, the estimated coefficient associated with possession of a particular certification is $728.00. However, because this coefficient is not statistically significant, it is not statistically different from zero (i.e., we cannot reject the null hypothesis that its true value is 0). From a statistical perspective, we cannot infer that a relationship exists between annual salary and possession of this certification. This has particular importance for evaluating the protected group effects on compensation. If an estimated effect is not statistically significant, no adverse inference can or should be drawn regarding compensation discrimination.

Practical Significance

Statistical significance addresses the question of whether a true relationship between the independent variable and the dependent variable exists. Practical significance addresses the question of whether the relationship between the independent variable and the dependent variable is "big enough to matter." As noted by Paetzhold and Willborn:

> Some coefficients can be statistically significant but not practically different from zero. A sex coefficient of −$25 could, in some situations, represent a statistically significant salary shortfall for women. Depending on absolute wage levels, however, the amount may be so small as to be practically negligible.[50]

---

[49]*Hazelwood School District v. United States*, 433 U.S. 299 (1977).
[50]Paetzhold and Willborn, *The Statistics of Discrimination*, 280.

On the other hand, estimated coefficients can be statistically insignificant but practically different from 0. According to Paetzhold and Willborn:

> *The coefficient of a predictor variable may not be statistically significant, yet the predictor may play an important role in the employer's determination of compensation.*[51]

The U.S. Supreme Court also addressed the issue of practical significance. In the same decision that established the legal threshold of statistical significance, the Court stated that gross statistical disparities could, by themselves, constitute prima facie proof of a pattern or practice of discrimination.[52]

Unlike statistical significance, there is no critical value for determining whether an estimated coefficient is practically significant. Practical significance is a question of judgment.[53]

Sample Size

Sample size refers to the number of observations being examined in the analysis. Sample size is commonly denoted as N. Referring back to the example regression output given in Figure 3-14, the sample size is reported in the second line of output ($N = 78$). When evaluating the results of a regression analysis, it is important to consider sample size because it can directly influence the outcome of statistical analyses. In fact, sample size plays an important role in statistical significance.

When testing the hypothesis that the true value of an estimated parameter is 0 (as given in Equation 3.23), we cannot reject the null hypothesis if the result is statistically insignificant. As discussed, one reason for failing to reject the null hypothesis is that the null hypothesis is true (i.e., there is no relationship between the dependent and independent variables).

It is also possible, however, that we fail to reject the null hypothesis because even though it is false, the data set used in the analysis is consistent with the null hypothesis. The statistical concept of *power*—the probability of rejecting the null hypothesis when it is in fact false—is important in understanding this explanation.[54]

---

[51] Ibid., 281.

[52] *Hazelwood School District v. United States*, 433 U.S. 299 (1977).

[53] The issue of practical significance is discussed in more detail in Chapter 10.

[54] The power of a hypothesis test is calculated as $(1 - p(Type\ II\ error))$, one minus the probability that the null hypothesis will be accepted as true when it is in fact false.

The power of a test is a function of both the size of the effect that has been measured and the size of the data set (the sample size). Generally speaking, a larger measured effect and a larger sample size will lead to a more powerful test.

As noted by Pindyck and Rubinfeld:

> When a statistical analysis with relatively low power fails to show a significant p-value, one should not automatically conclude definitively that there is no effect. Rather, one must allow for the fact that the study may be inconclusive because the data set is not sufficient to allow one to distinguish between the null and alternative hypotheses.[55]

Sample size can directly influence the outcome of a statistical analysis. If an analysis involves a small sample size, it is not uncommon to get a statistically insignificant result simply because there is not enough information and the statistical test lacks power. When evaluating the results of a statistical analysis, consideration should be given to how the sample size affects the power of the tests and what role it plays in accepting or rejecting the null hypotheses.

Explanatory Power

When assessing the results of a multiple regression analysis, it is important to consider the estimated coefficients, their statistical and practical significance, and what role sample size plays in the results generated. It is also necessary to assess how well the model, as a whole, performs in terms of explanatory power. To see the importance of evaluating overall explanatory power, consider the following example.

Assume that compensation is determined by time in job and possession of a particular certification, and we are interested in assessing whether gender plays any role in compensation decision making. Instead of estimating the model given in Equation 3.22, we estimate the model given in Equation 3.25, in which annual salary is a function of seniority, educational attainment, and gender:

$$SALARY = \beta_0 + \beta_1 SENIORITY + \beta_2 EDU + \beta_3 F \qquad (3.25)$$

Figure 3-15 provides an example of what the regression output may look like when Equation 3.25 is estimated.

---

[55]Pindyck and Rubinfeld, *Econometric Models and Economic Forecasts*, 44.

```
Dependent Variable                |  SALARY
N                                 |  78
Adjusted Squared Multiple R       |  0.421
Standard Error of Estimate        |  698.851
```

Regression Coefficients B = $(X'X)^{-1}X'Y$

```
Effect        |Coefficient          t           p-Value
--------------------------------------------------------
CONSTANT      | 27642.881         2.391         0.026
SENIORITY     |   912.342         3.317         0.001
EDU           |   858.764         1.090         0.158
FEMALE        | -6404.121         2.494         0.023
```

Figure 3-15. Example regression output

When one compares the results shown in Figure 3-15 to those shown in Figure 3-14, it may appear as though there are no substantial differences. Coefficient estimates were generated for all of the variables, three of the four variables are statistically significant, the gender coefficient is negative and statistically significant, and so on.

However, the models differ markedly in their overall explanatory power. The model given by Equation 3.22 does a much better job of explaining the variation in annual salary than the model in Equation 3.25. This is evidenced by the R squared (R^2) statistics for the two models.

In essence, the R squared statistic (also referred to as the coefficient of determination) measures the proportion of variability in the dependent variable that is explained by the independent variables. R squared ranges in value from 0.0 to 1.0; a value of 0.0 implies that *none* of the variation in the dependent variable is explained by the independent variables, whereas a value of 1.0 implies that *all* of the variation in the dependent variable is explained by the independent variables.

There are two variants of the coefficient of determination: R squared and adjusted R squared ($\bar{R}^2$). Adjusted R squared adjusts for the number of independent variables in the model, and R squared does not.[56] Because of this, adjusted R squared is preferred to R squared.

Returning to the example regression output, we see that the adjusted R squared in Figure 3-14 (associated with the model in which compensation is a function of time in job, possession of the particular certification, and gender)

---

[56]R squared will automatically increase when an additional independent variable is added to the model. Unlike R squared, adjusted R squared only increases if the additional independent variable improves the model more than would be expected by chance.

is equal to 0.924. This means that 92.4% of the variation in annual salary is explained by time in job, possession of the particular certification, and gender, after adjusting for the number of independent variables. The adjusted R squared in Figure 3-15 (associated with the model in which compensation is a function of seniority, educational attainment, and gender) is 0.421. This means that 42.1% of the variation in annual salary is explained by seniority, educational attainment, and gender, after adjusting for the number of independent variables. Comparing these two models in terms of adjusted R squared, we see that the model given in Equation 3.22 has far greater explanatory power than the one in Equation 3.25.

Examining the explanatory power of a regression model is an essential piece of reviewing and interpreting analysis results. However, caution should be exercised in how much weight is placed on R squared measures. As noted by Paetzhold and Willborn:

> An R^2 value of 0.8 indicates that a relatively substantial amount of variability in compensation has been explained by the predictors; a much smaller value of R^2, however, can still indicate that the equation usefully explains variation in compensation level. R^2 measures explanatory power relative to a model containing no predictors. Thus, an R^2 value of even .4 can indicate substantial explanation of compensation relative to a model having no predictors.[57]

Furthermore, R squared measures do not provide any information about how well the model describes the data set. This can only be addressed with an analysis of the regression residuals.[58]

Inferences of Discrimination

The results generated by a multiple regression analysis of compensation can be used to draw inferences about the presence or absence of discrimination. To demonstrate how these inferences are made, we return to the example model of compensation in Equation 3.22 and the associated regression results shown in Figure 3-14.

---

[57]Paetzhold and Willborn, *The Statistics of Discrimination*, 279.
[58]Residual analysis is discussed in detail in Chapter 5.

Assuming that none of the assumptions of the classical linear regression model have been violated, a review of the regression results indicates the following:

1. The sample size is sufficient ($N = 78$) such that our statistical tests have adequate power.

2. A review of the adjusted R squared measure indicates that 92.4% of the variation in annual salary is explained by time in job, possession of the particular certification, and gender.

3. The estimated coefficient associated with the gender variable (i.e., the additional amount of annual salary we would expect an employee to receive as a result of being female, ceteris paribus) is –$7,158.33. This implies that there is a "penalty" for being female in terms of annual salary.

4. The estimated coefficient associated with the gender variable is statistically significant, meaning we reject the null hypothesis that there is no true relationship between gender and compensation.

5. The estimated coefficient associated with the gender variable is also large enough (in dollars) to be considered practically significant.

Based on these results, what can we say about the presence or absence of gender discrimination?

We can infer that the results of the analysis are consistent with the hypothesis of gender discrimination in compensation. We cannot conclusively establish, however, that gender discrimination is taking place. These results do not *prove* discrimination. The distinction between inferring the presence or absence of discrimination and proving discrimination may appear to be a matter of nuance; the distinction, however, is actually quite substantial.

Despite our best efforts, no model of compensation can be 100% accurate in describing how compensation is determined. No matter how diligently the model was constructed, there is the possibility that some explanatory factor has been omitted. As noted by Paetzhold and Willborn, "no statistical model of an organization's compensation levels can be entirely accurate in representing how those compensation levels are determined."[59] Because of this, the possibility of misspecification cannot be completely and permanently eliminated.

---

[59]Paetzhold and Willborn, *The Statistics of Discrimination*, 281.

When interpreting regression results, it is important to keep in mind that a coefficient can only be interpreted within the context of the full model. In our example, we can conclude that when time in job and possession of the particular certification are accounted for, females are paid $7,158.33 less on average than their male counterparts. Any interpretation of an individual coefficient must consider the other explanatory factors that are controlled for in the model.

Regression results cannot be interpreted in a causal manner. The fact that the relationship between compensation and gender is statistically significant does not mean that gender has a causal effect on compensation. Interpreting this relationship in such as manner (i.e., "gender causes compensation") is akin to interpreting the relationship between stork populations and birthrates as causal (i.e. "storks cause babies"). We simply cannot conclude that being female causes an employee to earn $7,158.33 less per year.

Finally, the nature of statistics themselves should be kept in mind when interpreting results. The results express the likelihood of certain outcomes, not whether certain outcomes can or will occur. For example, if we flip a coin ten times, the likelihood of getting ten heads is 1 out of 1,000. Getting ten heads in ten flips is a pretty rare occurrence, but it does happen. In fact, we would *expect* it to happen once out of every 1,000 sets of flips. Although the likelihood of seeing a $7,158.33 difference in compensation by gender as a result of chance may be small, it is not zero and it is possible.

Tools for Performing Multiple Regression

Multiple regression analysis is, with rare exception, performed using some type of statistical software package. Although the calculations involved are mathematically relatively simple, they are too complex to be carried out by hand. All of the calculations discussed in this chapter are standard features of commercially available statistical software packages.

A variety of software packages exist; some of the commonly used packages include EViews, Gauss, SAS, SPSS, STATA, and SYSTAT. Open-source alternatives to commercial packages include PSPP and R. Microsoft Excel also has some basic statistical functionality.[60]

There are numerous advantages of using statistical software to perform multiple regression analysis. The required calculations and algorithms are built into the software. Very large data sets can be manipulated and analyzed with

---

[60]This listing of software packages should not be construed or interpreted as endorsement by author or publisher.

relative ease. Scripts and programs can be written within the software so that model specifications and estimation routines can be saved for future use, applied to modified data sets, and so on.

The ease of use of statistical software can also be a drawback. Given that most packages have a graphical user interface, statistical tests can be performed in a "point and click" manner by selecting specific tests from drop-down menus. Specific knowledge of which test variants are appropriate and well suited for the data set and the questions being addressed is required to generate meaningful and reliable results. If a statistical software package is used without underlying statistical expertise, disastrous results can ensue. If inappropriate test variants and estimation procedures are chosen and/or results are interpreted incorrectly, any inferences drawn from those analyses cannot—and should not—be used to make business decisions.

The Data

On two occasions I have been asked, "Pray, Mr. Babbage, if you put into the machine wrong figures, will the right answers come out?" . . . I am not able rightly to apprehend the kind of confusion of ideas that could provoke such a question.

—Charles Babbage

A good data set is the foundation of a successful statistical review of compensation. The old adage of "garbage in, garbage out" could not be more fitting. Any quantitative analysis is only as good as the underlying data set. Inaccuracies and inconsistencies in the data not only can render the analysis inaccurate and unreliable but can also lead to incorrect inferences regarding the relationships being investigated. If these incorrect inferences are applied to business decisions, an employer could unintentionally create the very situation it was trying to remedy.

The keys to an accurate and reliable analysis encompass a clear understanding of what you are measuring, what relationships will be explored, and a thorough review of the data for completeness, accuracy, and consistency.

The purpose of this chapter is to discuss some common data points used in compensation analyses and potential pitfalls with respect to typical data error issues. This discussion is not intended to be exhaustive of all potential data points that could be used in compensation reviews, nor is it an encyclopedia of all possible data errors.

Before turning to a discussion of the data points, a discussion of grouping employees for comparison purposes is warranted.

Similarly Situated Employee Groupings

For any statistical examination of compensation to generate meaningful results, it is important that each employee's compensation is assessed against the appropriate peer group. Grouping employees for comparison purposes may seem like an easy task—we simply put everyone in a particular job title into the same grouping, or we put all employees in a given cost center or department into the same grouping. In most cases, however, it is not as simple as this. To see why, consider the following example.

Assume that we are interested in examining the annual salaries of a group of employees for the presence or absence of gender pay discrimination. Further assume that the group of employees to be studied is defined as all who are assigned to the "headquarters" cost center, and these employees' genders, job titles, and annual salaries are given in Table 4-1.

Table 4-1. Employees Assigned to "Headquarters" Cost Center

ID#	Sex	Job Title	Annual Salary($)
2017	M	CEO	250,000
3112	F	Exec. Assistant, CEO	80,000
3798	F	Admin. Assistant, CEO	65,000
4263	F	Admin. Assistant II	57,000
5590	F	Receptionist	30,000

A simple comparison of average annual salaries by gender for this group of employees would indicate a difference of $192,000 in favor of males.[1] Based on this difference, one may be tempted to make an inference of gender discrimination. However, in this case the difference in average annual salaries by gender is explained by the fact that the group of employees being compared against one another is improperly defined.

Irrespective of gender, one would expect that the annual salary of the CEO of an organization would be greater than that of a receptionist, administrative assistant, or executive assistant. The job duties and responsibilities of a CEO are very different from those of executive or administrative assistants and receptionists, as are the required skills and experience levels. The functions, responsibilities, and required skills corresponding to the job titles in Table 4-1 are the following, according to the *Occupational Outlook Handbook*:[2]

---

[1] The average male compensation is $250,000; the average female compensation is $58,000. The difference between these figures is $192,000.
[2] *2012–2013 Occupational Outlook Handbook*, Bureau of Labor Statistics, U.S. Department of Labor (www.bls.gov/ooh/).

- Chief Executive Officer: *Provide overall direction. Manage company operations, formulate policies and ensure goals are met. Collaborate with and direct work of other top executives and typically report to board of directors. Have a bachelor's or master's degree in business administration or in an area related to their field of work. Must have related work experience, including extensive managerial experience and experience in the organization's area of specialty.*

- Executive Admin Assistant: *Provide high-level administrative support for top executives of an organization. Often handle more complex responsibilities such as reviewing incoming documents, conducting research, preparing reports, and arranging meetings. May supervise clerical staff. May require bachelor's degree.*

- Admin Assistant: *Perform a variety of clerical and organizational tasks necessary to run an organization efficiently. Specific duties vary by experience and specialty. Generally need high school diploma or equivalent, may require specialized skills.*

- Receptionist: *Perform various administrative tasks such as answering telephones and giving information to customers and the public. Responsible for making a good first impression for the organization. Most receive training on the job.*

In the example shown in Table 4-1, the difference in average annual compensation by gender is not attributable to sex discrimination; it is due to the fact that we have grouped employees inappropriately for comparison purposes. Although simplistic, this example illustrates that any inferences of discrimination (on the basis of sex, race and ethnicity, or other protected characteristic) can be inaccurate and quite misleading if the employee groupings have been incorrectly structured.

Generally speaking, only employees that are "similarly situated" should be grouped together for comparison purposes. There are no definitive rules for creating similarly situated employee groupings. However, the Office of Federal Contract Compliance Programs (OFCCP) proposes the following definition: groupings of employees who perform similar work and occupy positions with similar responsibility levels and involving similar skills and qualifications.[3]

---

[3]Department of Labor, Employment Standards Administration, Office of Federal Contract Compliance Programs, "Voluntary Guidelines for Self-Evaluation of Compensation Practices for Compliance with Nondiscrimination Requirements of Executive Order 11246 with Respect to Systemic Compensation Discrimination Notice, Part V," *Federal Register* 71(116) (June 16, 2006): 35114.

The OFCCP notes that other "pertinent factors" should also be considered in the formulation of similarly situated employee groupings:

> *Otherwise similarly-situated employees may be paid differently for a variety of reasons: they work in different departments or other functional divisions of the organization with different budgets or different levels of importance to the business; they fall under different pay plans, such as team-based pay plans or incentive-based pay plans; they are paid on a different basis, such as hourly, salary or through sales commissions; some are covered by wage scales set through collective bargaining, while others are not; they have different employment statuses such as full-time or part-time.*[4]

In addition to those specifically mentioned by the OFCCP, other factors may be considered pertinent to the formation of similarly situated employee groupings. For example, geography (or some other measure of location) may be considered a pertinent factor if locality adjustments or cost of living adjustments are given to employees working in certain geographic locations, but not to those working in other locations.

In deciding whether employees really are similarly situated, it is useful to review job descriptions and what tasks are performed by the employees. It is also important to look at responsibility levels within the organization and chain-of-command issues, along with any general or specialized skills, abilities, and qualifications that may be required for the positions in question. Interviews with managers and employees are also used to evaluate whether two positions are similarly situated. Ultimately, the similarity of work performed, responsibility levels, and the required skills, abilities, and qualifications for the position remain a question of judgment.

Closely related to the concept of similarly situated employee groupings is the concept of *comparators*. Comparators are most often used within the compliance review and litigation contexts. Assume, for example, that a Hispanic employee claimed that he received a smaller increase in pay because of race and ethnicity discrimination. To evaluate whether race and ethnicity played a role in the pay increases, one first must identify the claimant's comparators: to whom is he similar? To whom should we compare his pay increase?

The appropriate comparators in this case may be other employees in the same job title and pay grade with similar time in job and seniority. In identifying the comparators, it would be important to know how pay increases were awarded in this case. If the increases were based on production, then one may want to limit the comparator set to only those individuals who had levels of production similar to that of the claimant. If the increases were based on

---

[4]Ibid.

possessing a certain certification or qualification, then one may want to limit the comparator set to only those who possessed the same certifications and qualifications as the claimant.

Within a litigation context, comparators are often drawn from the majority group. In this example, the Hispanic employee's comparators would most likely be white. In cases where women claim they have been discriminated against on the basis of their sex, males are commonly taken as the appropriate comparators. From a pure equity perspective, however, there is no reason to limit the comparators to one particular sex, racial, or ethnic characteristic.

From a pure equity perspective, it is important to know whether a particular white male is underpaid, for example, relative to other similarly situated white males. The demographics of the comparator set can differ based on the question(s) being addressed and what one hopes to learn from the analysis.

The way employees are grouped for comparison purposes is quite possibly the single most important aspect of any kind of workforce analytics. How employees are grouped can have a dramatic effect on the outcomes of the comparisons being made. Improperly grouped employees can render a comparison meaningless. Furthermore, aside from the analytical implications, the way employee groups are constructed serve as a memorialization of the organization's view of its workforce, and which employees are similar to one another.

Compensation Metrics

Virtually any type of compensation paid to an employee can be examined with a statistical review. Base salaries, hourly pay rates, overtime earnings, bonuses, incentive pay, and total compensation are among the common measures studied.

Choosing the appropriate measure(s) of compensation for a given group of similarly situated employees is central to the analysis. The choice will be guided by two factors: the types of compensation earned by the particular group of employees, and the questions addressed in the compensation review.[5]

Different types of employees receive different types of compensation. Generally speaking, all employees receive some form of base pay. Some types of compensation are applicable only to certain groups of employees. It would be pointless, for example, to attempt to study overtime earnings for a

---

[5]Because the employee groupings themselves influence the compensation metrics that can be studied, the construction of similarly situated employee groupings must precede any data collection efforts.

group of exempt employees.[6] Similarly, it would not make sense to attempt to study commission earnings among a group of employees who do not earn commissions.

Many employees receive different types of compensation. For example, a salesperson may receive a base rate of pay (either an hourly rate or a salary amount), commissions on sales made, and bonuses for meeting specific sales targets or quotas. In this case, there are a variety of compensation metrics to choose from: base rates of pay, commissions, and bonuses. The choice of which compensation metrics to examine is determined by the questions being addressed. If overall equity is a concern, then total compensation (base earnings plus commissions plus bonuses) may be an appropriate choice. If the employer is investigating claims of discriminatory pay-setting practices, then the base rate of pay may be the appropriate choice.

Note There is no reason the same compensation metrics must be studied across similarly situated employee groupings. Different compensation metrics can be selected for different groupings of similarly situated employees.

Each element of compensation has its own peculiarities with respect to data capture and retention and its own set of unique governing influences that must be considered.

Base Pay

Base pay is perhaps the most commonly examined compensation metric. It is nearly universally received by all employees and is routinely maintained in an organization's human resources and/or payroll databases.[7] Reviewing base pay for internal equity is a natural starting point, because many other elements of compensation are tied to or dependent on base pay in some fashion.[8]

The most commonly encountered difficulty with respect to base pay data is reporting in inconsistent units. This primarily takes one of two forms: mixtures of hourly and annual rates and failure to account for full-time equivalency.

---

[6]This is, of course, because exempt employees do not receive overtime pay.

[7]In some circumstances, an employee may receive only commission-type earnings with no guaranteed base rate of pay.

[8]For example, overtime earnings are calculated at 1.5 times the regular rate of pay; the regular rate of pay, in turn, is based in large part on the hourly rate of pay. Bonuses may be determined as a percentage of annual salary.

Depending on the human resources and payroll database software used by the organization, there is the potential for base pay to be recorded and maintained in inconsistent units for individuals within the same similarly situated employee grouping. In other words, base pay can possibly be captured in terms of an hourly rate for some employees and in terms of an annualized salary amount for others. This inconsistent reporting can create the appearance of problems in internal equity when in fact no such problem exists. For example, consider the compensation data shown in Table 4-2.

Table 4-2. Hypothetical Pay Rates Expressed in Annual and Hourly Amounts

ID#	Sex	Job Title	Pay ($)
0411	M	Analyst I	20,800.00
0573	M	Analyst I	20,800.00
0697	M	Analyst I	20,800.00
1042	F	Analyst I	10.00
1126	F	Analyst I	10.00

If these pay data were used in a regression analysis, assuming the only differences among these employees was gender, the analysis would indicate a statistically significant disparity in pay by gender.

The problem, however, is not gender discrimination; the problem is that the pay of some employees is expressed in terms of an annual amount and the pay of others is expressed in terms of an hourly rate. Assuming that all employees in this similarly situated employee grouping are paid for 2,080 hours per year, their annual pay and hourly rates are exactly identical.[9]

A similar problem can manifest if a similarly situated employee grouping contains a mixture of full-time and part-time employees. Assume, for example, that base pay is recorded in terms of an annual amount (hours multiplied by hourly pay rate) for a group of full-time and part-time employees, as shown in Table 4-3.

---

[9]$10 per hour multiplied by 2,080 hours per year is $20,800 per year. $20,800 per year divided by 2,080 hours per year is $10 per hour.

Table 4-3. Hypothetical Pay Rates for Full-Time and Part-Time Employees

ID#	Sex	Status	Job Title	Hours per Week	Annual Pay ($)
A117	M	FT	Cust Svc Rep	40	20,800
A121	M	FT	Cust Svc Rep	40	20,800
A134	M	FT	Cust Svc Rep	40	20,800
A137	F	PT	Cust Svc Rep	30	15,600
A139	F	PT	Cust Svc Rep	30	15,600
A206	F	PT	Cust Svc Rep	35	18,200

If these annual pay data were used in a regression analysis, assuming the only differences among these employees was gender, the analysis would indicate a statistically significant disparity in pay by gender.

Again, the problem is not gender discrimination. The problem is that there is a mixture of full-time and part-time employees in this similarly situated employee grouping, and differences in the number of hours worked per week have not been incorporated. If compensation is expressed in terms of an hourly pay rate, we see that all employees are earning $10 per hour.[10]

In the example shown in Table 4-2, a visual inspection of the data is likely to reveal the inconsistency in the units of measure of pay. It is unrealistic (and most likely a violation of minimum wage laws) that an employee earns just $10 a year.

The inconsistency in Table 4-3 is less likely to be revealed through visual inspection. All of the data points are plausible annual pay amounts, and the differences in values are not large enough to automatically trigger a red flag. Cases like those shown in Table 4-3 are not easily detected unless a review of full-time or part-time status, typical hours worked per week, and so on, are considered along with the annual pay. This makes these kinds of inconsistencies insidious because they can have a substantial impact on a review of internal pay equity but often remain undetected without a thorough review of the data.

Overtime Earnings

When studying overtime earnings for internal equity, there are two main issues that need to be considered. First, overtime earnings are directly related to the number of hours of overtime an employee works.

---

[10]$20,800 per year divided by 52 weeks per year divided by 40 hours per week is $10 per hour. $15,600 per year divided by 52 weeks per year divided by 30 hours per week is $10 per hour. $18,200 per year divided by 52 weeks per year divided by 35 hours per week is $10 per hour.

Among similarly situated employees, differences in overtime earnings by protected group status are typically explained by differences in overtime hours worked by protected group status.

Reasons for differences in overtime hours worked by protected group status are varied. For example, it may be the case that the number of overtime hours men choose to work is greater than the number of overtime hours women choose to work.[11] It some circumstances, overtime opportunities are granted according to seniority.[12] Any differences in seniority by protected group status may lead to differences in overtime hours worked by protected group status.

Generally speaking, because overtime earnings are dependent on overtime hours, examination of these earnings with respect to internal pay equity should include some measure of overtime hours worked.

Second, overtime earnings are determined—at least in part—by an employee's hourly pay rate. Under the Fair Labor Standards Act, most employees are entitled to receive time and one half the regular rate of pay for all hours worked over forty hours in a given work week.[13] In some cases, an employee's regular pay rate will be identical to the hourly rate of pay. In other cases, where an employee receives a shift differential, cost of living adjustments, discretionary bonuses, or other qualifying compensation, the regular rate of pay will be greater than the hourly rate of pay.

Generally speaking, the hourly rate of pay determines a substantial part of an employee's regular rate of pay and, therefore, the overtime rate. If inequities in overtime earnings are discovered that are not accounted for by differences in overtime hours worked, these may be attributable to inequities in hourly rates of pay. In cases like these, an examination of hourly rates of pay for inequities should be included in the follow-up investigations.[14]

Variable Pay

Variable pay programs are gaining in popularity, and more organizations are using these programs to reward employees. Companies are increasingly relying on incentive and bonus payments, technical achievement awards,

---

[11] There are varying reasons women may choose to work fewer overtime hours. Commonly cited reasons include child care and family responsibilities. This is discussed in more detail in Chapter 9.

[12] For example, if a limited number of overtime hours are available during a given time period, an employer may offer them to employees according to a seniority list, moving through the list until opportunities for the given period are exhausted.

[13] Section 13(a)(1) of the Fair Labor Standards Act provides an exemption from overtime pay for certain types of employees.

[14] Follow-up investigations are detailed in Chapter 7.

and profit-sharing plans to minimize risks associated with fixed labor costs and to maximize return on investment.

There is incredible variety among variable pay plans. Some types of variable pay—such as individual performance bonuses, commissions, or payments for skill and knowledge—are based on an employee's performance. Other types of variable pay, such as work group bonuses, incorporate group-based performance. Still other types of variable pay, such as profit sharing plans, are tied to overall organizational performance. In some cases, variable pay will be tied to an easily quantifiable metric, such as revenue generated, on-time completion of project milestones and deliverables, and attainment of profit goals. In other cases, variable pay may be based on more discretionary conditions, such as "exceptional performance."

Because of this variety, examining variable pay for internal equity can be challenging. It is important to have a thorough understanding of what form(s) of variable compensation are possible within a group of similarly situated employees and the criteria that must be met to receive the variable payment.[15]

In cases where the amount of variable pay is directly tied to easily quantifiable metrics, such as revenue generated or on-time completion of project milestones, the examination of variable pay takes on the form of an audit. Here, the analysis addresses whether the employee received the proper amount of variable compensation, as set forth in the compensation policy, based on the outcome of the metric in question (dollars of revenue, a "yes/no" condition for on-time completion, etc.).[16]

The potential for internal inequities is greatest within discretionary variable pay. Here it is useful to examine the amount of variable pay received by each member of the similarly situated employee grouping to assess whether meaningful differences exist. The analysis may examine the dollar amount of bonuses or incentives relative to performance ratings or other measures of employee performance used in the decision-making process.

In certain circumstances, it may also be of interest to examine the eligibility requirements of a variable pay program for discrimination. This is a fundamentally different question; rather than examining whether different groups were treated differently (disparate treatment), the analysis examines whether the eligibility criteria themselves have a disparate impact by protected group status.[17]

---

[15]For example, some groups of employees may be eligible for profit sharing based on job function, level of responsibility within the organization, and so on, whereas other groups are not. In most cases, if employees have been grouped appropriately for comparison purposes, all members of the group will be eligible for the same kinds of variable pay.

[16]This is essentially an audit of whether the variable pay policy was followed.

[17]Formal statistical tests of disparate impact are presented in detail in Chapter 6.

Total Compensation

Because total compensation is the summation of all types of pay earned by an employee, its examination includes the peculiarities and pitfalls mentioned for base pay, overtime earnings, and variable pay. There is one additional point that should be made. Because total compensation is made up of various elements, it is possible that inequities in any given type of pay can be masked in an examination of total compensation.

For example, assume that the total compensation for a given group of similarly situated employees consists only of base pay and overtime earnings, and all employees in this grouping are identical on all characteristics (e.g., education, seniority, time in job, and so forth) and that the only difference within this group is the race of the employee. Further assume that Table 4-4 represents base pay, overtime earnings, and total compensation for the employees in this grouping.

Table 4-4. Hypothetical Base Pay, Overtime Pay, and Total Compensation

ID#	Race	Base Pay ($)	Overtime Pay ($)	Total Compensation ($)
029959	W	68,000	3,000	71,000
419341	W	68,000	2,800	70,800
528251	NW	64,000	7,000	71,000
611475	W	68,000	3,500	71,500
716604	NW	64,000	6,800	70,800
980528	NW	64,000	7,500	71,500

A statistical review of total compensation indicates that there is zero differential by race. If, however, base pay is examined, there is a statistically significant differential by race of $4,000; the base pay rate of nonwhites is $4,000 less than the base pay rate of whites. There is also a statistically significant differential by race of $4,000 in overtime earnings; the overtime earnings of nonwhites are $4,000 greater than the overtime earnings of whites.

In this example, the differentials in base pay and overtime earnings cancel each other out when total compensation is examined. When looking only at the results of the total compensation analysis, one would infer that there are no equity problems by race. The opposite conclusion would be arrived at through an examination of base pay rates.

Because of just this type of occurrence, it is generally preferable to examine individual components of pay—or at a minimum, base pay—along with total compensation. Aggregating compensation to its highest levels can mask potential problems in its individual components. Only by examining the constituent pieces of total compensation in isolation will these potential problems be uncovered.

Rates vs. Raises

The question of whether to examine pay rates or pay raises is interesting. There is value in both; the selection of rates or raises is dependent on the questions addressed by the analysis and what the researcher hopes to learn from the results. If one is interested in examining whether annual base salary increases are granted equitably, then raises would be the appropriate compensation metric for analysis. If, on the other hand, the question to be addressed is whether base salaries of newly hired employees are set in a nondiscriminatory fashion, an examination of raises would be inappropriate; pay rates would be the appropriate compensation metric to examine.

It should be noted, however, that the results of a statistical review of raises does not provide any information about underlying compensation levels and vice versa. In fact, evaluating compensation solely in terms of raises may mask problems of internal pay equity.

For example, assume that within a given similarly situated employee grouping, employees differ only by gender and current year's performance evaluation rating and are identical on all other characteristics (e.g., past performance, education, seniority, time in job, and so forth). Further assume that Table 4-5 represents salary, performance rating, and raise information for this group of similarly situated employees:

Table 4-5. Hypothetical Salaries, Performance Ratings, and Raises

ID#	Sex	Old Salary ($)	New Salary ($)	Performance	Raise (%)
3070	M	56,000	57,680	8	3.0
5189	M	56,000	57,960	10	3.5
5563	F	45,000	46,575	10	3.5
5862	F	45,000	46,350	8	3.0
7743	F	45,000	46,575	10	3.5
9313	M	56,000	57,960	10	3.5

A statistical review of the raises indicates that there is no disparity by gender. The annual percentage increases for men and women in this similarly situated employee grouping were awarded equitably and reflected differences in performance evaluation rating: those rated 10 received a 3.5% increase and those rated 8 received a 3.0% increase, regardless of gender. Based on an analysis of annual percentage increases, one would infer that no gender discrimination exists.

However, an examination of annual salaries—whether "old" salaries before the raise or "new" salaries after it—reveals disparities by gender. The male salary was $56,000, and the female salary was $45,000. Because these employees differ only by gender and are identical on all other relevant characteristics, one would infer that gender discrimination may be present. If raises were the only metrics examined, then differences in salaries by gender would go undetected.

Factors Explaining Compensation

To examine the chosen compensation metric for internal equity, it is important to account for legitimate, nondiscriminatory factors affecting compensation. Only by incorporating those factors into the model and accounting for their effect on pay can we begin to explore questions of potential internal inequity.[18]

Within the context of a compensation review, the task at hand is to identify factors that explain why similarly situated employees are paid differently. For example, assume that we are interested in examining a similarly situated employee grouping defined as all bookkeeping, accounting, and auditing clerks within the company. Even though these employees are similarly situated (they perform similar work and occupy positions that require similar skills and qualifications and have similar responsibility levels), we would not expect the annual salary, for example, to be identical for all employees within the grouping. Some employees will earn more, and some will earn less, based on legitimate nondiscriminatory factors. Some factors relate to the employee's stock of human capital.

Human Capital

The conventional theory of labor markets says that an individual's wage is based on his or her human capital stock and reflects personal productivity.[19] *Human capital stock* is the stock of knowledge, skills, aptitudes, education, and training that an individual possesses.[20] In broad terms, human capital is the knowledge and characteristics a worker possesses that contribute to his productivity.

---

[18]For a review of why this is so, readers are referred to the example laid out in Table 3-1.

[19]Thomas Hyclak, Geraint Johnes, and Robert James Thornton, *Fundamentals of Labor Economics* (Cengage South-Western, 2005).

[20]Note that training is separate and apart from education. Training is the component of human capital that workers acquire after schooling. It is often associated with some set of skills useful for a particular industry or with a particular set of technologies.

Typically, differences in earnings between similarly situated employees are at least partly explained by differences in human capital. Differences in educational attainment, professional certifications, and licenses may account for variation in earnings among similarly situated employees. Within the similarly situated employee grouping defined as all bookkeeping, accounting, and auditing clerks, those with Certified Public Accountant designations may earn more than those without it. Those employees with payroll or tax certifications may earn more than those who do not possess these certifications.

Differences in training and skills acquired on the job may also account for variations in earnings among similarly situated employees. It is not uncommon for workers who are newly hired or promoted into a position to earn less than those who have years of experience in that job. Similarly, an employee who has no prior experience may be hired at a pay rate lower than that of a person hired into the same job at the same time who has years of prior relevant experience. Common measures of training used by employers include number of years of relevant prior experience, time in job, length of service, seniority, and completion of company-sponsored training and development programs.

Other factors contributing to differences in compensation among similarly situated employees may directly reflect productivity. For example, performance ratings are frequently used as part of the pay-setting process. Generally speaking, more productive employees receive better performance evaluations and higher performance ratings. This, in turn, typically translates into higher earnings.[21]

The factors explaining differences in compensation within each similarly situated employee grouping are likely to differ across groupings and may differ across employers. For example, within the bookkeeping, accounting, and auditing clerks grouping, possession of a CPA license or payroll or tax certification may lead to greater earnings. Within a similarly situated employee grouping defined as all outside salespersons, possession of a CPA license or payroll or tax certification is likely to have no bearing on compensation.[22] Similarly, the number of patents held by an individual within a similarly situated employee grouping of engineers may partly explain differences in earnings within the group. Within the outside salespersons grouping, compensation is unlikely to be influenced by the number of patents held.

---

[21] In some cases, performance ratings can be a tainted variable. Plaintiffs often contend that although their pay rates reflect their lower performance ratings, they were rated lower on performance because of discrimination. Tainted variables are discussed in detail in the next section.

[22] In certain circumstances, such as sales of accounting, bookkeeping and auditing products or services, possession of a CPA license or payroll or tax certification could have an impact on compensation.

Because the legitimate, nondiscriminatory factors that explain differences in compensation are likely to vary across similarly situated employee groupings, a thorough understanding of the relevant compensation policies and practices is critical. Without this understanding, it will be extremely difficult to identify which factors should be included in the model specification for a given group of similarly situated employees.

Tainted Variables

When identifying the legitimate, nondiscriminatory factors that explain differences within similarly situated employee groupings, consideration should be given to the possibility that the variable may be tainted. Courts have labeled certain explanatory factors tainted if they are contaminated in some fashion by an employer's discriminatory actions.[23] Examples of explanatory variables that courts have found to be tainted include academic rank, disciplinary history, marital status, and part-time work assignment.[24]

Ramona Paetzhold and Steven Willborn provide the following example of a tainted variable:

> *Academic rank could be considered tainted if a university is believed to set different standards for awarding rank to males than to females. If academic rank were to be used in a compensation equation for that university, some of any sex-based differences in compensation may be reflected in the rank variable instead, so that the coefficient of the sex variable would underestimate the degree of discrimination in compensation.*[25]

Tainted variables can pose substantial difficulty for detecting the presence or absence of discrimination using multiple regression analysis. The coefficient associated with the tainted variable may contain some of the discrimination

---

[23]Generally speaking, courts question the inclusion of a tainted variable in a regression model of pay only if it is subject to some degree of employer discretion in its measurement or use.

[24]According to Paetzhold and Willborn, courts have not appropriately viewed tainted variables. They argue that "tainted variables are often highly important proxies of productivity or performance that contribute significantly to the explanation of salary or wages. Because the adequacy of the regression equation and the reliability of the inferences based on it depend, in part, on the completeness of the model, it is important not to exclude key predictor variables. It is our position that tainted variable should not be routinely excluded from the regression equation. Instead, the effects of the inclusion of a tainted variable must be assessed and minimized." Ramona Paetzhold and Steven Willborn, *The Statistics of Discrimination: Using Statistical Evidence in Discrimination Cases* (West Publishing, 2011–2012), 298–300.

[25]Ibid., p. 299.

against the protected class. Because of this, the coefficient associated with protected class status will likely underestimate the degree of discrimination. In this case, examining only the protected class status variable could result in an incorrect inference regarding the presence or absence of discrimination.

It should be noted that a variable found to be tainted in one circumstance is not necessarily tainted in another. In the foregoing example, the fact that one employer used different standards for awarding academic rank to men and women does not automatically imply that *every* employer will do so. A given explanatory variable is not inherently tainted; it *becomes* tainted when it is infected by an employer's discriminatory actions.

Dummy Variables

Many of the factors explaining compensation are continuous variables.[26] For example, time in job is an example of a continuous variable. It can take on different values (e.g., 0.0 years, 0.1 years, 0.2 years, 0.3 years) along the continuum of a person's career. Other factors, however, are discrete and take on two or more distinct values.[27] For example, a person can possess a CPA designation, or he can possess no CPA designation. It is not possible to "half-possess" a CPA designation.

In cases where discrete factors are included into the equation describing compensation, they are typically incorporated through the use of dummy variables. A *dummy variable* can be used to express a "yes/no" condition. The possession of a CPA designation could be incorporated into the compensation equation by using a dummy variable named *CPA*.[28] This *CPA* variable would take on a value of 1 if the individual held a CPA designation and would take on a value of 0 if he or she did not.[29]

---

[26]A variable is said to be *continuous* if it can take on any value along a continuum. Age is an example of a continuous variable. An individual can be 18.0 years old, 18.2 years old, 18.7 years old, 19.0 years old, and so on.

[27]A variable is said to be *discrete* if it can take on a value from a set of distinct integers. For example, the number of children in a family is a discrete number. It is possible to have 1 child in a family or 2 children in a family, but it is not possible to have 1.5 children in a family.

[28]Dummy variables can be named whatever the researcher wishes. Typically, a name is chosen that is related to the factor being measured for convenience and ease of use.

[29]The values in this example could be reversed. There is no reason that a value of 1 has to be associated with possession of the CPA designation. A value of 0 could just as easily be associated with possession of the CPA designation. The point is, in cases of a "yes/no" condition, whatever value is assigned to the "yes" condition cannot be assigned to the "no" condition.

Dummy variables are particularly useful in expressing protected group status. Protected group status is essentially a yes/no condition. An employee is either a member of the protected group or a member of the nonprotected group; he cannot simultaneously be a member of both groups. The use of a dummy variable representing protected class status allows this status to be incorporated directly into the compensation equation.[30]

Dummy variables can also be used to express categorization of employees by discrete factors. Assume, for example, that an employee's educational attainment is a determinant of her compensation. Within a group of similarly situated employees, the educational attainment of those employees ranges from a high school diploma to a bachelor's degree, as shown in Table 4-6.

Table 4-6. Hypothetical Educational Attainment

ID #	Education Level
107-A	High school
112-A	Bachelor
126-A	Associate
134-A	High school
141-A	Bachelor

Educational attainment can be incorporated into the compensation equation through the use of dummy variables. A yes/no condition can be created for each of the unique values of the highest level of education achieved:

- Is a high school diploma the highest level of education completed by this employee?

- Is an associate's degree the highest level of education completed by this employee?

- Is a bachelor's degree the highest level of education completed by this employee?

Then, a dummy variable is created for each of the yes/no conditions, as shown in Figure 4-1.

---

[30]This point is discussed in detail in Chapter 5.

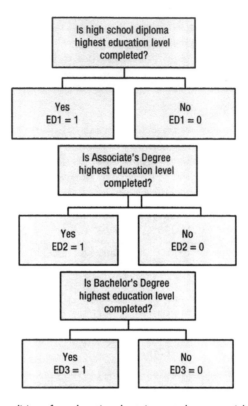

Figure 4-1. Yes/no conditions for educational attainment dummy variables

Because the yes/no conditions regarding educational attainment in this example are mutually exclusive, no employee can have more than one yes (coded as 1) value.

These yes/no conditions are used to create dummy variables ED1, ED2, and ED3 for maximum educational attainment. Table 4-7 shows the values each of these dummy variables takes for these five employees.

Table 4-7. Assignment of Dummy Variable Values by Educational Attainment

ID #	Education Level	ED1	ED2	ED3
107-A	High school	1	0	0
112-A	Bachelor	0	0	1
126-A	Associate	0	1	0
134-A	High school	1	0	0
141-A	Bachelor	0	0	1

This educational attainment example can be used to highlight a common mistake associated with the use of dummy variables. Less experienced practitioners may be tempted to create one dummy variable for educational attainment and assign values to it based on the array of unique values of the highest level of education achieved. For example, a value of 1 would be assigned to high school diploma, a value of 2 would be assigned to associate's degree, and a value of 3 would be assigned to bachelor's degree, as shown in Table 4-8.

Table 4-8. Incorrect Use of Dummy Variables

ID #	Education Level	ED
107-A	High school	1
112-A	Bachelor	3
126-A	Associate	2
134-A	High school	1
141-A	Bachelor	3

Assigning values in this manner makes the implicit assumption that the difference (in this case, in compensation) between those who earned a high school diploma and those who earned an associate's degree is the same as the difference between those who earned an associate's degree and those who earned a bachelor's degree. This is implicitly assumed because the mathematical difference between 1 and 2 and the mathematical difference between 2 and 3 is exactly equal.[31]

To see the effect on the regression analysis and associated results, consider the following example. Assume that the hourly pay rate for this group of employees is given in Table 4-9.

Table 4-9. Hourly Pay Rates

ID #	Education Level	Hourly Pay Rate ($)
107-A	High school	10.00
112-A	Bachelor	25.00
126-A	Associate	15.00
134-A	High school	10.00
141-A	Bachelor	25.00

In Table 4-9, we can see that the difference in hourly pay rates between individuals holding a high school diploma and an associate's degree is $5 per hour

---

[31] $(2 - 1) = 1$ and $(3 - 2) = 1$.

($10 versus $15); the difference in hourly pay rates between individuals holding an associate's degree and a bachelor's degree is $10 ($15 versus $25).

If dummy variables for educational attainment were assigned as in Table 4-8, and assuming these five employees were identical with respect to all other explanatory variables in the model, the estimated effect of "more" education (e.g., high school diploma compared to associate's degree and associate's degree compared to bachelor's degree) would be $7.50 per hour; the estimated intercept of this equation is $2.00 per hour.

Table 4-10 provides a comparison between actual hourly pay rates and predicted hourly pay rates based on the estimated effect of educational attainment at $7.50 per hour and an estimated intercept of $2.00 per hour.

Table 4-10. Estimated Hourly Pay Rates Using Incorrect Dummy Variables

ID #	Education Level	Hourly Pay Rate ($) Actual	Estimated	Difference
107-A	High school	10.00	9.50	(0.50)
112-A	Bachelor	25.00	24.50	(0.50)
126-A	Associate	15.00	17.00	2.00
134-A	High school	10.00	9.50	(0.50)
141-A	Bachelor	25.00	24.50	(0.50)

As can be seen from Table 4-10, the model underestimates the hourly pay rates for those employees holding high school diplomas and bachelor's degrees and overestimates the hourly pay rates for those holding an associate's degree.

The inaccurate estimation of hourly rates of pay in this example is completely attributable to the way the dummy variable was created and used. Because only one dummy variable was used and took on values of 1, 2, and 3 for the three levels of educational attainment, the regression model forced the difference in educational attainment to be the same across all levels of education.[32]

If educational attainment was incorporated into the compensation model as given in Table 4-5, and assuming that these five employees were identical with respect to other explanatory variables in the model, the intercept of the model is $10 per hour. The estimated effect of having earned an associate's degree is $5, and the estimated effect of having earned a bachelor's degree would be $15 per hour. The actual and estimated hourly pay rates for these employees is shown Table 4-11.

---

[32]Again, this is because $(2 - 1) = 1$ and $(3 - 2) = 1$.

Table 4-11. Estimated Hourly Pay Rates Using Correct Dummy Variables

ID #	Education Level	Hourly Pay Rate ($)		Difference ($)
		Actual	Estimated	
107-A	High school	10.00	10.00	0.00
112-A	Bachelor	25.00	25.00	0.00
126-A	Associate	15.00	15.00	0.00
134-A	High school	10.00	10.00	0.00
141-A	Bachelor	25.00	25.00	0.00

As can be seen from Table 4-11, the actual and estimated hourly pay rates are identical. Because multiple dummy variables were used to express education in a series of yes/no conditions, the effect of educational attainment on compensation was not constrained to be equal across all educational attainment levels.

One final point regarding dummy variables should be kept in mind. In cases where multiple dummy variables are created for a series of yes/no conditions, as in the educational attainment example, inclusion of *all* of those variables creates collinearity. As noted in Chapter 3, the fourth assumption of the classical linear regression model is that no exact linear relationship exists between two or more independent variables. If ED1, ED2, and ED3 were all included in the model, the fourth assumption would be violated, because:

$$ED1 + ED2 + ED3 = 1 \qquad (4.1)$$

This situation is easily remedied by dropping one of the three dummy variables from the model. In the example shown in Table 4-9, only ED2 (possession of an associate's degree) and ED3 (possession of a bachelor's degree) were included in the model; ED1 (possession of a high school diploma) was omitted to prevent collinearity. The model that was estimated generated the following results:

$$Hourly\ pay\ rate = \$10 + \$5\ (ED2) + \$15\ (ED3) \qquad (4.2)$$

In this example, those employees whose highest educational attainment was a high school diploma are said to be the reference group.[33] In terms of interpretation of the regression output, all estimated coefficients are relative to the reference group. Thus, the hourly pay rate of the reference group—those individuals with high school diplomas—is equal to the intercept of the equation: $10. The hourly pay rate of those individuals possessing associate's degrees is

---

[33] The *reference group* is defined as those individuals satisfying (i.e., those for whom the answer is "yes") the yes/no condition expressed by the dummy variable omitted from the model.

$5 per hour more than the reference group: $10 + $5 = $15. The hourly pay rate of those individuals possessing bachelor's degrees is $15 per hour more than the reference group: $10 + $15 = $25.

Dummy variables can be a very useful way to incorporate discrete variables and qualitative information into a model of compensation. However, as evidenced by the preceding discussion, care should be exercised in how those dummy variables are structured and the values assigned to them.

Data Measurability

Some of the factors explaining differences in compensation among similarly situated employees will be easy to measure and quantify. For example, company seniority may be maintained directly in an organization's human resources database. In other cases, it can be calculated using each employee's date of hire, a data point that is commonly maintained in HR databases.[34] In cases such as this, the factor is measured directly in the database itself and can be extracted for all similarly situated employees in the grouping.

Unfortunately, not all factors explaining differences in compensation among similarly situated employees can be measured directly. In these cases, measurement poses a difficulty. This difficulty is most commonly caused by data limitations. The employer may not maintain comprehensive information on the factor in its HR database, or the information may not be captured in a machine-readable format.[35] In other cases, the factor itself may be difficult to quantify. In these cases, proxy variables are often used.

Proxy variables are substituted for the original variable that is difficult to quantify or measure. A good proxy variable is easily measurable and is highly correlated with the factor for which it is being substituted. In some cases, a good proxy variable will be easily identifiable. In other cases, a good proxy variable may be difficult to identify.

For example, prior relevant work experience may be a critical factor in explaining differences in compensation within a similarly situated employee grouping. If information on prior relevant work experience is not quantified in a machine-readable format within an organization's HR database, a proxy

---

[34]In some cases, seniority is simple to calculate; it is the number of years between the current date and the employee's date of hire. The calculation becomes more complex in cases of breaks in service. For example, layoff and recall situations can complicate the calculation of seniority. An employee who is laid off and later recalled to work may or may not accrue seniority during the layoff period. Interruptions in service are not uncommon, and how those breaks in service are factored into each employee's calculation of seniority depends on the particular policies of each employer.

[35]These situations will be discussed in detail in a subsequent subsection of this chapter.

variable may be used. A commonly chosen proxy variable for prior relevant work experience is age at hire.

Age at hire may, on its surface, appear to be a good proxy for prior relevant work experience. Age is hire is easily measurable. It is calculated simply as the difference between an employee's date of hire and that employee's date of birth. Dates of birth and dates of hire are nearly universally maintained in an organization's human resources databases. Further, one would expect that age at hire would be correlated with prior relevant work experience— "older" workers typically have more prior experience than "younger" workers because they have spent more time participating in the labor force.

However, a number of assumptions are made when age at hire is used as a proxy for prior relevant work experience: all individuals in the grouping of similarly situated employees (1) began their education at the same age, (2) completed their education at the same age, (3) entered the labor force at the same age, (4) have been accruing the same level and amount of relevant experience since entering the labor force, and (5) have been participating in the labor force continuously since entry.

The assumptions regarding educational trajectories may pose potential problems, depending on the particular grouping of employees. It may not be unreasonable to assume that all employees started their education at the same age.[36] It may be unreasonable, however, to assume that all of them completed their education at the same age, particularly if differences in educational attainment are not controlled for separately in the model of compensation.[37]

It may also be unreasonable to assume that all employees entered the workforce at the same age. Differences in educational attainment aside, not everyone shares the same education-to-employment trajectory. Among those with bachelor's degrees, for example, some may complete high school at age eighteen, immediately enroll in college and earn a bachelor's degree at age twenty-two, and immediately enter the labor force. Some people may not immediately enroll in college after high school, instead choosing military service or entrance into the workforce before enrolling in college. This would, of course, delay their entrance into the labor force on completion of a bachelor's degree. Others may choose to delay entrance into the workforce after earning a bachelor's degree,

---

[36]In the United States, children typically begin school at the age of five. Some children may start a few months before their fifth birthday, and others may start a few months after. Generally speaking, these variations do not pose a substantial problem.

[37]If, for example, educational attainment was not explicitly included as an explanatory factor in the model of compensation, and educational attainment varied among employees in the grouping, age at hire would implicitly assume that the number of years spent earning a high school diploma and the number of years spent earning a bachelor's degree were identical. This is clearly an unrealistic assumption.

spending time traveling, exploring opportunities, and so on. Using age at hire as a proxy ignores these possibilities, leading to an inaccurate measurement of prior relevant work experience.

Even so, the experience gained in prior employment may not reflect *relevant* work experience. A person may change from one job to another and have completely different functional responsibilities or may change occupation, industry, and so on. The training and on-the-job skills acquired prior to the change may not be relevant to the current employment. Training and skills acquired through practical experience are not necessarily transferable to a new job, occupation, industry, and so on. If the skill sets and human capital requirements differ substantially between prior and current employment, then the use of age at hire as a proxy is likely to overstate actual prior relevant work experience.

The assumption that all individuals have been participating in the labor force continuously is likely to be inaccurate. Individuals routinely experience periods of absence from the labor force for reasons such as their own or a family member's illness or injury, personal or family obligations, maternity or paternity leave, child care issues, civic or military duty, and so forth. The use of age at hire as a proxy for prior relevant work experience does not and in fact cannot account for periods of absence from the labor force for any of these reasons. As such, age at hire is likely to overstate actual prior relevant experience for some individuals.[38]

As can be seen from this example, the use of proxy variables can introduce biases into the analysis. Caution should be exercised when using proxy variables, and careful consideration should be given to their choice, as they can have a considerable effect on the results of the statistical analysis and inferences drawn from it.

Accessibility of Data

Related to data measurability is the issue of data accessibility. As previously mentioned, difficulty in measurement of the factors explaining compensation is most commonly caused by data limitations. The employer may not maintain comprehensive information on the factor, or the information may not be captured in a machine-readable format.

---

[38]Perhaps of greater importance to the issue of internal pay equity is the fact that use of age at hire as a proxy for prior relevant work experience can introduce a gender bias into the compensation model. Women typically experience greater periods of absence from the labor force than do their male counterparts. Because age at hire cannot account for periods of absence, its use as a proxy may lead to a disproportionate overstatement of prior relevant work experience for women, introducing gender bias. This point is discussed in more detail in Chapter 9.

For example, assume that an employer is interested in examining its initial pay-setting practices to assess internal pay equity among newly hired employees. One of the factors influencing a newly hired employee's initial pay is salary history in previous employment. Assume that information regarding a candidate's salary history is captured only at the interview stage, in the form of interviewer notes; salary history is not requested or recorded on the job application.

This scenario presents several difficulties. First, this process requires that the notes created by the interviewer regarding the candidate's salary history in previous employment find their way into the candidate's personnel file. Although an employer may have a clearly stated policy mandating that interviewers record information on salary history and place that information into the file, it is always possible that the policy will be violated, perhaps unintentionally. If the notes are not included in the file, the salary history information will be missing, which poses a sizeable difficulty not only for an internal review of pay equity but also for defending the compensation decisions in the event of litigation or regulatory investigation.

The salary history information must be retained and maintained in a manner that allows for easy, on-demand future access. If an organization uses hard-copy personnel files, the interview notes typically would be placed in the file alongside other types of documentation. Retrieval of salary history in the future may involve sifting through the employee's file to find the appropriate documents. Although this is not necessarily resource-intensive or time-consuming for a single employee, the costs involved increase dramatically when salary history information for multiple individuals (e.g., all those within a similarly situated employee grouping) must be found.[39]

Even assuming that the salary history notes are placed appropriately in personnel files and are retrievable on demand, there is still the problem of consistency of information. Some interviewers may collect prior salary history for multiple years, whereas other interviewers may collect only the most recent figures. Some may collect salary history in a very detailed manner (e.g., 2011: $74,560, 2012: $77,925) and others may collect more general information (e.g., 2011: $75K, 2012: $78K).

Differences like these create inconsistencies in the data and can create barriers for performing an analysis of internal pay equity. For example, if some newly hired employees in a given similarly situated grouping have three years of salary history and others have only one, then only one year of salary history can enter into the analysis, because that is the extent of complete data for all newly hired employees within the grouping.

---

[39]This difficulty is compounded if there are multiple storage sites or repositories for information, because efforts between sites or repositories must be coordinated.

Even so, information that is collected and retained in hard copy is not in a machine-readable state. Some kind of data entry to convert the information into an electronic form is required before analysis can proceed. Contrary to popular conceptions, this process requires more than just scanning hard-copy documents into PDF files and using optical character recognition (OCR) to create a database.[40] Data entry processes—even those assisted by the latest technological advances—are time-consuming and very resource-intensive.

Most difficulties with data accessibility can be avoided through the use of a well-designed human resources information system (HRIS). An HRIS system has many advantages; they allow for standardized collection of information in a centralized repository. The information is maintained in an electronic format that can easily be searched via queries, which greatly facilitates on-demand information retrieval. Electronic retention of information also reduces storage costs associated with maintaining hard-copy files. Finally, an HRIS system retains data in an electronic format which, generally speaking, can be exported directly to a data file that can easily be read by commercially available statistical software. This can greatly reduce, if not completely eliminate, the need for costly data entry.

There is one additional issue with respect to the availability of data that should be discussed: availability of historical information. It is important that an employee's entire history, from earliest date of hire to the present (or, if applicable, to the most recent date of termination), is maintained. Overwriting historical values with current values or otherwise failing to preserve historical employment information in the organization's HRIS system can be extremely problematic, particularly for internal pay equity analyses. To see this, consider the following example.

Assume that a company is engaging in a multiyear retrospective equity review of the annual salaries of a similarly situated employee grouping containing program managers in a given geographic location. The retrospective review will encompass three years and examine pay rates as of April 1 of 2011, 2012, and 2013. Further assume that program managers' annual salaries are based on (among other factors) company seniority and time in job.

---

[40]Although advances in optical character recognition in recent years have been substantial, in most cases one cannot simply rely on OCR software to create a machine-readable database from PDF files. Layouts may differ from page to page, print quality and resolution may differ, some portions of the documents may be unreadable, and so on. It is necessary to verify that the OCR software has accurately captured the data, and fill in any data points missed by the software manually, if possible.

Since the time period encompassed by the analysis is April 1, 2011 through April 1, 2013, one might think that extracting all records for a given employee falling within this time period from the HRIS system would be sufficient. The data from such an extraction for one employee—ID # 4746—is shown in Table 4-12.

Table 4-12. Hypothetical Employment History Information 4/1/2011 through 4/1/2013

ID #	DOH	Eff. Date	ACT	RSN	TTL	Rate ($)
4746	06/01/2007	4/1/2011	PAY	MER	Pgm Mgr	50,184
4746	06/01/2007	4/1/2012	PAY	MER	Pgm Mgr	51,439
4746	06/01/2007	4/1/2013	PAY	MER	Pgm Mgr	52,982

As can be seen, these data provide the annual salaries of this employee for the time period in question. Because these data also contain the employee's date of hire, his company seniority can be calculated. It should be noted that this calculation assumes he had no leaves of absence during the June 1, 2007 to April 1, 2013 time period. We know with certainty that there were no periods of absence from April 1, 2011 through April 1, 2013, because there are no entries in the HRIS reflecting periods of absence. We do not know, however, whether there were any periods of absence from this employee's date of hire prior to April 1, 2011, because no HRIS information for this time period was extracted. A calculation of company seniority based solely on the information contained in this data set might not be accurate.

Time in job is one of the factors that determine an individual's annual salary. The data set shown in Table 4-12 does not contain sufficient information to calculate this person's time in job. Thus, it is not possible to determine when this employee commenced employment as a program manager. We know that it was prior to April 1, 2011, but the data set provides no further information. Without knowing this piece of information, there is no way to assess this individual's salary against his comparators accounting for all relevant factors determining annual salary.[41]

Table 4-13 presents this worker's complete employment history with the organization and provides the information required to properly calculate company seniority and time in job.

---

[41]If this person was the only one (or one of only a few employees) for whom time in job could not be calculated, one alternative is to omit him (or the small group) from the analysis. If time in job information is missing for a sufficient number of employees, the alternative may be to omit time in job as an explanatory factor from the model. Neither situation is ideal.

Table 4-13. Hypothetical Employment History Information (Complete)

ID #	DOH	Eff. Date	ACT	RSN	TTL	Rate ($)
4746	6/1/2007	6/1/2007	HIR	HIR	Pgm Analyst	35,000
4746	6/1/2007	4/1/2008	PAY	MER	Pgm Analyst	35,700
4746	6/1/2007	3/15/2009	PRO	PRO	Pgm Mgr	48,000
4746	6/1/2007	4/1/2010	PAY	MER	Pgm Mgr	48,960
4746	6/1/2007	4/1/2011	PAY	MER	Pgm Mgr	50,184
4746	6/1/2007	4/1/2012	PAY	MER	Pgm Mgr	51,439
4746	6/1/2007	4/1/2013	PAY	MER	Pgm Mgr	52,982

The data set shown in Table 4-12 is said to be *truncated*; it does not encompass *all* records for the employee contained in the HRIS system from the employee's earliest hire date to the current date.[42] Only a portion of the records—those whose effective dates fall within the April 1, 2011 to April 1, 2013 time period—have been extracted. Because of this, the data extraction does not provide all of the information necessary to complete the multi-year retrospective equity review of the annual salaries for this similarly situated employee grouping.

It is critical that a comprehensive, "cradle to grave" data set be provided that encompasses the entire employment histories of all employees within the similarly situated grouping. Failure to provide this comprehensive data set may prevent an accurate and complete analysis of internal pay equity.

Data Collection and Assembly

After assessing the measurability of the factors determining compensation and resolving any difficulties with the accessibility of these data points, data collection and assembly can proceed.

The goal for collecting and assembling data is to construct an employee-level data set that captures all information relevant to the compensation decision-making process for each person in the study population. The relevant information and data points will be defined by the factors that determine compensation within each similarly situated employee grouping.

---

[42]A data set encompassing all records for employees from earliest hire date through the current date is often referred to or characterized as a "cradle to grave" data set.

The way data collection and assembly will proceed depends on the information systems of the organization. If the organization maintains its HR and compensation information in an electronic database, then a query should be carefully constructed to extract the relevant information for the relevant employees. When constructing the query, ensure that all relevant job codes, departments, divisions, and so on are included so that all information for all individuals in the study population is captured.

Extracting all relevant information about each employee in each of the similarly situated employee groupings contained in the study population in the same query allows the creation of one comprehensive data set. If required information is missing from the initial query, if relevant job codes are inadvertently missing from the initial query, and so on, it will be necessary to either reextract all information or create a supplemental file that will then have to be appended to the original file. This can be a costly process, in terms of both financial cost and time. It also introduces the opportunity for mistakes to be made when appending supplemental files to the original. Take the time to formulate a complete and comprehensive query for extracting all relevant information for all relevant employees in one file.

If the organization does not maintain its HR and compensation information in an electronic database, it will be necessary to assemble the required information by hand; all of the foregoing guidelines hold for manual assembly of data. When manually constructing the data set for the compensation review, the financial cost and time required to repair an inaccurate or incomplete file is substantially increased. Ensure that all relevant information for all relevant employees is captured in the initial file construction.

Data Cleaning and Verification

Prior to performing the statistical analysis, the data sets must be cleaned and reviewed for gaps and missing data. All problems should be identified, and if possible, corrected. If, for example, the compensation rates for a given grouping of similarly situated employees contains a mixture of hourly rates and annual salary figures, it is necessary to convert the hourly rates to annual salaries or vice versa (refer to Table 4-2). Adjustments to full-time equivalents may be necessary if the standard number of hours per day or per week differs across employees (refer to Table 4-3). The point here is that the data should be internally consistent among employee groupings. It is not problematic from a statistical point of view to express compensation in terms of an hourly rate for some employee groupings and in terms of an annual salary amount for other employee groupings. The key here is consistency *within* groupings, because the groupings serve as the unit of analysis for the multiple regression analysis.

If there are any gaps in the data that can be filled, the additional data should be collected and integrated into the data set. For example, if date of birth is missing for some employees, and age at hire is to be used in the multiple regression analysis, the missing date of birth information should be collected and integrated. Entering 0 for those individuals with missing dates of birth can potentially have a strong impact on the estimated effect of age at hire on compensation.

If the gaps are sufficiently large and/or are unable to be filled, and no suitable proxy variable exists, it may be necessary to remove that factor from the analysis.

Aside from ensuring a correct and comprehensive data set for the compensation review, examining gaps in data can provide valuable insight into the organization's processes and procedures for data capture and retention. Missing pieces of information for one or two employees is probably not indicative of a larger problem. If the same piece of information is missing for many employees, however, this could be an indication of a systemic problem in the data capture and retention process. Systemic data gaps should be investigated and any deficiencies in data processes should be corrected so that future problems can be avoided.

Regression Models of Equal Pay

Since 1975 multiple regression analysis has been the preferred statistical technique for identifying compensation discrimination based on protected class status.[1] This technique is used by plaintiffs and defendants to demonstrate discrimination (or lack thereof), and was approved by the U.S. Supreme Court for analysis of pay discrimination in 1986.[2]

Traditional models for examining equal pay generally fall into the two forms suggested in the *Harvard Law Review.*[3]

---

[1]Note: "Beyond the Prima Facie Case in Employment Discrimination Law: Statistical Proof and Rebuttal," *Harvard Law Review* 89 (1975), 387–422, is credited as being the first scholarly work to address the statistical analysis of compensation discrimination.

[2]Bazemore v. Friday, 478 U.S. 385, 106 S. Ct. 3000, 92 L. Ed. 2d 315, 32 Ed. Law Rep. 1223, 41 Fair Empl. Prac. Cas. (BNA) 92, 40 Empl. Prac. Dec. (CCH) 36199, 4 Fed. R. Serv. 3d 1259 (1986).

[3]"Note: Beyond the Prima Facie Case in Employment Discrimination Law."

1. The classic model: Regressing the dependent variable (some measure of compensation) on legitimate, non-discriminatory factors and a dummy variable for protected status.

2. The separate equations model: Separating the sample into protected and nonprotected groups and then regressing the dependent variable (some measure of compensation) on legitimate, nondiscriminatory factors (excluding a dummy variable for protected status) for each of the two groups.

These two model structures are based on different underlying assumptions and lead to different kinds of inferences regarding the relationship between compensation and protected group status.

As will be discussed later, both approaches have distinct advantages and disadvantages. Researchers have proposed a third model structure that capitalizes on the advantages of the classical and separate equations approaches, referred to as an *interaction model*. The aim of the interaction model is to leverage the advantages of the classical and separate equations structures while reducing the impact of their disadvantages.

All three model structures classify individuals within the similarly situated employee grouping on the basis of protected group status. Although this is useful for assessing discrimination on the basis of protected group status, these structures are not ideal for assessing overall equity. Assessing whether similarly situated white males, for example, are paid equitably is better achieved through an alternate model structure in which protected group effects are not directly estimated. One such alternate model structure is referred to as the *overall equity* model.

The Classical Model

The classical model is the most commonly used structure for examining the relationship between protected group status and compensation. This is due largely to the fact that it is easy to understand conceptually, the calculations involved are simple, and the interpretation of results generated is straightforward.

The purpose of the classical model is to directly estimate the effect of protected group status on compensation, controlling for other relevant explanatory factors. Direct estimation of the protected group effect is achieved by including a dummy variable representing protected group status.[4]

---

[4]A detailed discussion of dummy variables is provided in Chapter 4.

Formally, the classical model of pay equity takes the following structure:

$$Y_i = \beta_0 + \beta_1 X_{1i} + \beta_2 X_{2i} + \ldots + \beta_k X_{ki} + \beta_{k+1} DI_i + \varepsilon_i \qquad (5.1)$$

where

k = number of independent variables

β_k = *kth* coefficient

β_{k+1} = coefficient associated with DI

X_{ki} = *ith* observation of the *kth* independent variable

DI_i = *ith* observation of the protected status dummy variable

ε_i = error term

This structure expresses compensation as a function of its determinants (seniority, time in job, education, prior relevant work experience, performance ratings, etc.) and whether the employee is a member of the protected group. The estimated coefficient of protected group status reflects the effect of protected group status after accounting for the effects of all the determinants of compensation. Because of this, the classical model directly estimates the effect of protected group status on compensation. This, in turn, means that the estimated protected group effect can be directly tested for statistical significance.

The classical model of pay equity contains several inherent assumptions. Just as for the classical linear regression model, we assume the following:[5]

1. The dependent variable (compensation) can be calculated as a linear function of a specific set of independent variables and an error term;

2. The error term has zero expected value for all observations;

3. Errors have constant variance for all observations and are not correlated;

4. No exact linear relationship exists between two or more independent variables; and

5. The independent variables are nonstochastic (i.e., can be considered fixed in repeated sampling).

Within the context of the classical model of pay equity, the error variances for the protected and nonprotected groups is assumed to be equal. This is

---

[5]A detailed discussion of the assumptions of the classical linear regression model is provided in Chapter 3.

an important assumption. Essentially, this means that the effects of the factors explaining compensation are constant across protected group status. If a one-year increase in seniority, for example, leads to a $2,000 increase in annual salary, this model structure assumes that this one-year-to-$2,000 relationship is identical for protected and nonprotected employees.

Herein lies the main disadvantage of this model structure. Because of this assumption, the classical model of pay equity cannot detect cases of discrimination in which the factors explaining compensation contribute differently to the compensation of different protected groups.

For example, it could be the case that an additional year of seniority leads to a $2,300 increase in annual salary for whites but only a $1,800 increase in annual salary for nonwhites as a result of discrimination. In essence, the classical model would combine these two effects across protected group status and generate an average effect for all employees, irrespective of protected group status. This would mask the discrimination created by providing larger increases for whites for additional years of seniority. Because of its underlying assumptions, the classical model structure cannot detect this type of compensation discrimination.

To see how the classical model of pay equity is applied, consider the following example. Assume that we are interested in examining whether there are differences in annual salary by gender for a similarly situated employee grouping. Within this grouping, there are eight individuals: four women and four men. Annual salaries are determined based on time in job and years of prior relevant experience.

Further assume that salary, gender, time in job, and years of prior relevant experience data for these employees are given in Table 5-1. This table also includes a dummy variable for gender.[6]

Table 5-1. Hypothetical Annual Salary, Time in Job, Prior Experience and Gender

ID #	Sex	Time in Job	Years Prior Exp	Annual Salary ($)	D1
422	M	4.0	5.2	42,000	0
491	M	3.5	4.0	36,000	0
461	F	3.0	3.4	30,000	1
463	F	3.5	3.5	30,000	1
510	M	2.5	3.0	30,000	0
479	M	3.0	2.5	27,000	0
507	F	3.0	1.0	25,000	1
464	F	2.0	0.0	24,000	1

[6]Note that the gender dummy variable is coded 0 for male employees and 1 for female employees.

The classical model structure for this example is provided in Equation 5.2.

$$Salary = \beta_0 + \beta_1 Time\ in\ Job + \beta_2 Yrs\ Prior\ Experience + \beta_3 DI \qquad (5.2)$$

Figure 5-1 provides the regression output when Equation 5.2 is estimated using the data shown in Table 5-1.

```
Dependent Variable                  |      SALARY
N                                   |      8
Adjusted Squared Multiple R         |      0.728
Standard Error of Estimate          |      3,104.194

Regression Coefficients B = (X'X)⁻¹X'Y

Effect      | Coefficient         t           p-Value
------------------------------------------------------------
Constant       18,666,636       2.396         0.075
TIJ             2,069.517       0.579         0.594
EXP             2,274.132       1.496         0.209
D1             -1,857.907       0.677         0.536
```

Figure 5-1. Regression output

As can be seen from Figure 5-1, the classical model of pay equity provides an estimate of the coefficients associated with all of the factors explaining compensation, including DI, the dummy variable for protected group status. The coefficient associated with DI is a direct estimate of the protected group effect. In this example, the protected group effect is the gender effect.

The estimated coefficient associated with DI is –$1,857.907. The interpretation of this coefficient is that there is a gender penalty for women equal to $1,857.907. Because the coefficient is negative, the effect of being female (DI = 1) is $1,857.907 *less* per year. In other words, a comparison of the annual salaries of two employees—one male and one female—with identical time in job and prior relevant work experience would reveal a $1,857.907 difference in favor of the male employee.

However, the gender effect is not statistically significant; the associated probability value of 0.536 indicates that chance is the likely explanation for the observed differences by gender.[7] Thus, we cannot reject the null hypothesis that the true effect of gender on compensation, after controlling for time in

---

[7]Under the generally accepted standard of 95% confidence (assuming a two-tailed test), the threshold for statistical significance is 0.05. Results with associated probability values less than or equal to 0.05 are considered to be statistically significant. Results with associated probability values greater than 0.05 are considered to be statistically insignificant (i.e., not statistically significant).

job and years of prior relevant experience, is zero. We would therefore infer that these compensation decisions are neutral with respect to gender.[8]

Had the estimated coefficient associated with D1 been a positive number, there would be a gender premium. A comparison of the annual salaries of one male and one female employee with identical time in job and prior relevant work experience would reveal a difference in favor of the female employee.

When assessing the magnitude of the protected group effect, it is critical to consider the way the dummy variable(s) representing protected group status was coded. In this example, D1 took on a value of 0 for male employees and a value of 1 for female employees. The equation is therefore measuring the effect of being female; a negative coefficient indicates a female penalty and a positive coefficient indicates a female premium.

If the coding had been reversed (1 for male employees and 0 for female employees), this same data set would generate an estimated D1 coefficient of +$1,857.907. The estimate is positive, rather than negative, because the equation would be measuring the effect of being male.

When evaluating the estimated protected group effect (and the effects of the variables explaining compensation as well), statistical significance and practical significance (i.e., the direction and magnitude of the estimated effect) should be viewed in light of the size of the sample being studied, as well as the explanatory power of the model.[9]

The classical model of pay equity can be expanded to include dummy variables representing more than one protected class definition. For example, assume that we are interested in examining whether there are differences in annual salary by gender and/or by race for a similarly situated employee grouping. Within this grouping, there are ten individuals: four women and six men, and five white and five nonwhite. Annual salaries for these employees are determined based on seniority.

Further assume that salary, seniority, gender, and race data for these employees are given in Table 5-2, which also includes dummy variables for gender and race.[10]

---

[8]Readers are reminded that if a coefficient is not statistically significant, the effect of that variable is not statistically different from zero. If a coefficient is not statistically significant, no adverse inference can or should be drawn. A basic overview of statistical significance is provided in the Appendix.

[9]This point is discussed in Chapter 3.

[10]DF is coded 1 for females and 0 for males; DNW is coded 1 for nonwhites and 0 for whites.

Table 5-2. Hypothetical Annual Salary, Seniority, Gender, and Race

ID #	Sex	Race	Seniority	Annual Salary ($)	DF	DNW
1201	M	NW	3	36,346	0	1
1872	M	W	4	43,051	0	0
3373	M	NW	4	42,540	0	1
4050	F	NW	3	32,457	1	1
4340	M	W	5	45,813	0	0
7361	F	W	2	28,914	1	0
7378	M	NW	1	25,770	0	1
8311	F	W	2	31,712	1	0
9332	M	W	1	26,690	0	0
9620	F	NW	2	27,156	1	1

The classical model structure for this example is provided in Equation 5.3.

$$Salary = \beta_0 + \beta_1 Seniority + \beta_2 DF + \beta_3 DNW \qquad (5.3)$$

Figure 5-2 provides the regression output when Equation 5.3 is estimated using the data shown in Table 5-2.

```
Dependent Variable              |     SALARY
N                               |     10
Adjusted Squared Multiple R     |     0.963
Standard Error of Estimate      |     1,444.879

Regression Coefficients B = (X'X)⁻¹X'Y

Effect      | Coefficient        t          p-Value
-------------------------------------------------------
Constant      22,339.199      16.096         0.000
SEN            5,017.280      13.291         0.000
DF            -2,878.957      -2.954         0.025
DNW           -1,378.744      -1.504         0.183
```

Figure 5-2. Regression output

As can be seen from Figure 5-2, the regression process has estimated two coefficients associated with the dummy variables. These estimated coefficients are interpreted the same way as in the previous example. The estimated coefficient associated with gender is negative (–$2,878.957), indicating that there is a gender penalty for women equal to $2,878.957. In other words, a comparison of the annual salaries one male and one female employee with identical seniority would reveal a $2,878.957 difference in favor of the man.

The gender effect here is statistically significant; the associated probability value of 0.025 indicates that chance is *not* the likely explanation for the observed differences by gender. We reject the null hypothesis that the true effect of gender on compensation, after controlling for time in job and years of prior relevant experience, is zero. Based on these results, we would infer that the compensation decisions represented in Table 5-2 are not neutral with respect to gender.

However, it would be incorrect to automatically assume that the cause of this difference by gender is the result of gender discrimination. Although gender discrimination *may* play a role, there are a variety of other explanations. For example, it is possible that the model has been misspecified via omission of a legitimate, nondiscriminatory determinant of compensation that happens to be correlated with gender. The observed difference by gender is possibly the result of chance (although it may be unlikely or rare, it is not impossible). In fact, over repeated sampling we would expect to see a difference as large—or larger—25 times out of 1,000 samples.

The estimated coefficient associated with the race dummy variable, DNW, is –$1,378.744. The interpretation of this coefficient is that there is a race penalty for nonwhites equal to $1,378.744. Because the coefficient is negative, the effect of being nonwhite (DNW = 1) is $1,378.744 *less* per year. A comparison of the annual salaries of one white and one nonwhite employee with identical seniority would reveal a $1,378.744 difference in favor of the white employee.

However, the race effect is not statistically significant; the associated probability value of 0.183 indicates that chance is the likely explanation for the observed differences by race. Thus, we cannot reject the null hypothesis that the true effect of race on compensation, after controlling for seniority, is zero. Based on these results, we would infer that the compensation decisions represented in Table 5-2 are neutral with respect to race.

It should be noted that in Equation 5.3, the effect of gender is estimated separately and apart from the effect of race and vice versa. The estimated coefficients provide only information about the effect on compensation of being female or of being nonwhite. They do not provide information about the effect on compensation of being *both* female *and* nonwhite. To measure this joint effect, it is necessary to incorporate an additional dummy variable that measures both gender and race.[11] This dummy variable (DCOMB) is given in Table 5-3.

---

[11] In this case, we create a dummy variable representing the interaction of gender and race. Interaction terms are discussed in more detail later in this chapter.

Table 5-3. Hypothetical Annual Salary, Seniority, Gender, and Race

ID #	Sex	Race	Seniority	Salary ($)	DF	DNW	DCOMB
1201	M	NW	3	36,346	0	1	0
1872	M	W	4	43,051	0	0	0
3373	M	NW	4	42,540	0	1	0
4050	F	NW	3	32,457	1	1	1
4340	M	W	5	45,813	0	0	0
7361	F	W	2	28,914	1	0	0
7378	M	NW	1	25,770	0	1	0
8311	F	W	2	31,712	1	0	0
9332	M	W	1	26,690	0	0	0
9620	F	NW	2	27,156	1	1	1

The classical model structure for estimating the individual effects of gender and race, as well as the joint effect of gender *and* race, is given in Equation 5.4.

$$Salary = \beta_0 + \beta_1 TSeniority + \beta_2 DF + \beta_3 DNW + \beta_4 DCOMB \qquad (5.4)$$

Figure 5-3 provides the regression output when Equation 5.4 is estimated using the data shown in Table 5-3. As can be seen, the regression process has estimated coefficients for the gender effect, the race effect, and the interacted gender and race effect.

```
Dependent Variable                  |    SALARY
N                                   |    10
Adjusted Squared Multiple R         |    0.972
Standard Error of Estimate          |    1,248.966

Regression Coefficients B = (X'X)⁻¹X'Y

Effect     | Coefficient        t          p-Value
---------------------------------------------------
Constant     21,333.703      16.022        0.000
SEN           5,155.289      15.352        0.000
DF           -1,331.281      -1.087        0.327
DNW            -195.807      -0.188        0.859
DCOMB        -2,888.337      -1.741        0.142
```

Figure 5-3. Regression output

These estimated coefficients are interpreted the same way as in the previous example. The estimated coefficient associated with gender is negative (–$1,331.281), indicating that there is a gender penalty for women equal to

$1,331.281. However, the gender effect is not statistically significant; the associated probability value of 0.327 indicates that chance is the likely explanation for the observed differences. Thus, we cannot reject the null hypothesis that the true effect of gender on compensation, after controlling for seniority, is zero. Based on these results, we would infer that the compensation decisions represented in Table 5-3 are neutral with respect to gender.

The estimated coefficient associated with race is −$195.807. The interpretation of this coefficient is that there is a race penalty for nonwhites equal to $195.807. However, the race effect is not statistically significant; the associated probability value of 0.859 indicates that chance is the likely explanation for the observed differences by race. Thus, we cannot reject the null hypothesis that the true effect of race on compensation, after controlling for seniority, is zero. Based on these results, we would infer that the compensation decisions represented in Table 5-3 are neutral with respect to race.

The estimated coefficient associated with the interaction of gender and race is −$2,888.337. The interpretation of this coefficient is that there is a nonwhite female penalty equal to $2,888.337. A comparison of the annual salaries of a white male and a nonwhite female employee with identical seniority would reveal a $2,888.337 difference in favor of the white male.

The effect of the interaction of gender and race is not statistically significant; the associated probability value of 0.142 indicates that chance is the likely explanation for the observed differences. Thus, we cannot reject the null hypothesis that the true effect of the interaction of gender and race on compensation, after controlling for seniority, is zero. Based on these results, we would infer that the compensation decisions represented in Table 5-3 are neutral with respect to the interaction of gender and race.

As previously noted, the classical model structure is favored for its ability to be easily understood, its simple calculations, and its straightforward interpretation. This model, however, cannot detect cases of discrimination in which the factors explaining compensation contribute differently to the compensation of different protected groups. To detect this kind of discrimination, the separate equations model structure is often used.

Separate Equations Model

The separate equations model structure has been used in compensation discrimination litigation as an alternative to the classical model structure.[12] The purpose of the separate equations model is to allow for the possibility that the factors determining compensation have different effects on compensation between the protected and nonprotected groups.

---

[12]For example, *Ottaviani v. State University of New York*, 875 F2d 365, 1989.

Formally, the separate equations model of pay equity takes the following structure:

$$Y_{NON} = \beta_{0NON} + \beta_{1NON}X_{1iNON} + \ldots + \beta_{kNON}X_{kiNON} + \varepsilon_{NON} \qquad (5.5)$$

$$Y_{PROT} = \beta_{0PROT} + \beta_{1PROT}X_{1iPROT} + \ldots + \beta_{kPROT}X_{kiPROT} + \varepsilon_{PROT}$$

where

NON = nonprotected group

$PROT$ = protected group

k = number of independent variables

β_k = kth coefficient

X_{ki} = ith observation of the kth independent variable

ε_i = error term

This structure expresses compensation as a function of the determinants of compensation (seniority, time in job, education, prior relevant work experience, performance ratings, etc.). Rather than including protected group status as a dummy variable, separate equations are estimated for the protected and nonprotected groups.

Unlike the classical model structure, the effect of protected group status on compensation is not directly estimated. Arriving at an estimation of the effect of protected group status (and its associated level of significance) is more complex. This point can best be illustrated using the following example.

Imagine that we are interested in examining whether there are differences in annual salary by gender for a given grouping of similarly situated university professors. Annual salary is determined based on semesters of seniority, semesters of prior teaching experience, the number of courses currently taught, the number of dissertation students supervised in the current semester, and the professor's educational attainment. Further assume that among the male professors, there is a mixture of educational attainment (PhD and ABD degrees);[13] all female professors have doctoral degrees.[14]

The separate equations model structure for this example is provided in Equations 5.6A and 5.6B.[15]

---

[13]ABD refers to "all but dissertation" and is awarded in cases where the doctoral candidate has completed all of the required coursework but has not yet defended his dissertation.

[14]This hypothetical example is used for illustrative purposes only and is not intended to reflect or imply anything about the way dissertation students are supervised in reality.

[15]The dummy variable coefficient takes on a value of 0 for ABD and a value of 1 for a doctoral degree.

$$Salary_M = \beta_0 + \beta_1 Sen + \beta_2 PriorExp + \beta_3 Courses + \beta_4 Students + \beta_5 Education$$

$$(5.6A)$$

$$Salary_F = \beta_0 + \beta_1 Sen + \beta_2 PriorExp + \beta_3 Courses + \beta_4 Students + \beta_5 Education$$

$$(5.6B)$$

Figures 5-4A and 5-4B provide the regression output when Equations 5.6A and 5.6B are estimated, respectively. As can be seen, the estimated effect of protected group status on compensation is not immediately obvious, as it was under the classical model structure. This is the main disadvantage of the separate equations model structure. Comparison of individual coefficients may not reveal insights into the effect of gender on compensation. For example, comparing the coefficients associated with prior teaching experience, we see that men receive on average \$2,945 for each semester of prior teaching experience, whereas women receive \$1,303 on average. This indicates that women receive less pay than their male counterparts for the same prior teaching experience. This finding is consistent with the hypothesis of gender discrimination.

MALE EQUATION
Regression Coefficients B = $(X'X)^{-1}X'Y$

Effect	Coefficient	t	p-Value
Constant	19,421.631	10.906	0.000
SEN	2,017.280	3.711	0.001
PRIOREXP	2,944.787	2.892	0.011
COURSES	3,293.448	4.916	0.000
STUDENTS	1,582.440	7.642	0.000
EDUCATION	4,958.378	2.189	0.045

Figure 5-4A. Regression output, male equation

FEMALE EQUATION
Regression Coefficients B = $(X'X)^{-1}X'Y$

Effect	Coefficient	t	p-Value
Constant	21,023.224	11.403	0.000
SEN	2,217.801	4.021	0.001
PRIOREXP	1,302.948	2.426	0.028
COURSES	3,186.513	5.014	0.000
STUDENTS	1,923.158	7.882	0.000
EDUCATION	N/A	N/A	N/A

Figure 5-4B. Regression output, female equation

On the other hand, we see that men receive $2,017 (on average) for each semester of seniority, and women receive $2,218 (on average). This indicates that women receive *more* pay than their male counterparts for the same seniority. This finding is *inconsistent* with the hypothesis of gender discrimination.

Comparing each individual coefficient for protected and nonprotected individuals may not reveal any clear patterns of discrimination. It is often the case—as in the foregoing example—that neither group consistently experiences higher coefficients for all of the factors explaining compensation. One group has higher estimated coefficients on some variables, and the other group has higher estimated coefficients on other variables.

Additionally, as noted by Ramona Paetzhold and Steven Willborn, direct comparison of the estimated coefficients is warranted only if the coefficients in both equations are individually interpretable.[16] As can be seen from Figure 5-4B, education does not enter into the equation for female professors because there is no variation in educational attainment among them.

Because the separate equations model does not directly estimate the effect of protected group status on compensation, this effect must be estimated in a different way. A common method is to examine the residuals generated by fitting the protected group's data to the nonprotected group's fitted regression equation and vice versa. As noted by Paetzhold and Willborn:

> Since the average residual for the data on which the equation is based must be zero, any deviation from zero for the women's data indicates the extent to which the regression equation does not fit the women's data as well as it fits the men's data and could serve as a measure of salary discrimination based on sex. Thus, if the average residual for women (fit against the men's regression equation) were negative and large enough in magnitude, a legal inference of salary discrimination based on sex may be warranted.[17]

To see how this fitting process is conducted, we examine one female employee for illustrative purposes. Professor Jane Smith's annual salary and characteristics are given in Table 5-4.

---

[16]Ramona Paetzhold and Steven Willborn, *The Statistics of Discrimination: Using Statistical Evidence in Discrimination Cases* (West Publishing, 2011–2012), 284.
[17]Ibid., 285.

Table 5-4. Employment Characteristics for Jane Smith

ID# 7224	Name: Smith, Jane
Current Salary:	$50,000 Annual
Education:	Ph.D.
Semesters Seniority:	4
Semesters Prior Experience:	6
Current Course Load:	2
Ph.D. Students Supervised:	3

We can use information about her characteristics, along with the male parameter estimates shown in Equation 5.7, to predict what Jane Smith's annual salary would be if she were male.

$$Salary = \$19,422 + \$2,017\ Sen + \$2,945\ Prior\ Exp \\ + \$3,293\ Courses + \$1,582\ Students \qquad (5.7) \\ + \$4,958Education$$

Using Equation 5.7, we would predict her salary to be $61,452.[18] Her actual salary is $50,000. Her residual is equal to the difference between actual and predicted salary, as shown in Equation 5.8:

$$\$50,000 - \$61,452 = -\$11,452 \qquad (5.8)$$

As can be seen, Jane Smith's residual is equal to −$11,452. This means that had she been a man, given her seniority, prior experience, current course load, students supervised, and education, she would be expected to earn $11,452 *more* than she is currently earning.

To assess whether a legal inference of pay discrimination among this group of college professors based on sex is warranted, we would perform this same calculation for all women in the similarly situated employee grouping, generating an average residual. If the average residual is negative and large enough in magnitude, an inference of discrimination may be warranted.

As can be seen from this discussion, estimating the effect of protected group status on compensation using the separate equations approach is a complex process. Interpreting the results generated by analyzing compensation with this model is challenging. Because of this, it is often rejected in favor of the classical model structure.

---

[18]$19,422 + ($2,017 * 4) + ($2,945 * 6) + ($3,293 * 2) + ($1,582 * 3) + $4,958 = $61,452.

The Interaction Model

A third model structure, the interaction model, combines the advantages of the classical and separate equations structures while reducing the impact of their respective disadvantages. The interaction model preserves the simple calculations and straightforward interpretation of the classical model while allowing for the possibility that the factors determining compensation have different effects on compensation between the protected and nonprotected groups. It allows for the direct estimation of protected group effects on compensation, as well as an estimation of how factors explaining compensation contribute differently to the compensation of different protected groups.

Formally, the interactive model of pay equity takes the following structure:

$$Y_i = \beta_0 + \beta_{11}X_{1i} + \beta_{12}X_{1i}DI_i + \ldots + \beta_{k1}X_{ki} + \beta_{k2}X_{ki}DI_i + \beta_{k+1}DI_i + \varepsilon_i \quad (5.9)$$

where

k = number of independent variables

β_{k1} = coefficient associated with X_{ki}

β_{k2} = coefficient associated with X_{ki} interacted with DI_i

X_{ki} = ith observation of the kth independent variable

DI_i = ith observation of the protected status dummy variable

β_{k+1} = coefficient associated with DI

ε_i = error term

The interaction terms—the factors determining compensation multiplied by the dummy variable representing protected group status—are known as cross-products. Assuming that the dummy variable representing protected group status is coded as 1 for protected employees and 0 for nonprotected employees, these cross-products enter the equation for observations for protected employees but not for those observations for nonprotected employees.[19]

---

[19] This is because any number multiplied by 0 is equal to 0.

Returning to the previous example regarding compensation of college professors, and assuming we are interested in examining the effect of race on compensation, the interaction model is given by Equation 5.10:

$$Salary = \beta_0 + \beta_{11}Sen + \beta_{12}Sen * NW + \beta_{21}PriorExp$$
$$+ \beta_{22}PriorExp * NW + \beta_{31}Courses$$
$$+ \beta_{32}Courses * NW + \beta_{41}Students \qquad (5.10)$$
$$+ \beta_{42}Students * NW + \beta_{51}Education$$
$$+ \beta_{52}Education * NW + \beta_6 NW$$

This model provides estimates of the individual effects of the factors determining compensation (semesters of seniority, semesters of prior teaching experience, the number of courses currently taught, the number of dissertation students supervised during the current semester, and educational attainment) on compensation, irrespective of race, via β_{11}, β_{21}, β_{31}, β_{41}, and β_{51}, respectively. The model also estimates the extent to which the factors determining compensation contribute to the compensation of nonwhites via the coefficients associated with the cross-protect terms, β_{12}, β_{22}, β_{32}, β_{42}, and β_{52}. In essence, this is equivalent to estimating two separate equations and allowing the factors determining compensation to affect compensation differently by protected group status.

Finally, the model estimates the effect of race on compensation, controlling for the effects of semesters of seniority, semesters of prior teaching experience, number of courses currently taught, number of dissertation students supervised during the current semester, and educational attainment, both overall and by race, via the β_6 parameter estimate.

Figure 5-5 provides example regression output when Equation 5.10 is estimated.

INTERACTION MODEL STRUCTURE
Regression Coefficients B = $(X'X)^{-1}X'Y$

Effect	Coefficient	t	p-Value
Constant	20,575.442	9.765	0.000
SEN	1,992.078	3.412	0.002
SEN*NW	54.337	0.866	0.393
PRIOREXP	3,051.848	3.189	0.003
PRIOREXP*NW	-695.031	2.451	0.020
COURSES	3,246.229	5.933	0.000
COURSES*NW	-102.695	1.472	0.151
STUDENTS	1,582.440	4.834	0.000
STUDENTS*NW	29.834	0.021	0.983
EDUCATION	5,257.387	3.552	0.001
EDUCATION*NW	N/A	N/A	N/A
NW	-244.402	1.684	0.103

Figure 5-5. Regression output

Interpretation of the results generated from the interactive model structure is very similar to interpretation of the classical model. For example, from Figure 5-5 we see that one semester of seniority is worth, on average, $1,992, all else equal. Based on the calculated probability value of 0.002, this effect is statistically significant. We would infer that seniority is a statistically significant predictor of compensation within this similarly situated employee grouping.

The effect of the cross-product of seniority and race on compensation is $54. This means that on average, one semester of seniority is worth an additional $54 for a nonwhite professor than for a white professor, all else equal. However, this effect is not statistically significant. The associated probability value of 0.393 indicates that chance is the likely explanation for the observed difference.

The only cross-product that is statistically significant is the interaction of race and semesters of prior experience. Based on the regression results shown in Figure 5-5, we see that the estimated coefficient of this cross-product is –$695. This means that on average, one semester of prior experience is worth $695 *less* for a nonwhite professor than for a white professor, all else equal. This effect is statistically significant; the associated probability value is 0.020. This result is consistent with the hypothesis that the employer may be engaging in race discrimination by valuing prior experience for whites and nonwhites differently.

The interaction model is useful because it allows for the direct estimation of protected group effects while simultaneously allowing each factor explaining compensation to differ in its effect on compensation by protected group status. The main disadvantage of this model is that because the number of explanatory variables is nearly double that of the classical model structure, a larger sample size is required.

The Overall Equity Model

The three model structures presented thus far are used primarily for detecting compensation discrimination. As such, they all classify individuals within the similarly situated employee grouping on the basis of protected group status. Classifying individuals by protected group status is necessary for examining questions of compensation discrimination on the basis of protected group status.

However, classification in this manner may generate little, if any, information about pay inequities *within* protected group status. For example, to assess whether similarly situated white men are paid equitably, an alternative model structure ignoring protected group status may be more useful.

One such alternative model structure is the overall equity model structure. This structure examines residuals for all individuals within the similarly situated employee grouping, providing insight into whether employees are under- or overpaid vis-à-vis their comparators.

The overall equity model structure is similar to the classical model structure, with the exception that no dummy variables representing protected group status are included. Formally, the overall equity model of pay equity takes the following structure:

$$Y_i = \beta_0 + \beta_1 X_{1i} + \beta_2 X_{2i} + \ldots + \beta_k X_{ki} + \varepsilon_i \qquad (5.11)$$

where

k = number of independent variables

β_k = kth coefficient

X_{ki} = ith observation of the kth independent variable

ε_i = error term

This structure expresses compensation as a function of the determinants of compensation (seniority, time in job, education, prior relevant work experience, performance ratings, etc.) and assumes that this functional relationship is the same for all individuals within the similarly situated employee grouping, irrespective of protected group status.

The model is estimated via multiple regression, just like the classical, separate equations, and interactive model structures. Similar to the separate equations approach, the estimated model structure is used to calculate residuals for all individuals within the similarly situated employee grouping. The residuals are examined for directionality (positive or negative) and magnitude. Sufficiently large positive or negative residuals may indicate situations of inequity within the similarly situated employee grouping.

To see how the overall equity model is applied, consider the following example. Assume that we are interested in examining the similarly situated employee grouping of college professors for overall pay equity. Further assume that Table 5-5 represents a sampling of data from this employee grouping:

Table 5-5. Sampling of Data for College Professor SSEG

ID #	Name	Sex	Race	Sen	Exp	Classes	Stud	Ed	Sal ($)
5676	Miller, James	M	W	8	10	3	4	Ph.D.	88000
5972	Wilson, John	M	B	8	4	2	2	ABD	70000
7224	Smith, Jane	F	W	4	6	2	3	Ph.D.	50000
7495	Moore, Robert	M	B	4	4	2	1	Ph.D.	54000
8709	Taylor, Michael	M	W	4	3	2	2	ABD	48000
9250	Hobbs, William	M	W	4	4	3	4	Ph.D.	48000
9292	Garcia, Mary	F	H	4	2	2	2	Ph.D.	48000

Figure 5-6 provides the regression output when compensation is estimated for all individuals within the similarly situated employee grouping as a function of semesters of seniority, semesters of prior teaching experience, the number of courses currently taught, the number of dissertation students supervised during the current semester, and the professor's educational attainment.

```
Regression Coefficients B = (X′X)⁻¹X′Y

Effect      | Coefficient       t          p-Value
-------------------------------------------------------
Constant     20,042.409       10.906       0.000
SEN           2,117.024        4.021       0.001
PRIOREXP      3,000.116        2.892       0.011
COURSES       3,300.143        4.916       0.000
STUDENTS      1,600.227        7.882       0.000
EDUCATION     5,000.378        2.189       0.045
```

Figure 5-6. Regression output

This estimated model is then used to fit each employee's compensation.[20] The results of this fitting process are given in Table 5-6.

Table 5-6. Predicted Compensation for Sampling of College Professors within SSEG

ID #	Name	Sex	Race	Actual ($)	Predicted ($)	Difference ($)
5676	Miller, James	M	W	88,000	88,281	−281
5972	Wilson, John	M	B	70,000	58,780	11,220
7224	Smith, Jane	F	W	50,000	62,913	−12,913
7495	Moore, Robert	M	B	54,000	53,712	288
8709	Taylor, Michael	M	W	48,000	47,312	688
9250	Hobbs, William	M	W	48,000	61,813	−13,813
9292	Garcia, Mary	F	H	48,000	49,312	−1,312

On review of the differences between actual and predicted salaries shown in Table 5-6, three employees stand out: John Wilson, Jane Smith, and William Hobbs. Wilson's annual salary is $70,000. When the estimated model is fitted using his employment characteristics, his predicted compensation is $58,780. The difference between his actual and predicted salary amounts is $11,220—he is earning $11,220 *more* than would be expected based on his employment characteristics.

---

[20]This fitting process is the same as that discussed in the separate equations approach.

Smith and Hobbs, on the other hand, are earning less than would be expected based on their employment characteristics. Smith is earning nearly $13,000 a year less and Hobbs is earning nearly $14,000 a year less than would be expected based on the estimated model and employment characteristics.

When we look at Hobbs's current salary and characteristics, we see that he is closest to Taylor (in terms of current salary and characteristics). Table 5-7 shows salary and employment characteristics for both professors.

Table 5-7. Employment Characteristics for William Hobbs and Michael Taylor

ID# 9250 Name: Hobbs, William Current Salary: $48,000 Annual		ID# 8709 Name: Taylor, Michael Current Salary: $48,000 Annual	
Education:	Ph.D.	Education:	ABD
Semesters Seniority:	4	Semesters Seniority:	4
Semesters Prior Experience:	4	Semesters Prior Experience:	3
Current Course Load:	3	Current Course Load:	2
Ph.D. Students Supervised:	4	Ph.D. Students Supervised:	2

As can be seen, both Hobbs and Taylor are currently earning $48,000 per year. Both have four semesters of seniority, three or more semesters of prior experience, and are currently teaching an average course load. However, they differ in that Hobbs holds a Ph.D., whereas Taylor is ABD; Hobbs is also supervising more Ph.D. students than Taylor is.

Based on this direct comparison, we would expect that Hobbs's annual salary would exceed that of Taylor (because Hobbs has a higher level of educational attainment and is supervising more Ph.D. students). In fact, they are both earning an annual salary of $48,000.

Based on the results of the overall equity model, there is reason to believe that Hobbs is underpaid relative to his similarly situated counterparts. Had the analysis focused on conventional definitions of protected group status based on gender, race and ethnicity, and so on, the possibility of Hobbs being underpaid by nearly $14,000 a year may have remained undiscovered. As noted in Chapter 1, *any* inequity in compensation, irrespective of protected group status, can be problematic. The overall equity model is particularly useful for detecting these inequitable situations and for improving overall internal pay equity.

Other Models

The models presented in this chapter represent those most commonly used in the context of compensation discrimination and internal pay equity analysis. The discussion is by no means exhaustive, and it is not intended to be encyclopedic in scope. The models presented are intended to provide the reader with an overview of some of the basic structures used to examine questions of compensation discrimination and internal pay equity.

The choice of model structure will depend on the goals of the analysis, the context in which the analysis is being conducted, and how compensation is determined. Statistical consultants are best positioned to choose the appropriate model structure for the pay equity question(s) under investigation.

Other Tests of Equal Pay

Although multiple regression analysis is the preferred statistical technique for examining questions of internal pay equity, a variety of other statistical and nonstatistical techniques are often used. Some common tools for examining disparate treatment in compensation include a comparison of means and medians, t-tests, cohort analyses, and tipping point and threshold tests.

Questions of disparate impact in compensation are frequently examined within the context of contingency tables. Common tools for evaluating contingency tables include the four-fifths rule, chi square test, Fisher's exact test, and the Mantel-Haenszel test. Logistic regression, a special form of multiple regression, can also be useful in evaluating the presence or absence of disparate impact as it relates to compensation.

Other Disparate Treatment Tests

The majority of other statistical and nonstatistical tests for disparate treatment in compensation focus on comparing aggregate descriptive statistics, such as means and medians, by protected group status for a given employee grouping. One technique, however, focuses on comparing individual compensation data points by protected group status within a given employee grouping.

Comparison of Means and Medians

As mentioned in Chapter 3, our first inclination when looking for the presence or absence of discrimination in pay data may be to turn to a comparison of average rates of pay for different groups. The calculations involved are simple, and interpretation is straightforward. Frequently businesses—and regulatory agencies—follow this inclination and base an assessment of compensation discrimination on a comparison of means.[1]

Sometimes, this comparison is extended to include a comparison of medians. The *median* is the numerical value separating the upper and lower halves of a data set. The median is found by arranging all of the observations from lowest value to highest value and selecting the middle number. If there is an even number of observations, there will be no middle number; in this case, the median is calculated as the mean of the middle two numbers.

The comparison of means and medians is typically done by protected group status (male versus female, white versus nonwhite, etc.) for a group of "similar" employees.[2] Example comparisons of mean and median compensation by gender by pay grade are given in Table 6-1 and Table 6-2, respectively.[3]

Table 6-1. Comparison of Mean Compensation by Gender and Grade

Grade	# of Employees			Means Analysis			
	All	M	F	M	F	Diff	
4	2	2	0	$32,781	N/A	N/A	
5	25	12	13	$33,367	$33,334	$33	*
6	53	37	16	$35,178	$34,417	$761	*
7	33	25	8	$37,414	$39,210	($1,769)	
8	24	18	6	$40,773	$41,392	($619)	
9	87	85	2	$43,938	$43,914	$24	*

Flagged as potential problem area for discrimination.

---

[1] In this case, we refer to the arithmetic mean, rather than the harmonic mean or geometric mean. Formally, the calculation of the arithmetic mean is given by the following:

$$\bar{x} = \frac{1}{n} * \sum_{i=1}^{n} x_i$$

[2] Note that "similar" may or may not be equivalent to similarly situated. Means and medians comparisons are frequently performed on the basis of EEO-1 category, pay grade, or other broad grouping variable that may group together employees who are not similarly situated.

[3] The examples shown in Tables 6-1 and 6-2 were excerpted from a sample compensation analysis report produced by Office of Federal Contract Compliance Programs (OFCCP). This sample report can be found at www.ofccp.com/PDF/Sample_Compensation_Analysis_Report.pdf.

Table 6-2. Comparison of Median Compensation by Gender and Grade

Grade	# of Employees			Means Analysis			
	All	M	F	M	F	Diff	
4	2	2	0	$32,781	N/A	N/A	
5	25	12	13	$34,720	$34,224	$496	*
6	53	37	16	$35,630	$34,731	$899	*
7	33	25	8	$37,495	$38,581	($1,086)	
8	24	18	6	$40,529	$41,308	($779)	
9	87	85	2	$43,887	$43,914	($27)	

Flagged as potential problem area for discrimination.

In the example comparison of means given in Table 6-1, pay grades 5, 6, and 9 would be flagged as potential problem areas for discrimination under the methodology used by the Office of Federal Contract Compliance Programs (OFCCP) and other regulatory agencies. In the example comparison of medians given in Table 6-2, pay grades 5 and 6 would be flagged as potential problem areas for discrimination.

Note that this flagging for potential discrimination is based solely on a positive difference between male and female average compensation. Under this methodology, no consideration is given to statistical significance or practical significance. Even though the differences of $33 per year and $24 per year between average compensation for men and women in pay grades 5 and 9, respectively, are not practically significant (and would likely not be statistically significant either), this analysis flags these two pay grades for potential discrimination.

As noted in Chapter 3, however, a comparison of simple average or median compensation by protected group status cannot account for legitimate, non-discriminatory factors that affect compensation. Because of this, in most cases a simple comparison of average or median compensation cannot provide an appropriate assessment of the presence or absence of discrimination.

One additional problem associated with a comparison of average compensation by protected group status is that averages can be influenced by extreme observations. To see how this happens, consider the two distributions of compensation shown in Table 6-3.

Table 6-3. Example Distributions of Compensation

Employee ID	Salary ($)	Employee ID	Salary ($)
101	74,000	201	30,000
102	74,000	202	30,000
103	74,000	203	30,000
104	74,000	204	30,000
105	74,000	205	250,000
Average:	$74,000	Average:	$74,000

As can be seen from Table 6-3, both distributions have mean compensation of $74,000. When we look at the individual compensation amounts, however, we see that there are dramatic differences. Employees 101–105 are all paid the same salary: $74,000. The average rate of compensation for employees 201–205 is also $74,000, but this average is influenced by employee 205, who is paid an annual salary of $250,000. If employee 205 were removed from the analysis, the average annual salary for employees 201–204 would be $30,000. Looking only at the averages for these two groups of employees masks the variation in compensation among employees 201–205. Based solely on the average rates of pay, one may conclude that there is no difference in the annual salaries of these two groups. If, however, employee 205 was removed from the analysis, a completely different picture emerges. Because of the manner in which means are calculated, this issue cannot be avoided.

t-Test

As previously noted, a simple comparison of means is an informal test, because no consideration is given to the issue of statistical significance. There is, however, a formal test for assessing whether a difference in means is statistically significant. This test is known as the *t-test*.[4] The *t*-test is a commonly used tool for testing the hypothesis that the sample means of two groups are equal.

---

[4]The *t*-test was introduced in 1908 by William Sealy Gossett. Gossett developed the test as an inexpensive way to monitor the quality of stout while working as a chemist at the Guinness brewery in Dublin, Ireland. The test was published in *Biometrika* in 1908 under the pen name Student because his employer considered the fact that statistics were being used in Guinness brewing as a trade secret.

Specifically, the hypothesis test takes the following null hypothesis/alternate hypothesis form:[5]

$$H_0 : \bar{X}_1 = \bar{X}_2$$
$$H_A : \bar{X}_1 \neq \bar{X}_2$$

(6.1)

In the context of internal pay equity, the null hypothesis would be that the average rates of pay for protected and nonprotected employees are the same, whereas the alternate hypothesis would be that the average rates of pay for protected and nonprotected employees are different.

There are a variety of forms of the *t*-test that make differing assumptions about how the samples were drawn and the sampling variances of each group. For example, different forms of the *t*-test are warranted when examining paired samples versus overlapping samples.[6] The form assuming independent samples is most commonly used for performing *t*-tests within the context of compensation analysis.[7]

Within the independent samples form, there are two variants that differ based on the assumption one makes about the variances of the two groups being studied. The first variant assumes equal variance of the groups and

---

[5]Note that this expresses the null and alternate hypotheses for a two-tailed test. In a one-tailed test, the alternate hypothesis is constructed such that the sample mean for the second group is either (a) greater than or (b) less than the sample mean for the first group:

$$(a)\ H_A : \bar{X}_1 < \bar{X}_2$$

$$(b)\ H_A : \bar{X}_1 > \bar{X}_2$$

The choice of one-tailed or two-tailed test depends on the question being addressed.
[6]The assumption of paired samples is appropriate when comparing matched pairs of observations, or "before" and "after" observations on the same group of individuals. Paired samples are sometimes referred to as "dependent samples." The assumption of overlapping samples is used in the case of paired samples with missing data in one of the samples.
[7]The independent samples *t*-test is used when two separate sets of independent and identically distributed samples are drawn, one from each of the two populations under comparison. Within the context of internal pay equity, we are looking at, for example, annual pay rates for protected group members and nonprotected group members.

uses a pooled variance. The second variant allows for differing variances of the groups.[8]

Independent Samples and Equal Variances

Assuming independent samples and equal variances between the two groups, the t-test statistic is given by the following:

$$t = \frac{\bar{X}_1 - \bar{X}_2}{S_{x_1 x_2} * \sqrt{\dfrac{1}{n_1} + \dfrac{1}{n_2}}}$$

(6.2)

where

$$S_{x_1 x_2} = \sqrt{\frac{(n_1 - 1)s_{x_1}^2 + (n_2 - 1)s_{x_2}^2}{n_1 - n_2 - 2}}$$

$\bar{X}_1$ = sample mean of group 1

$\bar{X}_2$ = sample mean of group 2

s_1^2 = sample variance of group 1

s_2^2 = sample variance of group 2

n_1 = number of observations in group 1

n_2 = number of observations in group 2

---

[8]Levene's test can be used to assess the equality of variances in different samples. Levene's test statistic is given by:

$$W = \frac{(N - k)}{(k - 1)} * \frac{\sum_{i=1}^{k} N_i (Z_{i.} - Z_{..})^2}{\sum_{i=1}^{k} \sum_{j=1}^{N_i} (Z_{ij} - Z_{i.})^2}$$

The distribution of the test statistic, assuming equal variances, is approximated by the Student's t-distribution with degrees of freedom calculated using the following:

$$d.f. = (n_1 - 1) + (n_2 - 1) \qquad (6.3)$$

If the calculated t-statistic is greater than or equal to the critical value obtained from the Student's t-distribution, we reject the null hypothesis and infer that the means of the groups are different. If the calculated t-statistic is less than the critical value, we cannot reject the null hypothesis that the means of the groups are the same.[9]

Independent Samples and Unequal Variances

Assuming independent samples and unequal variances between the two groups, the t-test statistic is given by the following:

$$t = \frac{\bar{X}_1 - \bar{X}_2}{\sqrt{\dfrac{s_1^2}{n_1} + \dfrac{s_2^2}{n_2}}} \qquad (6.4)$$

where

$\bar{X}_1 = $ sample mean of group 1

$\bar{X}_2 = $ sample mean of group 2

$s_1^2 = $ sample variance of group 1

$s_2^2 = $ sample variance of group 2

$n_1 = $ number of observations in group 1

$n_2 = $ number of observations in group 2

---

[9]As noted by Snijders, a common misinterpretation of the results of a t-test is that nonrejection implies support for the null hypothesis. Snijders argues that nonrejection should be interpreted as an undecided outcome; there is not enough evidence to reject the null hypothesis, but this does not mean that there is evidence for it. T. A. B. Snijders, "Hypothesis Testing: Methodology and Limitations," *International Encyclopedia of the Social & Behavioral Sciences* (2001), 7125.

The distribution of the test statistic, assuming unequal variances, is approximated by the Student's t-distribution with degrees of freedom calculated using the following:

$$d.f. = \frac{\left[\dfrac{s_1^2}{n_1} + \dfrac{s_2^2}{n_2}\right]^2}{\dfrac{\left(\dfrac{s_1^2}{n_1}\right)^2}{(n_1 - 1)} + \dfrac{\left(\dfrac{s_2^2}{n_2}\right)^2}{(n_2 - 1)}} \qquad (6.5)$$

If the calculated t-statistic is greater than or equal to the critical value obtained from the Student's t-distribution, then we reject the null hypothesis, and infer that the means of the groups are different. If the calculated t-statistic is less than the critical value, then we cannot reject the null hypothesis that the means of the two groups are the same.

Calculation

To see how the t-test can be used to examine differences in average rates of pay for different groups, consider the following example. We are interested in examining total annual compensation for differences by gender among a group of 590 employees. Of them, 470 are male and 120 are female. The average total annual compensation for male employees is $117,408.17, and the average total annual compensation for female employees is $107,982.62. The difference in average total annual compensation for men and women is $9,425.55. The t-test will assess whether this difference is statistically significant.

Table 6-4 provides a sample of the output produced by a statistical software package when a t-test is performed using the data described.[10]

---

[10]The exact format and layout of the output, including what summary statistics are included, varies by software. The sample output in Table 6-4 is intended to illustrate the nature of information commonly provided by most packages.

Table 6-4. Sample *t*-Test Output

H0: Mean1 = Mean2 vs. H1: Mean1 ≠ Mean2

Grouping Variable: SEX

Variable	SEX	N	Mean	Standard Deviation
ANNUAL	F	120	107,982.62	18,565.30
	M	470	117,408.17	22,811,41

Separate Variance

Variable	SEX	Mean Difference	*t*	*p*
ANNUAL	F	−9,425.55	−4.725	0.000
	M			

Pooled Variance

Variable	SEX	Mean Difference	*t*	*p*
ANNUAL	F	−9,425.55	−4.185	0.000
	M			

As can be seen, two different *t*-tests were performed: one assuming separate variances and one using a pooled variance (which assumes equal variances).[11]

Irrespective of the assumption regarding sample variance, the *t*-tests indicate that the difference of $9,425.55 in annual total compensation by gender is statistically significant. Assuming separate variances, the calculated *t*-statistic is equal to −4.725, with an associated *p*-value of 0.000.[12] Based on this *p*-value, we would conclude that the difference of $9,425.55 is statistically significant. Assuming equal variances, the calculated *t*-statistic is equal to −4.185, with an associated *p*-value of 0.000. Again, based on this *p*-value, we would conclude that the difference of $9,425.55 is statistically significant.

---

[11] It is not uncommon for statistical software to generate results for both *t*-tests. Some also provide a calculation of Levene's test to assist in interpreting which assumption is appropriate.

[12] As discussed in Chapter 3, the *p*-value is the probability of obtaining a test statistic at least as extreme as the one actually observed, assuming that the null hypothesis is true.

There are several advantages to *t*-tests. First, unlike a simple comparison of mean compensation by protected group status, a *t*-test allows one to associate a probability value with the difference, making an assessment of statistical significance possible. Second, *t*-tests are relatively easy to calculate and are a standard feature of statistical software packages. This makes them accessible to a wide range of users. Finally, the interpretation of results is straightforward.

The main disadvantage of *t*-tests, in the context of internal pay equity, is that like simple comparisons of mean compensation by protected group status, *t*-tests cannot account for legitimate, nondiscriminatory factors that affect compensation within similarly situated employee groupings.

Tipping Points and Threshold Tests

Tipping points and threshold tests are another kind of nonstatistical test frequently used to assess internal pay equity. The idea behind tipping points and threshold tests is that if differences in compensation by protected group status exceeds a certain threshold—either in percentage terms or in absolute dollars—then compensation discrimination is suspected.

These kinds of tests were popularized by OFCCP. Prior to 2010, OFCCP used tipping point tests based on simple mathematical calculations. Under this methodology, a federal contractor would fail the tipping point test of internal pay equity if each of the following conditions were found in its compensation data:

1. A 5% or larger difference in pay between protected and nonprotected employees grouped by job title;

2. At least thirty protected employees are in employed in the job titles favoring nonprotected employees;

3. The number of protected employees employed in the job titles favoring nonprotected employees represents at least 10% of the total number of protected individuals in the contractor's affirmative action plan;

4. The percentage of protected employees in job titles favoring nonprotected employees is at least three times the percentage of nonprotected employees in job titles favoring protected employees.

To see how this tipping point test is performed, consider the following example. Assume that a contractor's workforce is employed across five different job titles, and headcounts and average hourly rates of pay by gender are those shown in Table 6-5.

Table 6-5. Hourly Pay Rates by Job Title and Gender

Job Title	# of Employees M	F	Avg. Hourly Pay Rate ($) M	F	Percentage Difference
Title A	20	17	12.60	12.00	5.0
Title B	15	8	10.00	9.50	5.3
Title C	30	34	15.50	14.75	5.1
Title D	10	13	11.75	11.25	4.4
Title E	5	10	10.00	10.50	−5.0

As can be seen, all job titles except Title E favor men (that is, the average hourly pay rate for men is greater than the average hourly pay rate for women).

Using the tipping point methodology, Titles A, B, and C satisfy criterion 1. There are seventy-two women employed in job titles that favor men; this satisfies criterion 2. Criterion 3 is also satisfied: seventy-two out of eighty-two women, or 87.8% of the total female workforce, work in job titles that favor men. Finally, the percentage of the total female workforce employed in jobs favoring females is 12.2%. Since 87.8% is more than three times 12.2%, criterion 4 is satisfied. Based on these results, OFCCP would move forward with a compensation audit on the basis of suspected compensation discrimination against women.

As noted by Jana Moberg, in 2010 contractors noticed that OFCCP was inconsistently analyzing compensation data. At the 2010 National Industry Liaison Meeting, OFCCP publicly denied ever using the tipping point test and refused to respond to requests from contractors asking for identification of compensation screening procedures.[13]

In summer 2010, it is believed that OFCCP released a new directive internally, giving the agency's compliance officers new guidance on reviewing compensation data for potential discrimination. Under this new guidance, OFCCP will move forward with a compensation audit if pay differences of $2,000 or 2% in average compensation in at least one job grouping are found.

To see how this new $2,000/2% test differs from the tipping point test, consider the following example. Assume that a contractor's workforce is employed across five different job titles, and headcounts and average hourly rates of pay by gender are those shown in Table 6-6.

---

[13]Jana Moberg, "The New OFCCP Tipping Point Test," DCI Consulting, available at http://ofccp.blogspot.com/2011/02/new-ofccp-tipping-point-test.html.

Table 6-6. Annual Compensation by Job Title and Gender

| Job Title | # of Employees | | Avg. Compensation ($) | | Difference | |
---	M	F	M	F	Percent	Dollar
Title A	20	17	24,960	26,208	−5.0	1,248
Title B	15	8	19,980	20,800	−4.1	820
Title C	30	34	31,030	32,240	−3.9	1,210
Title D	10	13	23,400	24,440	−4.4	1,040
Title E	5	10	21,840	21,410	2.0	430

As can be seen, all job titles except Title E favor women (that is, the average compensation for women exceeds the average compensation for men).

Using the pre-2010 tipping point methodology, Title A has a 5% or larger difference in pay *in favor of women*; this satisfies criterion 1. There are seventy-five men employed in job titles that favor women; this satisfies criterion 2. Criterion 3 is also satisfied: seventy-five out of eighty men, or 93.8% of the total male workforce, work in job titles that favor women. Finally, the percentage of the total male workforce employed in jobs favoring females is 6.3%. Since 93.8% is more than three times 6.3%, criterion 4 is satisfied. Based on these results, OFCCP would move forward with a compensation audit on the basis of suspected compensation discrimination against men.

In contrast, when the same data are reviewed using the $2,000/2% tipping point test, Titles A, B, C, and D satisfy the test criteria treating men as the protected group. Interestingly, Title E also satisfies the test criteria treating women as the protected group. Based on this data set and the application of the $2,000/2% tipping point test, OFCCP would move forward with a compensation audit on the basis of suspected compensation discrimination against *women and men*.

The main problem with tipping points and threshold tests is that they are arbitrary in nature and lack scientific basis.

Cohort Analysis

All of the previous tools study compensation in the aggregate for a particular group of employees, meaning that summary statistics such as medians and means for different groups of employees are compared.

Cohort analysis is a nonstatistical technique that qualitatively compares the compensation of similarly situated employees to identify the cause(s) of pay differences. Conventional application of cohort analysis is to identify potential explanations for differences in compensation by gender, race, or other protected characteristic. Within this context, the analysis compares the compensation of the lowest paid protected member of one group with the compensation of his or her comparators.[14] The purpose of the comparison is to determine whether there are factors other than protected status that may account for differences in pay.

For example, assume that we are interested in examining compensation by gender among those individuals employed as Customer Service Rep III in Pay Grade 21. These employees' compensation is determined by total company tenure, time in job, and performance. Table 6-7 provides an example of a cohort analysis by gender among those employees.

Table 6-7. Example Cohort Analysis

						Performance	
Cohort	ID	Sex	Salary ($)	Tenure	Time in Job	2012	2011
Sarah	192	F	46,570	15	12	4	4
Comparators							
James	301	M	50,613	7	5	4	4
Salary difference:			(4,043)				
Bennett	337	M	50,430	13	9	4	4
Salary difference:			(3,860)				

As shown, the female employee, Sarah, earns $4,043 less than the male comparator James and $3,860 less than the male comparator Bennett. A review of these three workers' tenure and time in job reveals that Sarah has longer tenure and more time in job than either of the two male comparators. All three have identical performance ratings for the current and previous year.

Given that Sarah has longer tenure and greater time in job and performance ratings equal to the male comparators, we would expect her compensation to be greater than the two male comparators. The opposite, however, is true.

Cohort analysis can be a useful tool when the groupings of similarly situated employees are too small for formal statistical analysis. For example, assuming that the three people shown in Table 6-7 represent the totality of this similarly situated employee grouping, it would not be mathematically possible to

---

[14]Here, comparators are defined as nonprotected individuals who receive greater compensation than the protected individual but have what appears to be less qualifying experience, time in job, education, and so on.

estimate a regression in which compensation is a function of gender, tenure, time in job, and performance ratings in the current year and past year.[15] A cohort analysis is a reasonable alternative to multiple regression analysis in the event that small sample sizes or other issues prevent multiple regression analysis.

Cohort analysis can also be a very useful method of follow-up for any statistically significant differences in compensation between two groups of similarly situated employees identified by multiple regression analysis.[16]

Note that although cohort analysis traditionally has been used within the context of protected versus nonprotected status, it can be a useful tool for examining overall equity. Rather than defining the set of possible comparators as those nonprotected individuals who are receiving greater compensation than the protected individual in question but have what appears to be less qualifying experience, time in job, education, and so on, possible comparators could be defined as those people who are of the same gender, race, age, and so on, who receive greater compensation than the individual in question but have what appears to be less qualifying experience, time in job, education, and so on. Using cohort analysis in this way would allow the identification of men, for example, who are underpaid relative to other similarly situated men.

Disparate Impact Models

Questions of disparate impact examine whether a challenged employment policy or practice has a disproportionate effect on different groups of people. Both the effect of the employment policy or practice and the groups of individuals being studied can be expressed in terms of a dichotomous variable.[17]

The outcomes of the challenged policy or practice can be framed in terms of a yes/no question, such as "eligible for bonus" and "not eligible for bonus." Typically, the effect of the challenged employment policy or practice on two different groups will be examined: protected and nonprotected. In this case, protected status can be expressed in terms of yes (protected) or no (nonprotected).

---

[15]As discussed in Chapter 3, if the number of independent variables exceeds the number of observations, there are insufficient degrees of freedom and it is not mathematically possible to generate coefficient estimates.

[16]The use of cohort analysis for follow-up is discussed in Chapter 7.

[17]A dichotomous variable takes on one of two possible values (e.g., gender: male or female).

If both the outcome of the challenged policy or practice and protected group membership can be expressed in terms of a dichotomous variable, then the disparate impact question can be framed in terms of a two-by-two contingency table.[18]

A two-by-two contingency table cross-classifies observations across two variables. Each cell in the table contains the counts of the combinations of the two variables:

	Outcome 1	Outcome 2
Protected	A	B
Nonprotected	C	D

The counts within the contingency table are interpreted as follows:

- A = number of protected individuals experiencing employment outcome 1;

- B = number of protected individuals experiencing employment outcome 2;

- C = number of nonprotected individuals experiencing employment outcome 1;

- D = number of nonprotected individuals experiencing employment outcome 2.

Both the employment outcomes and groups are mutually exclusive; that is, a person cannot belong to both the protected and nonprotected groups, nor can a person experience both employment outcomes 1 and 2.

For example, assume we are looking at the number of female employees who are eligible to participate in a bonus program. Females would be considered protected and males would be considered nonprotected. Those eligible to participate in the bonus program would experience employment outcome 1, and those not eligible to participate in the bonus program would experience employment outcome 2.

The groups are mutually exclusive, because an employee cannot be both male and female at the same time. The employment outcomes are also mutually exclusive, because an employee cannot be eligible and ineligible to participate in the bonus program simultaneously.

---

[18]There are statistical tests designed to examine tables larger than two by two (e.g., three by three, two by n). The current discussion is limited to two-by-two contingency tables.

The Four-Fifths Rule

The predominant nonstatistical method for examining questions of disparate impact is known as the *four-fifths rule*.[19] This rule, also known as the *80% rule*, is described by the Equal Employment Opportunity Commission (EEOC) as follows:

> *A selection rate for any race, sex or ethnic group which is less than four-fifths (4/5) (or eighty percent) of the rate for the group with the highest rate will generally be regarded by the Federal enforcement authorities as evidence of disparate impact, while a greater than four-fifths rate will generally not be regarded by Federal enforcement agencies as evidence of disparate impact.*

Origin of the Four-Fifths Rule

The four-fifths rule was originally framed in 1971 by the Technical Advisory Committee on Testing (TACT). Assembled by the State of California Fair Employment Practice Commission (FEPC), TACT consisted of a panel of thirty-two professionals from various labor, employment and technical fields. TACT was tasked with outlining the specific methodology for evaluating disparate impact. The four-fifths rule was the methodology they proposed for disparate impact analysis.

The origin of this rule was described by one of the committee members as follows:

> *During the negotiations of the FEPC Guidelines (which went on for months), one session had a significant debate on an appropriate statistical tool for determining adverse impact. We wanted to put an operational definition to some words defining what constituted adverse impact. There were about twenty of the committee members in the room. The members agreed that a statistical test was appropriate, but not enough. They also agreed that those who would implement these guidelines (the FEPC consultants) would never have the appropriate training to implement statistical tests (prior to the common use of computers, calculating probability statistics was a difficult task only completed by the technically savvy). Therefore, we needed an administrative guideline as well as a technical one for cases. I recall a heated debate that went on for way too long (as usual) with two camps: a 70% camp and a 90% camp. The 80% Test was born out*

---

[19]Ramona Paetzhold and Steven Willborn, *The Statistics of Discrimination: Using Statistical Evidence in Discrimination Cases*, Thompson/West (2006).

of two compromises: (1) a desire expressed by those writing and having input into the Guidelines to include a statistical test as the primary step but knowing from an administrative point of view a statistical test was not possible for the FEPC consultants who had to work the enforcement of the Guidelines, and (2) a way to split the middle between two camps, the 70% camp and the 90% camp. A way was found to use both. In the way the 80% Test was defined by TACT, if there was no violation of the 80% Test, then there would be no reason to apply statistical significance tests. This hopefully would eliminate many calculations and many situations where TACT would not be necessary and the decision could be made in the field. So from a practical point of view, the 80% Test became a first step. If there was no 80% Test violation, there was no need to go further and use a statistical test. If there was a violation of the 80% Test, statistical significance was needed and the 80% Test then became a practical significance test for adverse impact.[20]

The four-fifths rule was published by the FEPC in October 1972 and was later codified in the 1978 Uniform Guidelines for Employee Selection Procedures (UGESP), which is used by the EEOC, Department of Labor, and Department of Justice in enforcing the nondiscrimination requirements of Title VII.

Calculation

As laid out in the UGESP, disparate impact is determined by a four-step calculation:

1. Calculate the rate of selection for each group—divide the number of persons selected from a group by the total number of persons in that group;

2. Observe which group has the highest selection rate;

3. Calculate the impact ratios by dividing the selection rate for a group by the selection rate for the highest group;

4. Observe whether the selection rate for any group is substantially less (i.e., usually less than 4/5 or 80%) than the selection rate for the highest group. If it is, disparate impact is indicated in most circumstances.

---

[20]Dan Biddle, *Adverse Impact and Test Validation: A Practitioner's Guide to Valid and Defensible Employment Testing* (Burlington, VT: Ashgate Publishing Company, 2006), 3.

The actual calculations proceed as follows. Assume that we are interested in applying the four-fifths rule to assess whether the eligibility requirements for an incentive pay program have a disparate impact by race among a group of 10,000 employees. Of those, 5,000 are white and 5,000 are nonwhite. Further assume that 4,500 white and 4,000 nonwhite employees satisfy the eligibility requirements.

The contingency table for this example is as follows.

	Eligible	Not Eligible
Nonwhite	A	B
	4,000	1,000
White	C	D
	4,500	500

The eligibility rates for whites and nonwhites are calculated as follows:

Nonwhite Eligibility Rate	White Eligibility Rate
$= A / (A + B)$	$= C / (C + D)$
$= 4{,}000 / (4{,}000 + 1{,}000)$	$= 4{,}500 / (4{,}500 + 500)$
$= 4{,}000 / 5{,}000$	$= 4{,}500 / 5{,}000$
$= 80\%$	$= 90\%$

Ratio of Eligibility Rates:
80% / 90% = 89%

In this example, because the ratio of eligibility rates is 89% (which is greater than four-fifths, or 80%), we would infer that the eligibility requirements do not have a disparate impact by race.

Limitations of the Four-Fifths Rule

The four-fifths rule is a relatively straightforward calculation and is easy to implement. Because of this, it has gained popularity for determining disparate impact in employment discrimination matters. However, there are three serious limitations of the rule that make it less than ideal for assessing disparate impact.

Insensitivity to Sample Size

First, the four-fifths rule is insensitive to sample size. It does not take into account the number of decisions being studied. To see why this matters, consider the following example.

We are interested in applying the four-fifths rule to assess whether the eligibility requirements for an incentive pay program have a disparate impact by race among a group of six employees: three whites and three nonwhites. All three white employees and two of the three nonwhite employees satisfy the eligibility requirements. The contingency table for this example is as follows.

	Eligible	Not Eligible
Nonwhite	A	B
	2	1
White	C	D
	3	0

The eligibility rates for whites and nonwhites are calculated as follows.

Nonwhite Eligibility Rate	White Eligibility Rate
= A / (A + B)	= C / (C + D)
= 2 / (2 + 1)	= 3 / (3 + 0)
= 2 / 3	= 3 / 3
= 67%	= 100%

Ratio of Eligibility Rates:

67% / 100% = 67%

In this example, the ratio of eligibility rates is 67% (less than four-fifths, or 80%), so we would infer that the eligibility requirements do have a disparate impact by race. However, because of the small sample size of six employees, the observed result could have occurred due to chance. In fact, this disparity is equivalent to approximately 1.1 units of standard deviation. This is well below the "two or three units" standard of statistical significance. If we were using a formal statistical tool to examine these eligibility rates by race, we would not infer that disparate impact existed.

Going back to the original example of 5,000 nonwhites and 5,000 whites, we saw that the eligibility ratio was 89%. Based on the four-fifths rule, we inferred that no disparate impact by race existed. However, the disparity in this example is equivalent to approximately fourteen units of standard deviation, well above the threshold of two or three units.

As discussed earlier, sample size affects statistical significance. By its very construction, the four-fifths rule cannot account for sample size. In the example, the four-fifths rule led to the conclusion that disparate impact existed, whereas the statistical analysis indicated no disparate impact.

Insensitivity to Magnitude of Disparity

The four-fifths rule is insensitive to the magnitude of the disparity. To see why this matters, consider the following example.

Assume that we are interested in applying the four-fifths rule to assess whether either of the two eligibility requirements for an incentive pay program has a disparate impact by race among a group of 10,000 nonwhite and 10,000 white employees. Assume that 7,000 nonwhites and 10,000 whites satisfy the first eligibility criterion, and that 7 nonwhites and 10 whites satisfy the second eligibility criterion.

The contingency tables for these two eligibility criteria are as follows.

	Eligibility Criterion 1	
	Eligible	**Not Eligible**
Nonwhite	A	B
	7,000	3,000
White	C	D
	10,000	0

The eligibility rates for whites and nonwhites for criterion 1 are calculated as follows.

Nonwhite Eligibility Rate	**White Eligibility Rate**
= A / (A + B)	= C / (C + D)
= 7,000 / (7,000 + 3,000)	= 10,000 / (10,000 + 0)
= 7,000 / 10,000	= 10,000 / 10,000
= 70%	= 100%

Ratio of Eligibility Rates:

70% / 100% = 70%

	Eligibility Criterion 2	
	Eligible	Not Eligible
Nonwhite	A	B
	7	9,993
White	C	D
	10	9,990

The eligibility rates for whites and nonwhites for criterion 2 are calculated as follows.

Nonwhite Eligibility Rate	White Eligibility Rate
$= A / (A + B)$	$= C / (C + D)$
$= 7 / (7 + 9,993)$	$= 10 / (10 + 9,990)$
$= 7 / 10,000$	$= 10 / 10,000$
$= 0.07\%$	$= 0.10\%$

Ratio of Eligibility Rates:
$0.07\% / 0.10\% = 70\%$

Using the four-fifths rule, both eligibility criteria appear to be identical in that they both result in an eligibility ratio of 70%.

However, the criteria are quite different in terms of the number of nonwhite employees affected. Under criterion 1, there are 3,000 more nonwhite employees than white employees who have been adversely affected (i.e., did not satisfy eligibility requirements). Under criterion 2, there are three more nonwhite employees than white employees who have been adversely affected. Even though the eligibility rates of both criteria are the same (70%) there is certainly a difference of practical significance in the number of nonwhite employees affected (3,000 versus 3). The four-fifths rule cannot account for this.

Arbitrariness and Lack of Statistical Basis

The final shortcoming of the four-fifths rule is its arbitrariness and lack of statistical basis. The choice of four fifths, or 80%, has no scientific or empirical basis. In fact, as one of the TACT committee members stated, the choice of 80% was simply a compromise between the 70% camp and the 90% camp.

Though all threshold rules have some degree of arbitrariness, some are more arbitrary than others. For example, in *Hazelwood School District v. United States* (433 U.S. 299, 1977), the court determined that two or three units of standard deviation was considered to be statistically significant. The court could have chosen one unit, or five units, but they chose "two or three units." This presumably is because these are the values associated with probabilities of 5% and 1%, respectively, which are widely accepted within the statistics and social sciences communities. In the case of the four-fifths rule, there is no such general acceptance.

The arbitrary nature of the four-fifths rule has been questioned by U.S. courts since 1980. In fact, the EEOC suggested that a "more defensible standard" would be based on a comparison of the selection rate of a particular protected group with the rate that would occur if the organization simply selected people at random.

Formal Statistical Tests of Disparate Impact

The suggestion made by the EEOC of selecting people at random is essentially the basis of formal statistical tests of disparate impact. The central assumption underlying all of the formal tests that are discussed in this section— the chi square test, Fisher's exact test, the Mantel-Haenszel test, and logistic regression—are all premised on the assumption of no relationship between protected status and the outcome of a given employment policy or practice.

The Central Assumption

When studying questions of disparate impact, the central assumption used is that if the challenged employment policy or practice is neutral with respect to protected status, then the rates for protected and nonprotected employees experiencing the same employment outcomes should be equal.

For example, if eligibility for a bonus program does not have a disparate impact by gender, then we would expect the percentage of men who are eligible for the program to be the same as the percentage of women who are eligible for the program. In other words, if 75% of men are eligible for the bonus program, we would expect that 75% of women would also be eligible for the bonus program if the criteria for eligibility do not have a disparate impact by gender.

In this example, we would expect that the eligibility rates for men and women would be equal: 75%. The actual female eligibility rate for women may be 76% or 74%. We can use statistics to assess whether the protected group "success" rate is different from the nonprotected group "success" rate in a statistically meaningful way. There are numerous statistical tools that can perform this assessment.

Hypothesis Testing

In a disparate impact analysis, the expected "success" rate for protected group members is based on the assumption that under a neutral policy or practice, the success rates for protected and nonprotected people would be the same. In terms of a contingency table, the underlying assumption is that there is no association between the row variable (protected status) and the column variable (employment outcome).

To statistically test this assumption, a hypothesis test is used. In the disparate impact context, the null hypothesis is that there is no relationship between protected status and the outcome of the challenged policy or practice. The alternate hypothesis is that such a relationship does exist.

If there is no statistically significant difference between the actual and expected outcomes experienced by protected and nonprotected individuals, the null hypothesis cannot be rejected. One would infer that the null hypothesis is true, and conclude that there is no relationship between protected status and the outcome of the challenged policy or practice.

If, however, there is a statistically significant difference between actual and expected outcomes experienced by protected and nonprotected individuals, the null hypothesis is rejected. One would infer that the alternate hypothesis is true and conclude that there is a relationship between protected status and the outcome of the challenged policy or practice.

Choosing an Appropriate Test Statistic

There are a variety of statistical tests that can be used to examine claims of disparate impact. Each implicitly contains some assumptions. Choosing the appropriate statistical test depends on the nature of the selection process. There are two basic forms of selection processes: those with a variable number of selections, and those with a fixed number of selections.

Within the compensation context, a common example of a process with a variable number of selections is participation in an incentive compensation plan. In the case where employees must meet some eligibility criteria, and what constitutes satisfaction of those criteria is determined prior to employee evaluation, the number of employees who satisfy those criteria is not fixed.[21] It could be the case that 50% of employees are eligible to participate. It could just as easily be the case that 25% or 75% are eligible to participate. If the

---

[21] If the eligibility for participation was determined after reviewing employees' eligibility criteria—for example, to ensure that 25% of employees were eligible for participation— then the number of employees eligible for participation in the incentive compensation plan is fixed.

particular employment policy or practice being challenged has a variable success rate, both the composition of successes (e.g., male versus female) and the overall number of successes can vary. When examining these kinds of policies and practices for disparate impact, the appropriate test statistic is based on the binomial distribution.[22]

In contrast, when there are a fixed number of overall successes, the appropriate test statistic is based on the hypergeometric distribution.[23] An example of this type of policy or practice within the compensation context might be a year-end bonus that is awarded to the top five salespersons based on ranking those salespersons by total revenue generated during the calendar year. In this type of scenario, the composition of successes can vary (five men, four men and one woman, three men and two women, etc.), the overall number of successes is fixed.

Variable Number of Selections

The calculation of statistical significance in a process with a variable number of selections is based on the binomial distribution. To see how the calculation is performed, assume that we are interested in examining whether bonus eligibility criteria have a disparate impact by gender. Five hundred employees were evaluated, and of them, 125 satisfy the bonus eligibility criteria. Of those 125 employees who are eligible, 20 are female and 105 are male, as shown in Table 6-8.

Table 6-8. Eligibility Rates by Gender

	Total	Eligible	Not Eligible	Eligibility Rate
Women	150	20	130	13.3%
Men	350	105	245	30.0%
Total	500	125	375	25.0%

---

[22]The binomial distribution is the discrete probability distribution of the number of successes in a series of independent yes/no experiments, each of which has a probability of success equal to p. One common example of the binomial distribution is coin-flipping. You flip a coin 10 times. What is the probability of getting 6 heads in 10 flips? The binomial distribution is used to calculate the likelihood of seeing x heads out of n flips.

[23]The hypergeometric distribution is the discrete probability distribution that describes the probability of k successes in n draws without replacement. The common example used to illustrate the hypergeometric distribution is the "urn model"; you draw 10 marbles from an urn containing 5 red and 20 blue marbles without putting any drawn marbles back into the urn (without replacement). What is the probability that exactly 4 of the 10 marbles you draw are red? The hypergeometric distribution is used to calculate this probability.

As can be seen, the overall eligibility rate for all employees is 25%. The eligibility rate for men is 30%, and the eligibility rate for women is slightly more than 13%.

The null hypothesis is that there is no relationship between gender and eligibility for participation. If the null hypothesis is true, then the difference between male and female eligibility rates will be statistically insignificant. The test for statistical significance is drawn from the binomial distribution. The formula for computing the z-statistic—the measure of units of standard deviation—of the difference in eligibility rates by gender is as follows:

$$z = \frac{(p_f - p_m)}{\sqrt{p * (1 - p) * \left(\dfrac{1}{N_f} + \dfrac{1}{N_m} \right)}} \tag{6.6}$$

where

$$p_f = \text{female pass rate}$$

$$p_m = \text{male pass rate}$$

$$p = \text{overall pass rate}$$

$$N_f = \text{number of female selections}$$

$$N_m = \text{number of male selections}$$

In our example, the required variables for the test statistic are as follows:

$$p_f = \frac{20}{150} = 13.3\%$$

$$p_m = \frac{105}{350} = 30.0\%$$

$$p = \frac{125}{500} = 25.0\%$$

$$N_f = 150$$

$$N_m = 350$$

The calculation of the z-statistic is as follows:

$$z = \frac{(0.133 - 0.300)}{\sqrt{0.25 * (1 - 0.25) * \left(\dfrac{1}{150} + \dfrac{1}{350}\right)}} = -3.95$$

To determine whether the difference in male and female eligibility rates is statistically significant, one examines the absolute value of the z-statistic. In this case, because the z-statistic (the units of standard deviation) is greater than the threshold of two units, we reject the null hypothesis of no relationship between gender and eligibility. We infer that the eligibility criteria have a disparate impact with respect to gender.

This testing procedure is appropriate for any kind of employment policy or practice where there are a variable number of successes.

Fixed Number of Selections

The calculation of statistical significance in a process with a fixed number of selections is based on the hypergeometric distribution. To see how the calculation is performed, imagine that we are interested in examining whether the selection process of fifty employees to receive a year-end bonus has a disparate impact by gender. Assume that 125 employees were considered for selection and 50 were actually selected. Further assume that among the 50 selected, 10 were women and 40 were men, as shown in Table 6-9.

Table 6-9. Selection Rates by Gender

	Total	Selected	Not Selected	Selection Rate
Women	20	10	10	50.0%
Men	105	40	65	38.1%
Total	125	50	75	40.0%

The overall selection rate for all employees is 40%. The selection rate for men is 38.1%, and that for women is 50%.

The null hypothesis is that there is no relationship between gender and selection. If the null hypothesis is true, then the difference between male and female selection rates will be statistically insignificant. The test for statistical significance is drawn from the hypergeometric distribution. The formula for computing the z-statistic of the difference in selection rates by gender is as follows:

$$z = \frac{(s_f - (p * N_f))}{\sqrt{\left[s * (N - s) * N_m * N_f\right] / \left[(N^2 * (N - 1)\right]}} \qquad (6.7)$$

where

$$s_f = \text{number of female selections}$$

$$s = \text{overall selection rate}$$

$$N_f = \text{number of female employees}$$

$$N_m = \text{number of male employees}$$

$$N = \text{total number of employees}$$

Based on our example, the required variables for the test statistic are as follows:

$$s_f = 10$$

$$s = 50$$

$$p = \frac{50}{125} = 40.0\%$$

$$N_f = 20$$

$$N_m = 105$$

$$N = 125$$

The calculation of the z-statistic is as follows:

$$z = \frac{(10 - (0.40 * 20))}{\sqrt{\dfrac{[50 * (125 - 50) * 105 * 20]}{[50 * (125 - 50) * 105 * 20] / \left[125^2 * (125 - 1)\right]}}} = +0.99$$

To determine whether the difference in male and female eligibility rates is statistically significant, one examines the absolute value of the z-statistic. In this case, because the z-statistic is less than the threshold of two units, we cannot reject the null hypothesis of no relationship between gender and selection. We infer that selection for year-end bonus does not have a disparate impact with respect to gender.

This testing procedure is appropriate for any kind of employment policy or practice where there are a fixed number of successes.

Chi Square Test

One of the most common formal statistical tools for hypothesis testing of disparate impact within the contingency table framework is the chi square test. To illustrate how the it can be used to examine questions of adverse impact, we return to one of our previous examples of eligibility for participation in an incentive compensation program.

	Eligible	Not Eligible	Total
Nonwhite	A	B	5,000
	4,000	1,000	
White	C	D	5,000
	4,500	500	
Total	8,500	1,500	10,000

This contingency table presents the actual eligibility outcomes. To formally test for the presence or absence of disparate impact, the actual outcomes are compared against the expected outcomes under a race-neutral process. The expected outcomes are calculated as follows:

$$\frac{row\ total * column\ total}{total\ number\ of\ employees}$$

Our expected values in this example are as follows:

	Eligible	Not Eligible	Total
Nonwhite	A'	B'	5,000
	4,250	750	
White	C'	D'	5,000
	4,250	750	
Total	8,500	1,500	10,000

$$A' = C' = \frac{5{,}000 * 8{,}500}{10{,}000} = 4{,}250$$

$$B' = D' = \frac{5{,}000 * 1{,}500}{10{,}000} = 750$$

The comparison of actual and expected eligibility among nonwhites is as follows:

$$A' - A = 4{,}250 - 4{,}000 = 250$$

Based on this comparison, we see that 250 fewer nonwhite employees were eligible than would have been expected under a race-neutral process.

To assess whether this difference is statistically significant, and thus determine whether an inference of disparate impact by race is warranted, the chi square test statistic is used.

The chi square test statistic is calculated as the sum of squares of the difference between the actual (A) and expected (E) counts divided by the expected count. Mathematically, the chi square test statistic is expressed as follows:

$$\chi^2 = \sum \frac{(A - E)^2}{E} \qquad (6.8)$$

If there is no association between the column and row variables in the contingency table—that is, if there is no association between race and eligibility—then the actual and expected counts will be equal or approximately equal. This will lead to a zero (or approximately zero) numerator, and the test statistic will be zero or very small. However, if there is an association between the column and row variables, the difference between actual and expected counts will be large, leading to a large numerator and a large calculated value of the test statistic.

The chi square test statistic follows a chi square distribution with one degree of freedom.[24] A larger value of the test statistic results in a smaller probability of the actual outcome occurring due to chance. This smaller probability, in turn, translates into more units of standard deviation.

---

[24] A two-by-two contingency table has one degree of freedom. The number of values in the final calculation that are free to vary—that is, the number of independent pieces of information—is referred to as the degrees of freedom. In a two-by-two contingency table, if we know the row and column totals (in this case, the number of white and nonwhite employees and the numbers eligible and not eligible for participation), only one number—either A, B, C, or D—is required to fill in the remainder of the cells.

In this example, the calculated chi square test statistic is equal to 196.08. Based on this value, the probability of a difference of this size occurring under a race-neutral process is less than 0.0001. This probability, when translated into units of standard deviation, satisfies the "two or three units" standard set forth in *Hazelwood*.[25]

Because the disparity—the difference between actual and expected—is statistically significant, the null hypothesis that there is no relationship between race and eligibility would be rejected. One would infer that there is a relationship between race and eligibility, and therefore make an inference of disparate impact.

The advantage of using the chi square test to study contingency tables is that it is relatively simple to calculate. However, there are two main disadvantages of this test. It provides only an approximate probability. There are other tests, such as Fisher's exact test, that provide an exact probability. Furthermore, the chi square test is inappropriate for small sample sizes.[26] If the expected cell counts are small, Fisher's exact test is preferred.

Fisher's Exact Test

Fisher's exact test is another formal statistical tool for hypothesis testing. The null hypothesis here is that the relative proportions of one variable (i.e., protected and nonprotected individuals) are independent of the second variable.

Fisher's exact test is based on the hypergeometric distribution. It therefore assumes that the number of selections is fixed. It calculates the probability of seeing the actual outcomes, and all other outcomes with more extreme deviations, under the null hypothesis.

To illustrate what is meant by "more extreme deviations," assume that a study population consists of twenty individuals, ten of whom are protected and ten of whom are nonprotected. Further assume that ten of the twenty individuals will receive a year-end bonus based on their relative rankings with respect to a given criterion. When all individuals are ranked, three protected and seven nonprotected people are selected to receive the year-end bonus.

Based on the composition of the twenty employees with respect to protected status (i.e., 50% protected and 50% nonprotected) we would expect have expected five protected and five nonprotected individuals to be selected

---

[25]The translation of the chi square test statistic into a probability, and hence into units of standard deviation, is not discussed here. Readers are encouraged to consult any elementary statistics text for a discussion of this translation process.

[26]In this context, a small sample size refers to an expected value in the contingency table cells of less than five.

(50% of all selections would be protected and 50% of all selections would be nonprotected). In this case, more "extreme deviations" from the expected outcome would be given by the following selections:

- two protected and eight nonprotected selections;

- one protected and nine nonprotected selections;

- zero protected and ten nonprotected selections.

To illustrate how Fisher's exact test can be used to examine questions of disparate impact, assume a study population containing ten protected individuals and ten nonprotected individuals. Three protected and seven nonprotected individuals are selected for a positive employment outcome. The two-by-two contingency table for this example would be as follows.

	Eligible	Not Eligible	
Protected	A	B	10
	3	7	
Nonprotected	C	D	10
	7	3	
	10	10	20

The null hypothesis is essentially the same as in the chi square test: there is no relationship between protected status and the likelihood of being eligible. The expected number of eligible protected employees is calculated in the same way as previously discussed. Because 50% of the total population of employees is protected, one would expect 50% of the eligible employees—or a total of five people—to be protected individuals.

Unlike the chi square test, Fisher's exact test has no test statistic; the probability is calculated directly. The probability is given by the following hypergeometric rule:[27]

$$\frac{\dfrac{(A+C)!}{A!C!} + \dfrac{(B+D)!}{B!D!}}{\dfrac{N}{(A+B)!(C+D)!}} \tag{6.9}$$

---

[27]Note that the symbol ! refers to the factorial. The factorial of a positive integer N is the product of all positive integers less than or equal to N. For example, $5! = 5 * 4 * 3 * 2 * 1 = 120$.

For computational purposes, this reduces to:

$$\frac{(A+B)!(C+D)!(A+C)!(B+D)!}{N!A!B!C!D!} \qquad (6.10)$$

Applying this formula to our example data, we have the following calculation:

$$\frac{(3+7)!(7+3)!(3+3)!(7+7)!}{20!3!7!7!3!} = 0.3715$$

Using this formula, the exact probability is equal to 0.3715. Because the probability is not small enough to be statistically significant, the null hypothesis that there is no relationship between protected status and the employment outcome cannot be rejected.[28] One would infer that there is no relationship between protected status and the employment outcome. One would therefore not make an inference of disparate impact.

Mantel-Haenszel Test

The chi square and Fisher's exact tests are useful in cases where selection decisions are examined as a group. If the selection decisions were made at one point in time, such as one evaluation of bonus eligibility, examining the decisions collectively in an aggregated analysis may be appropriate. It is often the case, however, that we want to study multiple occurrences of the same selection process.

For example, assume that bonus eligibility is determined on a quarterly basis—that is, four times per calendar year. One could perform four separate statistical tests in which eligibility rates by protected group status are examined individually for each round of eligibility evaluation. Alternatively, the four rounds could be statistically combined together to assess whether a pattern of disparate impact over time exists.

The Mantel-Haenszel test can be used to statistically combine groups of selection events. The Mantel-Haenszel test statistic is calculated as the squared sum of deviations between observed and expected values divided by the estimate of variance of the squared differences. Note that 0.5 is subtracted from the squared sum of deviations between observed and expected values

---

[28]To reject the null hypothesis, the probability would have to be less than or equal to 0.05 under standard statistical assumptions.

as a continuity correction.[29] Mathematically, the test statistic can be expressed as follows:

$$\chi^2_{MH} = \frac{\left\{\left|\sum\left[A - \frac{(A+B)(A+C)}{N}\right]\right| - 0.5\right\}^2}{\sum(A+B)(A+C)(B+D)(C+D) / (N^3 - N^2)} \qquad (6.11)$$

The Mantel-Haenszel test statistic follows the chi square distribution with one degree of freedom.

To see how the Mantel-Haenszel test can be used, consider the following example. We are interested in examining whether a bonus eligibility criterion has a disparate impact by gender. Assume that the eligibility criterion was applied at four different times throughout the year. Further assume that the results of the eligibility analyses were as shown in Table 6-10.

Table 6-10. Eligibility Rates

	Total	Eligible	Not Eligible	Eligibility Rate (%)
January 1				
Women	150	20	130	13.3
Men	350	105	245	30.0
Total	500	125	375	25.0
April 1				
Women	160	40	120	25.0
Men	480	152	328	31.7
Total	640	192	448	30.0
July 1				
Women	132	14	118	10.6
Men	244	88	156	36.1
Total	376	102	274	27.1
October 1				
Women	235	36	199	15.3
Men	537	154	383	28.7
Total	772	190	582	24.6

---

[29] A *continuity correction* is incorporated when a continuous function is used to approximate a discrete distribution. For example, if the normal distribution is used to approximate the binomial distribution, a continuity correction is used.

The results of the four instances of the application of the eligibility criterion can be statistically combined via the Mantel-Haenszel test to determine if the eligibility criterion has a disparate impact on women over time.

In this example, the calculated Mantel-Haenszel test statistic is equal to 51.05. Based on this test statistic, the probability of these results occurring under a gender-neutral process is less than 0.0001. The units of standard deviation in this example satisfy the two or three units standard set forth in *Hazelwood*. There is a statistically significant shortfall of women eligible for the bonus— that is, statistically significantly fewer women are eligible for the bonus than would be expected under a gender-neutral process.

Because the female shortfall is statistically significant, the null hypothesis that there is no relationship between gender and the likelihood of being eligible for the bonus is rejected. One would infer that there is a relationship between gender and the likelihood of bonus eligibility and that the eligibility criterion has a disparate impact with respect to gender.

Logistic Regression

All of the test statistics discussed up to this point have focused on examining disparate impact within the context of a two-by-two contingency table. By definition, the two-by-two contingency table framework can only examine two variables at a time. In the context of disparate impact, a two-by-two contingency analysis can only examine (1) protected group status and (2) selected or not selected.

There may be some cases in which one would want to incorporate more than just two dimensions of information. For example, assume that when selecting individuals for a year-end sales bonus, the decision maker considers each employee's total annual sales, the percentage of target sales volume achieved, and the employee's performance rating from the prior evaluation period. For the model to reflect the role that sales volume, percentage of target achieved, and performance play in the selection process, it is necessary to move away from the two-by-two contingency table framework and use a multiple regression analysis.

A multiple regression analysis examines the relationship between a dependent variable and two or more independent variables. In this example, the dependent variable would be whether the employee was selected for the year-end sales bonus, and the independent variables would be protected group status, total annual sales, percentage of target sales volume achieved, and performance.

There are numerous variations of the multiple regression model for the general linear and nonlinear forms. When the question being investigated can be expressed as a binary dependent value—essentially a "yes" or "no" value—a special form of a generalized linear model can be used: the *logistic model*.

Formally, the logistic model takes the following general form:

$$\log\left[\frac{p}{1-p}\right] = \alpha + \beta_1 X_1 + \beta_2 X_2 + \cdots + \beta_i X_i \qquad (6.12)$$

where

$$p = \text{probability of selection}$$

$$\alpha = \text{intercept}$$

$$\beta_1 = \text{coefficient of independent variable I}$$

$$X_1 = \text{independent variable I}$$

$$\beta_2 = \text{coefficient of independent variable 2}$$

$$X_2 = \text{independent variable 2}$$

$$\beta_i = \text{coefficient of independent variable } i$$

$$X_i = \text{independent variable } i$$

If one was interested in examining disparate impact with respect to gender of eligibility for a year-end sales bonus that considered protected group status, total annual sales, percentage of target sales volume achieved, and performance, the logistic model would be as follows:

$$\log\left[\frac{P_{selection}}{1-P_{selection}}\right] = \alpha + \beta_1 salesvol + \beta_2\,\% \text{ of target} + \beta_3 perf + \beta_4 F$$

After estimation of the logistic regression model, the results are be interpreted to determine if there is a statistically significant relationship between selection for a year-end sales bonus and gender. The interpretation and evaluation of results is the same as that for multiple regression analysis.

Other Statistical Tests

The statistical tests described in this chapter represent some of the most commonly used statistical tools for examining adverse impact. This discussion is by no means exhaustive and is not intended to be encyclopedic in scope. The tests presented are intended to provide the reader with an introduction and overview to the kinds of statistical tools available, how those tools work, and how they can be applied within the context of disparate impact.

Statistical consultants are best positioned to choose the appropriate statistical testing methodology for the disparate impact question(s) under investigation.

Analysis Follow-Up

Follow-through is the bridge between good planning and good results.

—Unknown

Analysis follow-up is a crucial step in the compensation review process. If the results of a given analysis indicate the possibility of a disparity, either by protected group status or within the context of overall equity, that disparity should be investigated. Without proper follow-up, the opportunities to learn from the analysis and correct potential problem areas are lost.

In fact, performing the analyses and then failing to follow up on the findings can do more harm than not conducting the analyses in the first place. Consider the case of *Dukes v. Wal-Mart Stores, Inc.* (N.D. Cal. No C-01-2252). The lawsuit, filed in June 2001, was the largest gender discrimination suit in the history of the United States; the claim sought to represent 1.6 million women employed by Wal-Mart since December 26, 1998.[1]

Six years before this suit was filed, Wal-Mart retained a well-known law firm to examine its vulnerability to gender discrimination claims. According to an article in the *New York Times*, the firm issued a report in 1995 indicating that female employees earned less than male employees in numerous job categories; women in salaried positions earned 19% less than their male

---

[1] Wal-Mart Stores, Inc., Form 10-Q for the Quarterly Period Ended October 31, 2005.

counterparts.[2] Specific actions for remedying the widespread gender disparities in compensation at Wal-Mart and Sam's Club stores were recommended.[3]

According to the article:

> The report, which [Wal-Mart] asserted was "confidential and privileged," was made available to The New York Times by someone not involved in the lawsuit who said that Wal-Mart had not done enough to address the issues [the report] raised.[4]

As pointed out by Steven Greenhouse, "company documents and depositions in the lawsuit suggest that Wal-Mart's initial adoption of the report's recommendations was fitful and incomplete."[5]

Had Wal-Mart engaged in proper follow-up on the identified gender disparities in pay, the litigation—as well as the public relations problems created by the release of the report—may have been avoided.

The manner in which the follow-up investigation proceeds depends on several elements, including what factors determine compensation, how the compensation decisions were made, and who made them, among others.

Typically, follow-up investigations begin with a deeper examination of the compensation and employment characteristics data and analysis results, a review of personnel and employment files, an examination of current and historical performance rating information, and discussions with managers, supervisors, and human resources personnel.

Follow-up is important because it can reveal areas of potential discrimination and/or inequity, highlight structural flaws in the model of compensation, and identify deficiencies in data capture and document retention. For example, when speaking with a manager or supervisor about a potential pay disparity for a given similarly situated employee grouping, you may learn that some of the employees in that grouping were red circled.[6] Red circling—rather than discrimination—may be the reason for what would appear to be a disparity.

---

[2]Steven Greenhouse, "Report Warned Wal-Mart of Risks Before Bias Suit," New York Times, June 3, 2010.

[3]The report also discussed specific recommendations for gender disparities in promotion rates that were identified by the analysis.

[4]Greenhouse, "Report Warned Wal-Mart of Risks."

[5]Ibid.

[6]Red circling, also known as red lining, is maintaining an employee's pay rate above the established range maximum for that employee's classification. An employee's pay rate may, at the discretion of management, be red circled when his or her position is downward reclassified and the current salary is above the pay range maximum for the new classification. Occurrences of red circling are most commonly found in cases of reclassification of jobs, personnel redeployment following a reduction in force, and so on.

In this case, information regarding which employees in the grouping were red circled should be incorporated into the statistical model. The model should then be reestimated to assess how the incorporation of red-circle information affected the estimated pay disparity.

A conversation with a manager or supervisor may also reveal that there are nondiscriminatory factors considered when making compensation decisions that were not included in the original model because no information is recorded or maintained regarding these factors. This kind of conversation should be an impetus to begin collection and retention of the necessary data so that they can be incorporated in future examinations of compensation.

Before turning to a discussion of the various methods of follow-up investigation, it is important to have an understanding of how to identify which similarly situated employee groupings require it. Groupings requiring follow-up are identified via analysis red flags and problem indicators.

Red Flags and Problem Indicators

Analysis red flags come in an array of forms. Some, like measures of statistical significance, are based in probability theory. Others, such as a collection of results across different groups of similarly situated employees that are directionally adverse to a given protected group, are pattern-driven. When examining the results of the compensation analysis, it is essential to consider and look for a variety of red flags. Relying solely on only one type of indicator is not recommended, because it can lull one into a false sense of security regarding pay equity and the risk of compensation discrimination litigation.

To facilitate the discussion of common red flags and problem indicators, and differences in the inferences they generate, a uniform data set will be used. Assume that we are interested in examining compensation for the presence of gender discrimination among ten similarly situated employee groupings.[7] We are examining total annual compensation among those employees assigned to the sales department and hourly rates of pay among those employees assigned to the installation department.

Our quantitative examination of pay for each similarly situated employee grouping will consist of multiple regression analysis. A review of the compensation policies and practices for the sales department indicates that annual salary is based on an employee's total company seniority, relevant prior experience, and performance, as shown in Equation 7.1:

$$salary = \beta_0 + (\beta_1 * sen) + (\beta_2 * prior\,exp) + (\beta_3 * perf) \qquad (7.1)$$

---

[7]Though the current discussion is framed in terms of gender equity, it is equally applicable to the examination of results for all protected class definitions.

A review of the compensation policies and practices for drivers, installers, and repair personnel assigned to the installation department indicates that an employee's hourly rate of pay is based on total company seniority, performance, and possession of a commercial driver's license (CDL), as shown in Equation 7.2:

$$rate = \beta_0 + (\beta_1 * sen) + (\beta_2 * perf) + (\beta_3 * DUMMY_{CDL}) \qquad (7.2)$$

A review of the compensation policies and practices for forklift operators and receiving personnel indicates that an employee's hourly rate of pay is based on total company seniority, performance, and possession of a forklift certification, as shown in Equation 7.3:

$$rate = \beta_0 + (\beta_1 * sen) + (\beta_2 * perf) + (\beta_3 * DUMMY_{FORKLIFT}) \qquad (7.3)$$

The following data points are collected for all of the employees in each of the ten similarly situated groupings:

> **Sales Department**: total annual compensation, seniority, prior relevant experience, and performance ratings
>
> **Drivers, Installers, and Repair**: hourly pay rate, seniority, performance ratings, and CDL status
>
> **Forklift Operations and Receiving**: hourly pay rate, seniority, performance ratings, forklift certification status

These data are then used to estimate ten regression models derived from Equations 7.1, 7.2, and 7.3, one for each similarly situated employee grouping. Table 7-1 represents the results of the multiple regression analyses.

Table 7-1. Hypothetical Regression Analysis Results

		# EEs		Gender Pay Effect		
Dept.	Job Title	M	F	β_F	t	p
(1)	(2)	(3)	(4)	(5)	(6)	(7)
Sales	Call Ctr Agent	64	57	(1,040)	2.28	0.0226
	Cust Svc Rep	36	19	(624)	2.12	0.0340
	Equip Sales Rep	43	12	(520)	0.63	0.5287
	Pricing Spec	24	21	(312)	0.55	0.5823
	Purch Agent	20	16	(520)	1.36	0.1738
Installation	Driver	30	5	(0.25)	0.71	0.4777
	Installer	48	6	(0.25)	8.69	0.0000
	Repair	33	3	(0.35)	0.80	0.4237
	Forklift Op	19	1	(1.00)	N/A	N/A
	Receiving	21	9	(0.10)	1.53	0.1260

Columns 1 and 2 in Table 7-1 represent the departments and job titles for the similarly situated employee groupings. Columns 3 and 4 show the number of men (M) and women (F) employed in each grouping. Column 5 presents the estimated gender effect (in terms of annual salary for the sales department and in terms of hourly pay rates for the installation department) from the regression analysis.[8] Columns 6 and 7 present the t-statistics and p-values (probability values) associated with each of the estimated gender effects.

Statistical Significance

As mentioned in Chapter 3, statistical significance addresses the question of whether an observed outcome is "sufficiently rare" such that it is unlikely to occur due to chance variation. The statistical significance of the estimated gender effects shown in Table 7-1 is assessed via the t-statistics and p-values.

---

[8]In each of the equations, gender was represented by a dummy variable taking on a value of 1 for women and a value of 0 for men. Estimated gender effects that are negative are directionally adverse to women (there is a penalty for being female); estimated gender effects that are positive are directionally favorable to women (there is a premium for being female).

On reviewing the results presented in Table 7-1, we see that among the ten similarly situated employee groupings, only two of the estimated gender effects—call center agent and customer service representative—are statistically significant. The estimated gender effect among call center agents is –$1,040 a year. Under a gender-neutral process, we would expect to see an estimated gender effect of –$1,040 or greater only 2.3% of the time over repeated sampling. We therefore infer that chance is not the likely explanation for the difference in hourly pay rates by gender among call center agents and that some other process is at work.

Similarly, the estimated gender effect among customer service representatives is –$624 a year. Under a gender-neutral process, we would expect to see an estimated gender effect of –$624 or greater only 3.4% of the time over repeated sampling. We therefore infer that chance is not the likely explanation for the difference in hourly pay rates by gender among customer service representatives and that some other process is at work.

It is important to keep in mind that, as noted in Chapter 5, we cannot automatically infer that the statistically significant gender disparities among call center agents and customer service representatives are the result of gender discrimination. There are a variety of other potential explanations for the observed disparities. The purpose of follow-up investigations is to identify these potential explanations and assess their validity.

The estimated gender effects for the remaining eight similarly situated employee groupings are not statistically significant. As such, they are not statistically different from zero and are consistent with the hypotheses of gender-neutral compensation practices. This does not mean, however, that we can automatically rule out the possibility of gender discrimination for these remaining groupings.

Consider, for example, the similarly situated employee grouping consisting of forklift operators. There are twenty individuals employed as forklift operators: nineteen men and one woman. As can be seen from Table 7-1, the estimated gender effect among forklift operators is –$1.00 per hour, but no measures of statistical significance (*t*-statistic and *p*-value) are calculated for this similarly situated employee grouping. Calculation of these statistics is not possible because there is only one woman within the grouping.[9]

---

[9]Because there is only one female in the similarly situated employee grouping, there is only a single observation on which the estimated gender effect is based. Because of this, there is no variation among observations of the estimated gender effect. As a result, the *t*-statistic and its associated probability value cannot be calculated.

Also consider the similarly situated employee grouping consisting of repair personnel. There are thirty-six people employed as repair personnel: thirty-three men and three women. As can be seen from Table 7-1, the estimated gender effect among repair personnel is −$0.35 per hour, but it is not statistically significant; the associated probability value is 0.4237. This result should not be interpreted as indicative of no gender discrimination. One must keep in mind that statistical significance is a function of both the size of the disparity and the sample size.[10] It is possible that the estimated gender effect failed to attain statistical significance because of the small number of women in this similarly situated grouping. One should not take comfort in an analysis indicating no statistically significant disparities in pay by protected group status in cases of small sample sizes.

Practical Significance

In addition to reviewing statistical significance, one should also review the estimated gender effects for practical significance. As noted in Chapter 3, practical significance addresses the question of whether the estimated effect is big enough to matter.

Among the five similarly situated employee groupings within the sales department, the estimated gender effects range from $312 to $1,040 a year. The estimated $312 differential by gender among pricing specialists is likely to be practically insignificant. Assuming that the average annual salaries for men and women are $36,712 and $36,400, respectively, the estimated differential is less than 1% of women's salary in this similarly situated employee grouping.[11] In most cases, this differential would not be practically significant.[12]

The estimated gender differential in annual salary among call center agents is $1,040. This differential is likely to be practically significant. Assuming that the average salary rates for men and women are $30,680 and $29,640, respectively, the estimated differential is 3.5% of women's annual salary in this similarly situated employee grouping.[13] In most cases, this differential may be considered practically significant.

---

[10]This concept is explained in the Appendix.

[11]The difference of $312 per year is 0.86% of the women's average annual salary (0.0086 = $312 / $36,400).

[12]Whether this estimated differential is in fact practically significant will depend upon its interpretation within the organization. Risk tolerances vary by organization, and each employer will have its own unique level of acceptable risk, thresholds for practical significance, etc.

[13]The difference of $1,040 per year is 3.5% of the women's average annual salary (0.035 = $1,040 / $29,640).

Among the five similarly situated employee groupings within the installation department, the estimated gender effects range from –$0.10 to –$1.00 per hour. The estimated ten-cent-per-hour differential by gender among receiving personnel is likely to be practically insignificant. Assuming that the average hourly rates of pay for men and women are $11.50 and $11.40, respectively, the estimated differential translates into an annual difference of $208; this is less than 1% of women's annual earnings in this similarly situated employee group-ing.[14] In most cases, this differential would not be practically significant.[15]

The estimated gender differential in hourly rates of pay among forklift opera-tors is –$1.00. This differential is likely to be practically significant. Assuming that the average hourly rates of pay for men and women are $13.85 and $12.85, respectively, the estimated differential translates into an annual dif-ference of $2,080; this is more than 7% of women's annual earnings in this similarly situated employee grouping.[16] In most cases, this differential would be practically significant. Even though the estimated gender effect is not statisti-cally significant, its practical significance warrants follow-up.

Directionally Adverse Results

Though it is important to examine the estimated gender effect for each simi-larly situated employee grouping individually, it is equally important to exam-ine the estimated effects collectively. A review of Table 7-1 reveals that all of the estimated gender effects for the ten similarly situated employee groupings are negative, meaning that they are all directionally adverse to women. A pattern like this may be indicative of systemic disparate treatment within the sales and installation departments.[17] Follow-up investigations on these depart-ments as a whole, and the similarly situated employee groupings contained

---

[14]Assuming that receiving personnel are paid for 2,080 hours per year, we expect a woman in this similarly situated employee grouping to earn $23,712 annually ($23,712 = $11.40 per hour * 2,080 hours per year). We would expect a man in this similarly situated employee grouping to earn $23,920 annually ($23,920 = $11.50 per hour * 2,080 hours per year). The difference of $208 annually ($208 = $23,920 − $23,712) is 0.88% of the woman's annual salary (0.0088 = $208 / $23,712).

[15]Whether this estimated differential is in fact practically significant will depend on its interpretation within the organization. Risk tolerances vary by organization, and each employer will have its own unique level of acceptable risk, thresholds for practical significance, and so on.

[16]Assuming that forklift operators are paid for 2,080 hours a year, we expect a woman in this similarly situated employee grouping to earn $28,808 annually ($28,808 = $12.85 per hour * 2,080 hours per year). We expect a man in this similarly situated employee grouping to earn $30,888 annually ($30,888 = $13.85 per hour * 2,080 hours per year). The difference of $2,080 annually ($2,080 = $30,888 − $28,808) is 7.2% of the woman's annual salary (0.072 = $2,080 / $28,808).

[17]Systemic disparate treatment is discussed in Chapter 2.

within them, is required. Possible explanations for the universally directionally adverse gender effects include discriminatory intent on the part of the decision maker(s) within these departments, compensation policies and practices creating a disparate impact on women, or misspecification of the models for these employee groupings. Further investigation is required to determine the underlying cause(s) of the estimated gender disparities.

One should not take comfort in an analysis indicating no statistically significant disparities in pay by protected group status when the majority of similarly situated employee grouping examined has an outcome that is directionally adverse to the protected group. Failing to investigate a collection of directionally adverse results can create substantial exposure to a "pattern or practice" discrimination claim.

Raw Differentials

As noted in previous chapters, multiple regression analysis is the preferred statistical technique for examining questions of internal pay equity. There are cases, however, in which multiple regression analysis is inappropriate or impossible.[18] In such cases, alternative techniques for the comparisons of pay rates are required. Chapter 6 illustrates several of these alternative techniques, such as comparison of means or medians, tipping point tests, and threshold tests.

Generally speaking, these alternative comparisons generate "raw" differentials by protected group status, meaning that they focus on two dimensions only: compensation and protected group status. These techniques are incapable of directly incorporating additional information regarding the determinants of compensation. Because of this, the two-dimensional comparison of compensation by protected group status may yield numerous false positive cases in which there appears to be a disparity by protected group status but that disparity is explained when factors explaining compensation are considered.

All groupings of employees for which these alternative techniques indicate disparities must be investigated. An increase in false positive cases increases the volume of follow-up investigations that must be performed. However, it is not possible to determine whether the result for a particular group of employees can be explained by legitimate nondiscriminatory factors or is unexplained. From a risk management perspective, failing to follow up on all disparities leaves the organization vulnerable to lawsuits alleging discriminatory differentials in compensation were detected but not remedied.

---

[18]For example, the similarly situated employee grouping may contain too few employees to allow for multiple regression analysis.

Systemic versus Individual Follow-Up

Follow-up investigations can be broadly classified into two categories: systemic and individual. The necessity of systemic and/or individual follow-up will be determined largely by the analysis results and to a lesser extent by the type of analysis performed (e.g., multiple regression, comparison of means, threshold test). Regardless of the type(s) of follow-up performed, the purpose of the investigation is to identify explanations for any differences in compensation within the similarly situated employee grouping that appear to be attributable to protected group status. Ideally, these explanations should relate to factors outside of the model.[19]

Systemic Follow-Up

In some cases, broad patterns will be evident in the analysis results. Table 7-1 is an example of this; the estimated gender effect is directionally adverse to women for all ten similarly situated employee groupings studied. This indicates that a systemic follow-up investigation is warranted.[20]

To illustrate how a systemic follow-up investigation might proceed, consider the following hypothetical example. The investigation begins with a review of the organizational structures of the sales and installation departments. Figures 7-1A and 7-1B illustrate the organizational structures for these two departments.[21]

---

[19]If a factor is included in the model, it has already been accounted for in the estimation process.

[20]The follow-up actions discussed in this chapter are meant to be illustrative of common scenarios. They are by no means exhaustive and should not be interpreted as such.

[21]The example companies, departments, job titles, employees, and supervisors referenced herein are fictitious. No association with any real companies, departments, job titles, employees, or supervisors is intended or should be inferred.

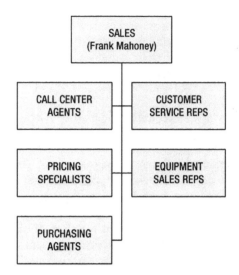

Figure 7-1A. Organizational chart for sales department

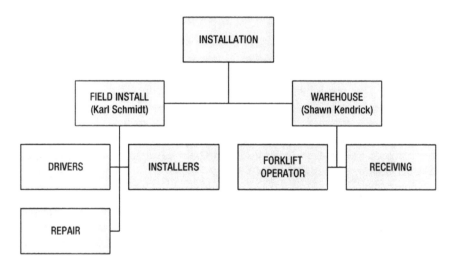

Figure 7-1B. Organizational chart for installation department

As can be seen from Figure 7-1A, Frank Mahoney has supervisory responsibility and decision-making authority over the 312 employees assigned to the sales department. Supervisory responsibility within the installation department is divided; Karl Schmidt has supervisory responsibility and decision-making authority over the 125 drivers, installers, and repair personnel. Shawn Kendrick has supervisory responsibility and decision-making authority over the fifty forklift operators and receiving personnel.

The next stage of the investigation entails conversations with Frank Mahoney, Karl Schmidt, and Shawn Kendrick regarding the compensation decisions they made for the employees under their supervision. Assume that these conversations reveal the following findings.[22]

Call Center Agents, Customer Service Representatives, and Equipment Sales Representatives

While talking to Frank Mahoney, you learn that the total compensation for call center agents, customer service representatives, and equipment sales representatives consists of a base salary and incentive compensation. Call center agents receive monthly bonus payments for meeting or exceeding the processing and completion of a target number of calls. Customer service representatives receive quarterly commission payments for product and service upsells and add-ons. Equipment sales representatives receive quarterly commission payments for meeting or exceeding their sales quotas.

Based on the conversation with Frank, a plausible explanation for the observed gender disparity is that the model for this similarly situated employee grouping is misspecified.

Among call center agents, customer service representatives, and equipment sales representatives, the model structure and the compensation metric are mismatched. The model structure, given by Equation 7.1, expresses annual salary as a function of seniority, prior relevant experience, and performance. However, during the data collection process, *total annual compensation*, not annual salary, was captured. Because these employees receive various forms of incentive compensation in addition to their base salary, total annual compensation is likely to exceed annual salary.

The observed gender disparity is likely attributable to the fact that our compensation metric includes bonus and commission payments, but our model structure is based solely on annual salary. This mismatch between the compensation metric and the model is a plausible explanation for the observed gender disparity if there are legitimate differences in earned incentive compensation by gender.

There are two approaches to resolving this mismatch. The first is to collect salary data and reestimate the models using annual salary, rather than total annual compensation. Alternatively, data regarding the factors determining incentive compensation could be collected, the models could be respecified to

---

[22]These scenarios are only a handful of an innumerable set of possible scenarios and should not be interpreted as an exhaustive listing of all possible outcomes. They are presented for illustrative purposes only.

incorporate these additional factors, and the respecified model could be reestimated using total annual compensation as the compensation metric under investigation.

The choice of approach will be determined by the question the analysis is intended to address. If one is interested in examining whether annual salaries are set equitably according to the relevant compensation policies and practices, then reestimation of the model using annual salary, rather than total annual compensation, is the preferred approach. Assuming that an analysis of annual salary does not indicate pay disparities by gender, then the gender disparities initially observed can be explained by the mismatch between the compensation metric and model misspecification. However, if gender disparities persist, then follow-up investigations are warranted.

On the other hand, if one is interested in examining whether differences in total compensation by gender exist, then respecification and reestimation is the preferred approach. The model structures for call center agents, customer service representatives, and equipment sales representatives could be respecified to account for incentive compensation as given in Equations 7.4, 7.5, and 7.6, respectively:

$$total\,comp = \beta_0 + (\beta_1 * sen) + (\beta_2 * prior\,exp) + (\beta_3 * perf) \\ + (\beta_4 * percent\,of\,target\,calls\,achieved) \tag{7.4}$$

$$total\,comp = \beta_0 + (\beta_1 * sen) + (\beta_2 * prior\,exp) + (\beta_3 * perf) \\ + (\beta_4 * \$value\,of\,upsells\,and\,add\text{-}ons) \tag{7.5}$$

$$total\,comp = \beta_0 + (\beta_1 * sen) + (\beta_2 * prior\,exp) + (\beta_3 * perf) \\ + (\beta_4 * percent\,of\,sales\,quota\,achieved) \tag{7.6}$$

Assuming that the estimation of these respecified models do not indicate pay disparities by gender, then the gender disparities initially observed can be explained by model misspecification. If gender disparities persist, then follow-up investigations are warranted.

It should be noted that even if the reestimation of the respecified models reveals no differences in total compensation by gender, it does not automatically follow that the employer is invulnerable to claims of discrimination. Although the analysis results do not support a claim of disparate treatment, there may be vulnerability to a claim of disparate impact.

The incentive compensation (i.e., bonuses and commissions) received by these employees is formula-based. As noted in Chapter 2, formula-based compensation systems are typically protected under Section 703(h) of Title VII. If a plaintiff were to make a claim and prove that the incentive compensation structure was adopted with actual discriminatory purpose, the employer could be found liable for discrimination. The recommended course of action, therefore, is to examine the formula-based elements of compensation for disparate impact to assess vulnerability to disparate impact claims.

Purchasing Agents

During the conversation with Frank, you learn that several of the purchasing agents were red circled following reassignment from more senior positions. Based on this, red circling of some employees may explain the observed gender disparity in compensation. The red-circled people should be identified, and the model should be respecified to incorporate a red circle dummy variable:

$$salary = \beta_0 + (\beta_1 * sen) + (\beta_2 * prior\,exp) + (\beta_3 * perf) \qquad (7.7)$$
$$+ (\beta_4 * RedCircled)$$

Assuming that the estimation of this respecified model does not indicate pay disparities by gender, then the gender disparity initially observed can be explained by red circling. If gender disparities persist, then an individual follow-up investigation is warranted.

Pricing Specialists

Your conversation with Frank reveals that he cannot think of a plausible explanation for the observed gender disparity in salary among pricing specialists. Therefore, individual follow-up investigation is required for this similarly situated employee grouping.

Drivers, Installers, and Repair Personnel

While talking to Karl Schmidt, you learn that the manner in which hourly pay rates are determined for new hires was changed three years ago. Previously, the initial rate of pay for a newly hired driver, installer, or repair person was based on the individual's prior relevant experience. Currently, the initial pay rate is fixed for new hires and no consideration is given to prior relevant experience.

A review of the driver, installer, and repair personnel indicates that all were hired three or more years ago. Hence, the model originally estimated is inconsistent with how the compensation of these individuals was determined. The model needs to be respecified to incorporate prior relevant experience as follows:

$$salary = \beta_0 + (\beta_1 * sen) + (\beta_2 * perf) + (\beta_3 * DUMMY_{CDL}) \qquad (7.8)$$
$$+ (\beta_4 * prior\,exp)$$

Assuming that the estimation of this respecified equation does not indicate pay disparities by gender, then the gender disparity initially observed can be explained by failing to incorporate prior relevant experience in the model. If gender disparities persist, then individual follow-up investigations are warranted.

Forklift Operators

During your conversation with Shawn Kendrick, the following exchange occurs:

> **You:** I've been looking at the pay rates for your direct reports. The compensation policy indicates that pay rates are determined by seniority, employee performance, and whether the individual has a forklift certification. After accounting for these factors, Janette—the only female forklift operator—earns $1.00 an hour less than her male counterparts. Can you think of anything that would explain that difference?
>
> **Shawn:** She's a poor performer.
>
> **You:** The $1.00 an hour difference accounts for performance, so that can't be the explanation.
>
> **Shawn:** She's not a good fit. Nobody wants her out here on the docks.
>
> **You:** Would you elaborate on that, please?
>
> **Shawn:** Look, there's a reason that she's the only girl working as a forklift operator. Everyone knows it's a man's job, and girls just shouldn't be running heavy equipment. It's bad enough I'm stuck with the girls in receiving. They don't belong in the warehouse, and they damn sure shouldn't be running forklifts and working the docks!

Based on the comments made during the conversation with Shawn, a possible explanation for the observed gender disparity among forklift operators is discrimination. A closer review of this similarly situated employee grouping at the individual level is required.

Receiving Personnel

Shawn's comments indicate that discrimination is also a possible explanation for the observed gender disparity among receiving personnel. A closer review of this similarly situated employee grouping at the individual level is also required.

Individual Follow-Up

If no broad patterns are evident in the analysis results, or if systemic follow-up investigations reveal a more detailed examination of the similarly situated employee grouping is warranted, individual follow-up investigations should be undertaken.

Following along with the hypothetical example from before, individual follow-up investigations are warranted for pricing specialists, forklift operators, and receiving personnel.

Pricing Specialists

As previously noted, the annual salaries of pricing specialists are determined by total company seniority, relevant prior experience, and performance. To identify the source of the observed gender disparity within this similarly situated employee grouping, personnel data on each of the pricing specialists should be collected. Assume that Table 7-2 presents a portion of this personnel data for four pricing specialists: two male and two female.[23]

---

[23]Personnel data should be collected on all individuals employed in this job title. For illustrative purposes, this example limits the data presented to only four employees.

Table 7-2. Sampling of Hypothetical Personnel Data for Pricing Specialists

ID # 1193		NAME: Williams, Linda		SEX: F		DOH: 01/16/85		SALARY: $41,000
	JOB TITLE: Pricing Specialist			SUPERVISOR: Mahoney, Frank				
	PRIOR EXPERIENCE: 9.5 years		PRIOR RELEVANT EXPERIENCE: 9.5 years					
	1.5 years		Customer Service Rep				WidgetCo.	
	5.0 years		Customer Service Mgr				WidgetCo.	
	3.0 years		Supervisor, Customer Service Manager				WidgetCo.	
ID # 1835		NAME: Hill, Daniel		SEX: M		DOH: 06/15/90		SALARY: $38,500
	JOB TITLE: Pricing Specialist			SUPERVISOR: Mahoney, Frank				
	PRIOR EXPERIENCE: 3.5 years		PRIOR RELEVANT EXPERIENCE: 3.5 years					
	3.5 years		Pricing Specialist				Omega Electrical Supply	
ID # 1960		NAME: Davis, Jennifer		SEX: F		DOH: 06/15/90		SALARY: $38,000
	JOB TITLE: Pricing Specialist			SUPERVISOR: Mahoney, Frank				
	PRIOR EXPERIENCE: 3.5 years		PRIOR RELEVANT EXPERIENCE: 3.5 years					
	0.5 years		Retail Sales Clerk				Retail Outlets, Inc.	
	2.5 years		Sales Representative				ABC Manufacturing	
	0.5 years		Pricing Specialist				ABC Manufacturing	
ID # 2291		NAME: Turner, Kevin		SEX: M		DOH: 09/01/95		SALARY: $36,000
	JOB TITLE: Pricing Specialist			SUPERVISOR: Mahoney, Frank				
	PRIOR EXPERIENCE: 6.0 years		PRIOR RELEVANT EXPERIENCE: 6.0 years					
	1.0 years		Equipment Sales Rep				Alpha Equipment Sales	
	3.0 years		Pricing Specialist				Alpha Equipment Sales	
	2.0 years		Pricing Specialist				Miller and Sons, Inc.	
	1.0 years		Pricing Specialist				Central Supply Co.	

A review of each employee's data leads to an interesting observation. In all four cases, the employee's prior relevant experience is equal to his or her *total* prior experience, which is incorrect. The effect of this on the analysis results is perhaps best illustrated through a comparison of Employees 1835 (Daniel Hill) and 1960 (Jennifer Davis).

Jennifer Davis and Daniel Hill appear to be identical on all characteristics reported in Table 7-2. They were hired on the same date, hold the same job title, and report to the same supervisor. Both have 3.5 years of total prior experience and 3.5 years of relevant prior experience. Based on this, we would expect their annual salaries to be identical. In reality, they are not; Daniel earns $500 a year more than Jennifer does.

A detailed review of each employee's prior experience information reveals the underlying cause of this difference. At the time he was hired, Daniel had 3.5 years of experience as a pricing specialist with Omega Electrical Supply. At the time she was hired, Jennifer had only six months of experience as a pricing specialist with ABC Manufacturing. The remainder of her experience was as a retail sales clerk and a customer service representative.

Given that Daniel has three more years of experience as a pricing specialist than Jennifer has, it is not surprising that his annual salary is greater than hers. It appears as though there is a disparity by gender, but this disparity is attributable to incorrect measurement of relevant prior experience. The model that was estimated for pricing specialists used as an input the relevant prior experience given in the data set. That information is incorrect in that it reflects *total* prior experience, not *relevant* prior experience. Assuming that the annual salaries for Jennifer and Daniel were determined based on a review of their employment histories—and therefore an accurate assessment of relevant prior experience—there is no disparity. The disparity indicated by the analysis results is simply an artifact of incorrect data measurement.

Forklift Operators

The similarly situated employee grouping containing forklift operators presents a unique challenge in that there is only one woman within the grouping. The ideal manner of follow-up is to identify male employees who have identical characteristics to the woman in the grouping and examine their characteristics vis-à-vis her characteristics.

A review of the forklift operators roster reveals that there are two male employees—Brian Mitchell and José Rodriguez—who have characteristics nearly identical to those of the lone woman, Janette Baker. Table 7-3 presents a portion of the personnel data for the three forklift operators.

Table 7-3. Sampling of Hypothetical Personnel Data for Forklift Operators

ID # 6214	NAME: Mitchell, Brian			SEX: M	DOH: 07/01/07	PAY RATE: $14.85
	JOB TITLE: Forklift Operator			SUPERVISOR: Kendrick, Shawn		
	FORKLIFT CERTIFICATION VALID THROUGH: 09/01/13					
	SENIORITY AS OF 01/01/13: 6.5 years			LAST PAY INCREASE: $0.20/HR		
	PERFORMANCE REVIEWS					
	07/01/12	4.0	Kendrick	Enjoy having this guy on the docks		
	07/01/11	4.0	Kendrick	Glad we got him to stay and not leave for competitor		
	07/01/10	4.0	Kendrick	Big asset to the warehouse environment		
ID # 6230	NAME: Baker, Janette			SEX: F	DOH: 07/01/07	PAY RATE: $13.85
	JOB TITLE: Forklift Operator			SUPERVISOR: Kendrick, Shawn		
	FORKLIFT CERTIFICATION VALID THROUGH: 09/01/13					
	SENIORITY AS OF 01/01/13: 6.5 years			LAST PAY INCREASE: $0.15/HR		
	PERFORMANCE REVIEWS					
	07/01/12	4.0	Kendrick	Meets expectations, but disruptive to working environment		
	07/01/11	4.0	Kendrick	Meets expectations, but not a good fit for warehouse		
	07/01/10	4.0	Kendrick	Suggested inside sales position may be a better fit		
ID # 6279	NAME: Rodriguez, José			SEX: M	DOH: 07/01/07	PAY RATE: $14.85
	JOB TITLE: Forklift Operator			SUPERVISOR: Kendrick, Shawn		
	FORKLIFT CERTIFICATION VALID THROUGH: 09/01/13					
	SENIORITY AS OF 01/01/13: 6.5 years			LAST PAY INCREASE: $0.20/HR		
	PERFORMANCE REVIEWS					
	07/01/12	4.0	Kendrick	Maintaining good performance		
	07/01/11	4.0	Kendrick	Performance has improved dramatically during year		
	07/01/10	3.5	Kendrick	Had a minor incident this year—needs to improve		

As can be seen, all three employees were hired on July 1, 2007. All three are certified to operate a forklift, and their certifications expire on the same date. All three received performance ratings of 4.0 for the evaluation periods ending on July 1, 2011, and July 1, 2012; Rodriguez had a slightly lower performance rating than Mitchell or Baker for the evaluation period ending July 1, 2010.[24]

Based on these characteristics, there appears to be no discernible differences between the employees. However, an examination of the performance evaluation comments reveals a difference. For the last three evaluation periods, Shawn Kendrick has commented that Janette was "not a good fit for the warehouse," "disruptive to the working environment," and may be better suited for an inside sales position. Neither of her two comparators received such comments.[25]

This finding, coupled with the views expressed by Shawn during the discussion ("everyone knows that it's a man's job, women don't belong in the warehouse," etc.), indicates that the likely cause of the observed disparity in hourly pay rates by gender is discriminatory pay-setting practices on the part of Shawn Kendrick.[26]

Receiving Personnel

Within the similarly situated employee grouping of twenty-one male and nine female receiving personnel, a ten-cents-per-hour difference by gender was observed. This difference cannot be attributed to seniority, performance, or possession of a forklift certification, because the model already accounts for these factors. A deeper investigation of the differential is required.

Table 7-4 presents a portion of personnel data for two men and two women from this similarly situated employee grouping (Ken Gonzales, Carol Harris, Joe Taylor, and Nancy Smith). As can be seen, all four employees were hired on August 16, 2010. Among them, all but Ken are certified to operate a forklift; the certifications for Carol, Joe, and Nancy expire on the same date. All four received performance ratings of 4.0 for the evaluation periods ending on July 1, 2012.

---

[24]Shawn Kendrick's comment that Janette Baker was a "poor performer" is in contradiction to her performance evaluation scores.

[25]In fact, a review of the performance evaluations for all of the forklift operators reveals that Janette was the only employee who received such comments on her performance evaluation.

[26]The appropriate way in which to deal with Shawn's comments regarding the role of women in warehouse positions and his potential gender discrimination in pay rates against women is beyond the scope of this discussion. Legal counsel should be consulted and should be involved in any disciplinary actions or other consequences imposed.

Table 7-4. Sampling of Hypothetical Personnel Data for Receiving Personnel

ID # 7181		NAME: Gonzales, Ken			SEX: M	DOH: 08/16/10	PAY RATE: $11.40
	JOB TITLE: Receiving				SUPERVISOR: Kendrick, Shawn		
	FORKLIFT CERTIFICATION VALID THROUGH: NOT CERTIFIED						
	SENIORITY AS OF 01/01/13: 2.4 years				LAST PAY INCREASE: $0.25/HR		
	PERFORMANCE REVIEWS						
	07/01/12		4.0	Kendrick	Big asset to the warehouse environment		
ID # 7293		NAME: Harris, Carol			SEX: F	DOH: 08/16/10	PAY RATE: $11.40
	JOB TITLE: Receiving				SUPERVISOR: Kendrick, Shawn		
	FORKLIFT CERTIFICATION VALID THROUGH: 09/01/13						
	SENIORITY AS OF 01/01/13: 2.4 years				LAST PAY INCREASE: $0.15/HR		
	PERFORMANCE REVIEWS						
	07/01/12		4.0	Kendrick	Uses too much of her paid time off		
ID # 7422		NAME: Taylor, Joe			SEX: M	DOH: 08/16/10	PAY RATE: $11.50
	JOB TITLE: Receiving				SUPERVISOR: Kendrick, Shawn		
	FORKLIFT CERTIFICATION VALID THROUGH: 09/01/13						
	SENIORITY AS OF 01/01/13: 2.4 years				LAST PAY INCREASE: $0.25/HR		
	PERFORMANCE REVIEWS						
	07/01/12		4.0	Kendrick	Big asset to warehouse environment		
ID # 7507		NAME: Smith, Nancy			SEX: F	DOH: 08/16/10	PAY RATE: $11.40
	JOB TITLE: Receiving				SUPERVISOR: Kendrick, Shawn		
	FORKLIFT CERTIFICATION VALID THROUGH: 09/01/13						
	SENIORITY AS OF 01/01/13: 2.4 years				LAST PAY INCREASE: $0.15/HR		
	PERFORMANCE REVIEWS						
	07/01/12		4.0	Kendrick	Won't work overtime because of her kids		

Based on these characteristics, there appears to be no discernible difference between Carol, Joe, and Nancy. We would expect their hourly pay rates to be the same. A review of their hourly pay rates indicates that Joe is paid $0.10 an hour more than his female counterparts. Additionally, we would expect Ken's hourly pay rate to be lower than the other three, because he does not possess a forklift certification. However, he is earning the same hourly rate as Carol and Nancy, both of whom possess a forklift certification.

An examination of the performance evaluation comments reveals a difference by gender. Even though all four employees received a score of 4.0, the tone of Kendrick's evaluation comments differ by gender. He noted that both Ken and Joe are "big assets to the warehouse environment," whereas Carol "uses too much of her paid time off," and Nancy "won't work overtime because of her kids." A review of the performance evaluation comments for the remaining nineteen men and seven women in this similarly situated employee grouping reveals a similar pattern.

Additionally, the pay increases granted to these four employees differ by gender. Even though all four are identical in terms of seniority and performance, the men received a $0.25 per hour increase on July 1, 2012, whereas the female employees received only a $0.15 an hour increase. There appears to be no justification for this $0.10 an hour difference by gender. A review of the pay increases granted to the remaining people in this similarly situated employee grouping reveals a similar pattern.

This, coupled with the views he expressed regarding women in the warehouse, indicates that the likely cause of the observed disparity in hourly pay rates by gender is discriminatory pay setting practices on the part of Shawn Kendrick.[27]

The Compensation Adjustment Process

Commonly, statistically significant disparities with no obvious explanation (or in cases where discriminatory pay setting practices are suspected or evident) are remediated via compensation adjustments. Regardless of how the employer chooses to investigate and remediate the statistically significant disparities, it is imperative that an investigation precedes remediation. As illustrated in the previous hypothetical example, follow-up investigation may reveal legitimate nondiscriminatory factors that were not considered in the statistical model but nonetheless explain variation in compensation. These factors, if they exist, should be identified and considered prior to contemplating or instituting any changes in compensation.

Though it is generally considered a best practice to involve legal counsel in any reviews of compensation for internal pay equity, any remediation to potential problem areas discovered during the review should *only* be done under the auspices of legal counsel. The implications of making remedies to compensation are significant, and legal counsel is best positioned to understand these implications and advise the organization on appropriate remedies.

The discussion of adjusting compensation to achieve internal pay equity in the following subsections is intentionally presented in general terms using overly simplistic examples. Each situation encountered in real life is unique and requires careful consideration. As such, it is simply not possible to present all variants of every scenario one may encounter. Similarly, it is not feasible to present every possible adjustment scenario. There are no definitive rules for adjusting compensation to achieve internal pay equity. No checklists or flowcharts exist; it is both science and art. The following discussion is intended only to provide a cursory introduction to the compensation adjustment process.

---

[27]As previously noted, the appropriate course of action for dealing with Mr. Kendrick's comments regarding the role of women in warehouse positions and his potential gender discrimination in pay rates against women is beyond the scope of this discussion. Legal counsel should be consulted and should be involved in any disciplinary actions or other consequences imposed on Mr. Kendrick.

Identifying Employees Requiring Adjustment

In some situations, the identification of employees whose compensation rates are out of line with their counterparts is very straightforward. In the case of the forklift operators in the previous example, it is obvious that the sole woman, Janette Baker, is paid $1.00 per hour less than her male counterparts, Brian Mitchell and José Rodriguez, who have identical characteristics to Janette.

Similarly, as can be seen from Table 7-4, the female receiving personnel are paid less than their male counterparts. Additionally, the annual increases in hourly pay rates received by these women are less than that of their male counterparts.[28] As previously discussed, the likely explanation for this disparity is discriminatory pay setting practices by the supervisor, Shawn Kendrick. In this case, all women within this similarly situated employee grouping should receive a pay adjustment to bring their hourly pay rates in line with those of their male counterparts.

In other situations, however, the identification of employees whose compensation rates are out of line with their counterparts is more challenging. Assume, for example, that we are interested in examining the annual salary amounts for a similarly situated employee grouping consisting of cost estimators. The factors determining the annual salary of a cost estimator are time in job (measured in whole years) and whether the individual holds a certification from the American Society of Professional Estimators. Among the incumbent cost estimators, time in job ranges from three to ten years. Table 7-5 shows that annual salaries for the incumbent cost estimators ranges from $53,000 to $62,225.

Table 7-5. Hypothetical Summary Statistics for Cost Estimator Salary by Time in Job

| Time in Job | # EEs | | Annual Salary ($) | | |
(years)	M	F	Min	Max	Avg
3	2	2	53,000	53,000	53,000
4	2	4	54,275	55,500	54,758
5	9	4	55,000	56,100	55,869
6	4	9	56,500	58,000	57,150
7	8	4	57,250	58,835	58,060
8	6	0	59,450	60,250	59,850
9	3	4	60,000	61,050	60,521
10	3	2	61,000	62,225	61,735

---

[28]Note that the combination of lower hourly rates and smaller annual increases will cause the gender disparity to increase over time, creating a greater divergence between the hourly pay rates of men and women.

Assume that the model given by Equation 7.9 is estimated for the similarly situated employee grouping consisting of cost estimators:

$$salary = \beta_0 + (\beta_1 * TIJ) + (\beta_2 * DUMMY_{CERT}) \qquad (7.9)$$

The results of this multiple regression analysis are given in Figure 7-2. As you can see, there is a statistically significant gender effect of −$703 per year.

```
Dependent Variable                    |      SALARY
N                                     |      66
Adjusted Squared Multiple R           |      0.977
Standard Error of Estimate            |      357.458

Regression Coefficients B = (X'X)⁻¹X'Y

Effect      | Coefficient        t           p-Value
----------------------------------------------------
Constant       50,079.282     253.934        0.000
TIJ             1,194.131      50.669         0.000
CERT             135.815       1.298          0.199
F               -703.271       -7.862         0.000
```

Figure 7-2. Regression output for cost estimators

Assume that follow-up investigations reveal no obvious explanation for the gender differential (i.e., there are no mismatches between the compensation metric and the explanatory variables, the model is properly specified, and so on).

Because there are no obvious causes of the gender disparity, compensation adjustments are warranted in this case. However, not all women in this similarly situated employee grouping should receive adjustments. Table 7-5 shows that all cost estimators with three years of time in job are earning $53,000, irrespective of gender. Therefore, increasing the salary amounts for the two female cost estimators with three years of time in job is neither appropriate nor warranted. In fact, if this adjustment was made, it would create a situation in which the male cost estimators were paid less than their female counterparts. Making this adjustment would not only fail to resolve the internal equity issue among cost estimators, it would also actually exacerbate the inequities among these four employees.

Among cost estimators with four years of time in job, however, the annual salaries range from $54,275 to $55,500; the average annual salary, as shown in Table 7-5, is $54,758. Employee-level detail for cost estimators with four years of time in job is given in Table 7-6.

Table 7-6. Hypothetical Data for Cost Estimators with 4 Years of Time in Job

ID#	Sex	TIJ (years)	Certified	Salary ($)
1496	F	4	Y	54,275
1502	F	4	Y	54,275
1513	F	4	Y	54,500
1521	F	4	Y	54,500
1523	M	4	Y	55,500
1527	M	4	N	55,500

A detailed review of the six cost estimators with four years of time in job indicates that all of the women receive a lower annual salary than their male counterparts. In fact, all four women—who possess certification from the American Society of Professional Estimators—receive a lower annual salary than the man in the employee grouping who does not possess this certification.

Aside from the gender disparity, there is an overall equity issue within this similarly situated employee grouping. The two male cost estimators both receive an annual salary of $55,000. Though both males have four years of time in job, only one is certified. Because certification factors in to the determination of annual salary, we would expect the man who is certified to have a greater annual salary than the man who is not. In actuality, their salaries are the same.

From a gender equity perspective, the four women in this similarly situated employee grouping require an upward adjustment of annual salary. Also, the four women and the one certified man require an upward adjustment of annual salary.[29]

To identify all individuals within this similarly situated employee grouping requiring an adjustment of annual salary, the above-described comparisons would be repeated for each of the subgroups defined by time in job.

---

[29]This, of course, assumes that all cost estimators with four years of time in job are identical in all other respects.

Determining the Magnitude of Adjustment

After identifying which employees require a compensation adjustment, the magnitude of the adjustment must be determined. In some situations the size of the required adjustment is self-evident. In the case of the forklift operators, the gender disparity can be rectified by increasing Janette Baker's hourly rate by $1.00. This adjustment would bring her hourly rate in line with the hourly rates of her male counterparts.

In other situations, the magnitude of the adjustment(s) will not immediately be self-evident. In many cases, different people within the similarly situated employee grouping will require different adjustment amounts. This is the case for the similarly situated employee grouping of cost estimators.

One obvious approach to eliminating the estimated −$703.27 gender effect on annual salary shown in Figure 7-2 would be to increase the annual salary of all female employees across the board by $703.27. If this adjustment were made, the gender disparity would be eliminated in the aggregate, as shown in Figure 7-3.

```
Dependent Variable              |    SALARY_ADJ
N                               |    66
Adjusted Squared Multiple R     |    0.976
Standard Error of Estimate      |    357.458
```

Regression Coefficients B = (X'X)⁻¹X'Y

Effect	Coefficient	t	p-Value
Constant	50,079.282	253.934	0.000
TIJ	1,194.131	50.669	0.000
CERT	135.815	1.298	0.199
F	−0.001	0.000	1.000

Figure 7-3. Regression output for cost estimators using adjusted salary amounts

Though there would be no evidence of a statistically significant gender disparity in annual salary among the similarly situated employee grouping of sixty-six cost estimators, this blanket adjustment to female salaries may create inequities *within subgroups* of the similarly situated employee grouping. For example, all cost estimators with three years of time in job are currently earning $53,000, as previously noted. If the salaries of the two women were increased by $703.27, they would be earning more than their two comparators. On the other hand, an increase of $703.27 would not remedy the gender disparities between cost estimators with six years of time in job, as shown in Table 7-7.

Table 7-7. Proposed Salary Adjustments for Cost Estimators with Six Years of Time in Job

ID#	Sex	TIJ(years)	Certified	Old Salary($)	Proposed Adjustment($)	Salary($)
121	F	6	N	56,500	+ 703	57,203
124	F	6	N	56,500	+ 703	57,203
125	F	6	Y	56,575	+ 703	57,278
129	F	6	Y	56,575	+ 703	57,278
131	F	6	Y	57,000	+ 703	57,703
133	F	6	N	57,000	+ 703	57,703
134	F	6	Y	57,000	+ 703	57,703
140	F	6	Y	57,000	+ 703	57,703
142	F	6	Y	57,000	+ 703	57,703
148	M	6	N	57,900	+ 0	57,900
150	M	6	Y	57,900	+ 0	57,900
156	M	6	Y	58,000	+ 0	58,000
158	M	6	Y	58,000	+ 0	58,000

Even after the adjustment, the female salaries are still below those of their male counterparts. The gender disparity is smaller, but internal equity has not been achieved. To do so, a more tailored approach is required, focusing on adjustments at the individual employee level.

Following this tailored approach, in the case of cost estimators with four years of time in job, one might be tempted to reset the annual salaries of all six employees to $54,500, the maximum of the female salary. As shown in Table 7-8, this adjustment process would involve a $225 increase in salary for Employees 1496 and 1502, and a $1,000 reduction in salary for Employees 1523 and 1527.

Table 7-8. Proposed Salary Adjustments for Cost Estimators with Four Years of Time in Job

ID#	Sex	TIJ (years)	Certified	Old Salary ($)	Proposed Adjustment ($)	Salary ($)
1496	F	4	Y	54,275	+ 225	54,500
1502	F	4	Y	54,275	+ 225	54,500
1513	F	4	Y	54,500	+ 0	54,500
1521	F	4	Y	54,500	+ 0	54,500
1523	M	4	Y	55,500	− 1,000	54,500
1527	M	4	N	55,500	− 1,000	54,500

Although it may eliminate the gender disparity within this subgroup, this adjustment violates the Equal Pay Act. As stated in Section 206 of the Equal Pay Act of 1963, reductions in compensation to achieve internal pay equity are prohibited:

An employer who is paying a wage rate differential in violation of this subsection shall not, in order to comply with the provisions of this subsection, reduce the wage rate of any employee.

A disparity in compensation by protected group status cannot be remedied by decreasing the compensation of the majority group. Therefore, this adjustment is not legally permissible.

The alternative is to leave the male salary at $55,500 and adjust the women's salaries upward. Table 7-9 illustrates the increase in annual salary for each female employee necessary to achieve gender pay equity.

Table 7-9. Proposed Salary Adjustments for Cost Estimators with Four Years of Time in Job

| | | | | | Proposed | |
ID#	Sex	TIJ (years)	Certified	Old Salary ($)	Adjustment ($)	Salary ($)
1496	F	4	Y	54,275	+ 1,225	55,500
1502	F	4	Y	54,275	+ 1,225	55,500
1513	F	4	Y	54,500	+ 1,000	55,500
1521	F	4	Y	54,500	+ 1,000	55,500
1523	M	4	Y	55,500	+ 0	55,500
1527	M	4	N	55,500	+ 0	55,500

This adjustment will eliminate the gender disparity; all cost estimators with four years of time in job will earn $55,500.

From an overall equity perspective, however, one issue remains. The one employee (ID 1527) who is not certified is earning the same annual salary as the other five employees who are certified. If certification carries a premium, then to achieve overall equity, the salaries of the certified employees must be greater than that of the one individual who is not certified. One possible adjustment scenario that would achieve overall equity is given in Table 7-10.[30]

---

[30] In order to maintain consistency in compensation within the entire similarly situated employee grouping, the "dollar value" of certification will – in most cases – take on a constant value irrespective of time in job.

Table 7-10. Proposed Salary Adjustments for Cost Estimators with Four Years of Time in Job

ID#	Sex	TIJ (years)	Certified	Old Salary ($)	Proposed Adjustment ($)	Proposed Salary ($)
1496	F	4	Y	54,275	+ 1,725	56,000
1502	F	4	Y	54,275	+ 1,725	56,000
1513	F	4	Y	54,500	+ 1,500	56,000
1521	F	4	Y	54,500	+ 1,500	56,000
1523	M	4	Y	55,500	+ 500	56,000
1527	M	4	N	55,500	+ 0	55,500

As evidenced by the preceding discussion, correcting a pay differential for a given protected group is, in most cases, more involved than simply increasing the compensation rate for members of the protected group by the magnitude of the estimated protected effect. Such blanket increases may yield a statistically insignificant estimated protected effect but can create situations of inequity among subgroups within the similarly situated employee grouping. Utmost care should be taken in determining the magnitude(s) of the compensation adjustments.

Equity versus Statistical Insignificance

Remediating situations of internal pay inequity can be a costly process, in terms of the resources spent on detection, investigation, and identification of appropriate corrections as well as payroll dollars. Making appropriate adjustments (which are typically upward adjustments) can lead to substantial increases in labor costs. Because of this, some employers are lured by the prospect of instituting only enough adjustment to generate statistically insignificant results. This may save some money in the short run, but in the long run it can lead to greater expenditures in the form of legal fees, damages, and fines and penalties.

For example, consider the case of the similarly situated employee grouping consisting of cost estimators. The estimated gender effect of −$703.27 is statistically significant, as shown in Figure 7-2. Providing a salary increase of 0.95% to every woman in this employee grouping would reduce the estimated gender effect to −$161.33; this effect is statistically insignificant ($t = 1.81, p = 0.075$), as shown in Figure 7-4. Because this result is statistically insignificant, it is not statistically different from zero, and no adverse inference can or should be drawn. Even though the estimated gender effect is directionally adverse to women, we cannot attribute this to anything other than chance. Therefore, this outcome is consistent with the hypothesis that the manner in which salaries of cost estimators are determined is neutral with respect to gender.

```
Dependent Variable              |      SALARY_NEW
N                               |      66
Adjusted Squared Multiple R     |      0.977
Standard Error of Estimate      |      356.350
```

Regression Coefficients B = (X'X)⁻¹X'Y

Effect	Coefficient	t	p-Value
Constant	50,052.195	254.585	0.000
TIJ	1,194.131	51.028	0.000
CERT	130.588	1.252	0.215
F	-161.330	-1.809	0.075

Figure 7-4. Regression output for cost estimators assuming a 0.0095% increase in female salary

Aside from eliminating the statistical significance of the estimated gender effect, making this 0.95% adjustment also results in an increase in payroll cost for these six people of only 0.6%, compared to the 2.1% increase associated with eliminating the differential, as shown in Table 7-11.

Table 7-11. Comparison of Adjustments for Cost Estimators with Four Years of Time in Job

ID#	Sex	TIJ(years)	Certified	Old Salary ($)	Adjusted Salary Tailored ($)	Adjusted Salary 0.96% Increase ($)
1496	F	4	Y	54,275	+ 1,725	56,000
1502	F	4	Y	54,275	+ 1,725	56,000
1513	F	4	Y	54,500	+ 1,500	56,000
1521	F	4	Y	54,500	+ 1,500	56,000
1523	M	4	Y	55,500	+ 500	56,000
1527	M	4	N	55,500	+ 0	55,500
Total Payroll Cost:				328,550	335,500	330,617
Increase in Payroll Cost as a Result of Salary Adjustments:					+ 6,950	+ 2,067
					+ 2.1%	+ 0.6%

We carry these adjustments through for all of the cost estimators in the similarly situated employee grouping and note there is a substantial difference in payroll costs associated with the two remedial approaches. As shown in Table 7-12, the statistical significance of the estimated gender effect—but not the gender effect itself—can be eliminated by increasing the salary of every woman in the similarly situated employee grouping by 0.95% for a modest increase of $15,672 in payroll costs. Achieving true pay equity within this similarly situated employee grouping would increase payroll costs by nearly $95,000.

Table 7-12. Comparison of Adjustments for All Cost Estimators

		Adjusted Salary	
	Old Salary	Tailored ($)	0.95% Increase ($)
Total payroll cost	3,797,940	3,892,890	3,813,612
Increase in payroll cost as a result of salary adjustments		+ 94,950	+ 15,672
		+ 2.5%	+ 0.4%

In some cases, achieving statistical insignificance of protected group effects is cheaper, in terms of payroll dollars, than achieving internal pay equity. However, statistical insignificance does not provide the competitive advantages and benefits of attraction and retention of top talent, increased employee engagement, and increased productivity that internal pay equity provides. As noted in Chapter 1, to fully leverage the competitive advantages provided, organizations must ensure that *all* employees are paid fairly.

Furthermore, achieving statistical insignificance of protected group effects may not successfully manage the risk of compensation discrimination litigation or regulatory investigation. If disparities exist, statistically significant or otherwise, employers can still face costly litigation and/or audits by regulatory agencies. In fact, pursing a course of eliminating statistical significance but not pay differentials can place an employer in a much worse position in litigation or regulatory investigation than failing to identify pay differentials in the first place. The Wal-Mart case discussed at the beginning of this chapter hints at the consequences of such a course of action; more detailed examples are provided in Chapter 10.

Making and Communicating Adjustments

Follow-up investigations culminate in making and communicating adjustments in compensation, where appropriate. The exact manner in which the adjustments are made will differ depending on the particular circumstances, but generally speaking, there are two approaches to making adjustments: immediate and extended.

Immediate adjustments proceed exactly as their name implies—the adjustments are made by making a one-time change in compensation. For example, granting one-time equity increases ranging from $500 to $1,725 among cost estimators with four years of time in job would be classified as an immediate adjustment. Typically, immediate adjustments are made in cases where the magnitude of the necessary adjustment is relatively small or the number of employees requiring adjustment is relatively small.

Extended adjustments occur over a period of time. Rather than granting a one-time equity adjustment, compensation is increased to the target level over the span of several evaluation periods. For example, employees warranting equity adjustments may be given larger annual increases than they would have otherwise received to bring compensation in line with other similarly situated employees. Typically, extended adjustments are made in cases where the magnitude of the necessary adjustment is relatively large or the number of employees requiring adjustment is relatively large.

It is not uncommon for employers to use a blended approach; one-time equity adjustments may be given to partially eliminate the pay differential between an employee and similarly situated counterparts, with the remainder of the differential eliminated over time via larger-than-typical annual increases.

Because pay equity adjustments have legal ramifications, the manner in which adjustments are made should be discussed with legal counsel. Legal counsel is best positioned to provide guidance on how to make the necessary compensation adjustments while minimizing any legal complications that may arise. This is particularly important if the employer is already involved in compensation-related litigation or regulatory investigation.

Legal counsel should also be involved in planning how the compensation adjustments will be communicated to employees. The preferred communication approach will vary depending on the number of employees receiving adjustments, the magnitude of the necessary adjustments, and whether the employer has been or is currently involved in compensation-related litigation or regulatory investigation, among other factors.

Generally speaking, communication with employees about pay equity adjustments should emphasize that the organization is committed to a fair and non-discriminatory workplace. In an effort to provide a fair workplace, a review of compensation practices was performed, and that review uncovered potential inequities. The adjustments are being made to address those potential problem areas and to ensure that everyone—irrespective of protected group status—is paid fairly and equitably.[31]

---

[31]As previously mentioned, the involvement of legal counsel in planning these communications is essential. Counsel should review and sign off on any verbal or written communication to employees regarding compensation adjustments.

The Changing Landscape of Pay Equity Enforcement

Since the late 2000s and early 2010s, there have been major changes in the legal and regulatory environment regarding compensation discrimination, and there are even more on the horizon. These changes encompass both individual claims and claims of systemic compensation discrimination.

Three of the most important changes affect the very nature of a compensation discrimination claim, the compensation information collected by the government, and the way employers are permitted to compensate their employees. These changes are the Lilly Ledbetter Fair Pay Act, the formation of the National Equal Pay Enforcement Task Force, and the introduction of the Paycheck Fairness Act.

The Ledbetter Fair Pay Act

Signed in to law on January 29, 2009, the Lilly Ledbetter Fair Pay Act amends the Civil Rights Act of 1964. It states that the 180-day statute of limitations for filing an equal pay claim resets with the issuance of each new discriminatory paycheck.[1]

Under this new law, an employee can potentially file a lawsuit for discriminatory pay decisions every time that decision is applied. This includes each time wages, benefits, or other compensation is paid, even if that decision occurred twenty or thirty years ago.

Compensation Decision Documentation

The reset provision of the Ledbetter Fair Pay Act presents a unique challenge to employers: without documentation, it is difficult to remember how pay increases were determined five or ten years ago. It is nearly impossible to remember how those decisions were made twenty or thirty years ago. Memories fade as time passes, and the people who made those compensation decisions are less and less likely to still be employed by an organization.

From a practical standpoint, each pay decision should be carefully documented, and that documentation should be retained. In addition to pay stubs, records of hours worked, and other records relating to the payment of wages, it is critical that compensation decision documentation is created and retained.

> *When you, as an employer, decide your employees' wages, salaries, pay increases . . . how do you arrive at a specific figure? I'm talking about performance reviews—what metrics were used—signed copies of the completed review, signed copies of the criteria at the start of the review period. Often companies will conduct or purchase industry statistics to ensure that they're paying people in the expected range for their industry. Employers are not "dart-boarding" compensation decisions. Record where these figures are coming from.*[2]

Specifically, compensation decision documentation should address the following kinds of questions.

- How were the compensation decisions made? What factors were considered?

---

[1] The genesis of the Ledbetter Fair Pay Act of 2009 is discussed in Chapter 1.
[2] "Ledbetter and Documentation LIVE with Philip Miles," *The Proactive Employer*, April 2, 2010, www.blogtalkradio.com/theproactiveemployer/2010/04/02/ledbetter-and-document-retention-live-with-philip-miles.

- How did the organization arrive at the specific compensation figures for employees?

- What metrics and criteria were used to evaluate employees' performance?

- Were the performance metrics and criteria validated?

- What compensation surveys or industry statistics were used to determine compensation amounts?

- If a specific employee's compensation was affected by special circumstances (e.g., red circling), what were the details of those circumstances?

It is important to create this compensation decision documentation contemporaneously, at the time they are made, while surveys, industry statistics, evaluations, and so on are easily accessible. Creating documentation for compensation decisions that occurred in the past is time-consuming and resource-intensive. The most effective way of creating compensation decision documentation is to do so on an ongoing basis.

This documentation should be not only created, but also retained. In the event that compensation decisions need to be re-created or justified at a future point in time, typically as a result of litigation or regulatory investigation, having access to appropriate documentation from the time these decisions were made will facilitate this process.

A common issue that arises with respect to compensation decision documentation relates to how long this documentation should be retained. The retention period of some types of compensation documentation is governed by law, but decision documentation typically falls outside of the scope of retention statues.[3] Thus, the retention period for compensation decision documentation is a matter of judgment.

The surefire method to eliminate concern about retention is to retain everything indefinitely. However, this is a very impractical solution. The appropriate retention period depends on, among other things, the type of document retention system in use by the organization. Paper-based retention systems can quickly become unwieldy and ineffective, and retaining information for extended periods of time can become cost-prohibitive. Retaining documentation in electronic form is an efficient and cost-effective alternative and in most cases allows more information to be retained at a lower cost with lower storage requirements.

---

[3] For example, the Internal Revenue Service and the Department of Labor have laws governing what types of compensation documentation and employee information must be retained and for how long. Some employment laws, such as the Fair Labor Standards Act, also have these requirements. A detailed discussion of these retention periods is given in Chapter 10.

▓ **Note**   Ask yourself the following question before destroying any compensation decision document: Without this document, what compensation decision(s) will go unsupported if we are involved in a lawsuit or regulatory investigation?

There is no universally correct answer to the question of document retention period. Each employer should arrive at a unique solution to document retention through a cost-benefit analysis.

"Other Practice" Language

As important as document retention is, it is not the only facet of the Ledbetter Fair Pay Act that poses potential difficulty for employers. The act states that the statute of limitations resets with each new "application of a discriminatory compensation decision or other practice, including each time wages, benefits or other compensation is paid." The potential difficulty lies in two words: *other practice*.

Despite the fact that the Ledbetter Fair Pay Act has been in effect since 2009, the meaning of "other practices" remains unclear. In their article "The Lilly Ledbetter Fair Pay Act of 2009: A Preliminary Report," Joanna Grossman and Deborah Brake state that "the plain meaning of the Act suggests that it encompasses employment practices that cause an employee to receive lower compensation than she should have received but for the discriminatory practice."[4]

From this perspective, an other practice could be any seemingly legitimate, nondiscriminatory factor that has an effect on compensation, such as pay grade, department, location, or shift.

For example, assume that employees in Pay Grade 9 are paid between $40,000 and $45,000 annually, and employees in Pay Grade 10 earn between $50,000 and $55,000 annually. A statistical analysis of employee compensation reveals no evidence of discrimination with respect to gender or race in either of the pay grades.

Even though compensation decisions within each pay grade are made equitably, an employee could make the claim that she should be in Pay Grade 10 but was assigned to Pay Grade 9 because of discrimination. In this case, the pay decision at issue is not that within the pay grade but the assignment to pay grade itself. Assignment to pay grade becomes the "other practice" under the Ledbetter Fair Pay Act.

---

[4]Joanna Grossman and Deborah Brake, "The Lilly Ledbetter Fair Pay Act of 2009: A Preliminary Report, Part One," http://writ.news.findlaw.com/grossman/20090928.html.

Other practice claims are a relatively new area, and it is not yet clear what kinds of claims will be made. It is also not yet clear how successful these claims will be when tried in a court of law. Although it may be difficult to prove, it is relatively easy for an employee to claim that she was assigned to the wrong pay grade, department, and so on, because of discrimination. Even if the claim is unfounded, employers will still need to launch a defense, which can be expensive and time-consuming.

From a risk management perspective, this means that compensation decisions cannot be examined in isolation. All of these other practices are in play and need to be considered and incorporated into studies of compensation equity.

■ **Note** Any kind of personnel decision—anywhere in the organization—likely will have a compensation component. In light of the other practice element of the Ledbetter Fair Pay Act, employers should take a big-picture perspective when analyzing compensation for internal equity.

It is critical that employers take a big-picture perspective and consider all of these potential other factors when examining compensation for internal equity.

The National Equal Pay Enforcement Task Force

In his 2010 State of the Union address, President Barack Obama stated, "We're going to crack down on violations of equal pay laws—so that women get equal pay for an equal day's work."[5] As a result of this renewed commitment to equal pay, the National Equal Pay Enforcement Task Force was created.[6] The interagency task force consists of members from four different agencies: the U.S. Department of Labor (DOL), the Office of Personnel Management (OPM), the U.S. Department of Justice (DOJ), and the U.S. Equal Employment Opportunity Commission (EEOC).

A number of laws exist to address equal pay; the task force, however, has identified five persistent challenges to the enforcement of these equal pay laws.[7]

---

[5] Remarks by President Barack Obama, State of the Union Address, January 27, 2010, www.whitehouse.gov/the-press-office/remarks-president-state-union-address.

[6] At the time of its creation, the interagency group was known as the National Equal Pay Enforcement Task Force. In recent months, however, the group has referred to itself as the Equal Pay Task Force. See, for example, "Equal Pay Task Force Accomplishments," White House, April 2012, www.whitehouse.gov/sites/default/files/equal_pay_task_force.pdf.

[7] National Equal Pay Enforcement Task Force, White House, www.whitehouse.gov/sites/default/files/rss_viewer/equal_pay_task_force.pdf.

1. Three federal agencies have responsibilities for enforcing laws prohibiting pay discrimination, but they do not consistently coordinate those responsibilities.

2. Employees and employers are insufficiently educated in their rights and obligations with respect to wage discrimination.

3. The Government Accountability Office (GAO) has identified an eleven-cent wage gap between the average salaries of men and women in the federal workforce.

4. The government's ability to understand the full scope of the wage gap and identify and combat wage discrimination can be improved by access to more data than are currently available.

5. Existing laws do not always provide federal officials with adequate tools to fight wage discrimination.

Since its formation, the task force has made a variety of recommendations regarding interagency cooperation, education and outreach, and understanding the full scope of the wage gap. The majority of these recommendations have resulted in proposed legislation and changes in the regulatory environment, all of which have implications for employers. The task force has also taken a strong position regarding the tools necessary for combating wage discrimination and the insufficiency of existing tools. As such, it is supporting a variety of proposed regulations and legislation, such as the Office of Federal Contract Compliance Programs (OFCCP) proposed compensation data collection tool and the Paycheck Fairness Act.

Interagency Cooperation

Interagency cooperation in enforcement of equal pay laws is a priority on the task force agenda, and member agencies are taking steps to streamline the sharing of information and coordinate enforcement efforts. In its Action Plan, the task force made the following recommendation:

> The EEOC, DOJ, and DOL will establish a standing working group to coordinate interagency enforcement of wage discrimination laws and to help implement Task Force recommendations. The agencies will focus on improving coordination and communication among the agencies, coordinating investigations and litigation, identifying areas in which they can issue joint guidance to employers and employees, and conducting

joint training as appropriate. The agencies will confer with one another to promote consistency in policy and litigation positions, including opportunities to file amicus briefs.[8]

As a result of this recommendation, cooperation and coordination between enforcement agencies has significantly increased, agreements between agencies have been created, and preexisting agreements have been reinvigorated.

EEOC–OFCCP Memorandum of Understanding

The EEOC and OFCCP have issued a Memorandum of Understanding that outlines a strategy to promote greater efficiency and coordination and to eliminate conflict and duplication of effort.

The terms of the memorandum indicate that procedures for notification and consultation during compliance activities will be established, and joint enforcement initiatives will be developed. The EEOC and OFCCP have agreed to establish compliance coordination committees to increase efficiency, minimize duplication of efforts, and ensure coordination of enforcement activities.

In addition, the memorandum provides OFCCP with the ability to act as an agent of the EEOC for purposes of accepting and investigating charges of discrimination, as well as providing for data sharing and referring individual charges of discrimination from OFCCP to the EEOC.

Specifically, the EEOC and OFCCP will share any information regarding the employment policies and/or practices of employers holding government contracts or subcontracts that will support the enforcement mandates of each agency and/or their joint enforcement efforts. This information includes (but is not limited to) affirmative action programs, annual employment reports, complaints, charges, investigative files, and compliance evaluation reports.

OFCCP–DOJ Cooperation

The DOJ and OFCCP are also working to improve coordination and cooperation in the enforcement of Executive Order 11246.[9] Specifically, these agencies are working collaboratively to improve enforcement efforts and develop criteria to determine when interagency referrals and/or enforcement partnerships

---

[8]Ibid.

[9]Executive Order 11246 was signed by President Lyndon Johnson on September 24, 1965. It established requirements for nondiscriminatory practices in hiring and in employment for federal contractors and subcontractors. Specifically, the order prohibits federal contractors and subcontractors from discriminating in employment decisions on the basis of race, color, religion, sex, or national origin. It also requires contractors and subcontractors to "take affirmative action to ensure that applicants are employed, and that employees are treated during employment, without regard to their race, color, religion, sex or national origin."

are appropriate in cases involving compensation discrimination. On the recommendation of OFCCP Director Patricia Shiu, the DOJ is authorized to initiate independent investigations and sue contractors it believes are in violation of the executive order. The DOL and the DOJ are evaluating whether this authority can be applied to improve enforcement efforts.

DOJ–EEOC Pilot Project

Since early 2010, DOJ attorneys have been working closely with EEOC district offices in Philadelphia, Chicago, Los Angeles, and San Francisco through a pilot project aimed at improved coordination in investigating discrimination charges against state and local public employees. Other EEOC district offices (Denver, New York, Indianapolis, and Washington, D.C.) have been informally involved in pilot project investigations. According to the task force report on its accomplishments, the EEOC and DOJ have consulted on more than 125 charges of discrimination under the auspices of the pilot project.[10]

EEOC Directed Investigations

Based on a recommendation from the task force, the EEOC is strengthening its emphasis to include systemic enforcement and litigation to address patterns of pay discrimination in particular industries, occupations, and geographic areas. Currently, the commission is focusing both on individual claims of pay discrimination with "strong litigation or educational potential" and patterns and practices of pay discrimination.

The EEOC is also using its authority to conduct directed investigations into suspected violations of the Equal Pay Act without individual charges of discrimination. In April 2012, the commission launched the Equal Pay Act Directed Investigation Pilot Program, based on a recommendation from the task force.

Many details of the pilot program are unknown at the time of writing. The EEOC has not released information on how employers are selected for a directed investigation, nor have they indicated the methodology used in the audit process or what enforcement actions would be taken in the event pay disparities are found.

Based on the information that is available, the directed investigation begins with a meeting between the EEOC and the employer. At this meeting, the EEOC gathers information about the employer's compensation practices: background on the types of compensation provided to employees, pay system(s) in use, compensation and review methods, retention and management of compensation data, and so on.

---

[10]"Equal Pay Task Force Accomplishments," White House, April 2012, p. 7, www.whitehouse.gov/sites/default/files/equal_pay_task_force.pdf.

After this meeting, the EEOC constructs discovery and data requests. These requests are specific to the employer and are based on the information gathered. The employer then responds with its data and document production.

Upon receipt of the data and document production, the EEOC reviews the information and performs the audit. If the audit reveals any violations, the commission will determine what enforcement actions (if any) will be pursued against the employer.

According to former EEOC Vice Chair Leslie Silverman, the tone of these meetings has been reported to be relaxed, cooperative, and nonadversarial.[11]

Currently, three district offices are participating in the pilot program and are actively auditing employers: New York, Chicago, and Phoenix. If the project is successful, it may be expanded nationwide.[12]

Federal–State–Local Cooperation

This interagency cooperation is also echoed in the DOL's Strategic Plan 2011–2016.[13] According to the plan, worker protection agencies such as the OFCCP are reforming their operations to increase collaboration with other federal, state, and local agencies to ensure compliance throughout the workplace and impose penalties and other remedies consistent with the seriousness of the violation.

Implications for Employers

The increased interagency cooperation on enforcement of equal pay laws means that information supplied to one agency could be turned over to another, leading to further scrutiny from additional regulatory bodies.

For example, federal contractors should be aware that information relating to their employment policies—affirmative action plans, annual employment reports, compliance evaluation reports, investigative files, and so on—may be turned over to the EEOC for investigation under the Memorandum of Understanding between the EEOC and OFCCP. Individual complaint files and other information obtained by the EEOC may be turned over to OFCCP, which could precipitate the launch of systemic investigations.

---

[11]"EEOC's Pilot Project to Combat Wage Discrimination," *The Proactive Employer*, July 12, 2012, www.blogtalkradio.com/theproactiveemployer/2012/07/12/eeocs-pilot-project-to-combat-wage-discrimination.

[12]The EEOC has not indicated how or on what criteria it will evaluate the "success" of the pilot program.

[13]*U.S. Department of Labor Strategic Plan Fiscal Years 2011–2016*, U.S. Department of Labor, September 30, 2010, www.dol.gov/_sec/stratplan/StrategicPlan.pdf.

Increased interagency referrals and an overall emphasis on cooperation in enforcement of equal pay laws have implications for employers. From a risk management perspective, employers should be engaging in proactive examinations of compensation with respect to internal pay equity. It is critical that employers understand what stories their compensation data sets tell. Employers should prepare for multidirectional scrutiny of their compensation policies and practices from regulatory agencies.

Education and Outreach

As articulated by the task force, education is critical to enforcement of equal pay laws:

> *Educating employers and employees about their rights and responsibilities under our nation's equal pay laws is essential to ending the pay gap. Many workers are unaware of their rights and of the fact that pay discrimination is still a problem in the twenty-first century American workplace.*[14]

To address the need of educating employers on their obligations and employees on their rights under equal pay laws, the task force made the following recommendation in its Action Plan:

> *Undertake a public education campaign to educate employers on their obligations and employees on their rights. In addition, agencies will work to develop enhanced training programs for their employees charged with identifying, investigating, and prosecuting wage discrimination and will improve the accessibility of publicly available information.*[15]

Public Education and Outreach

Since its formation, members of the task force have devoted considerable time and resources to educating the public about equal pay laws. For example, in January 2012, the DOL issued an Equal Pay App Challenge that invited developers to use publicly available data and resources to create applications that accomplished one of the following four goals:[16]

---

[14]"Equal Pay Task Force Accomplishments," p. 5.
[15]National Equal Pay Enforcement Task Force, White House, www.whitehouse.gov/sites/default/files/rss_viewer/equal_pay_task_force.pdf.
[16]"US Labor Department and National Equal Pay Task Force launch equal pay application development challenge," News Release, Office of Public Affairs, U.S. Department of Labor, January 31, 2012, www.dol.gov/opa/media/press/opa/OPA20120146.htm.

1. Provide greater access to pay data broken down by gender, race, and ethnicity that would be helpful to women throughout their careers as they negotiate starting pay, request a promotion or raise, or consider switching fields to a more lucrative career path;

2. Provide interactive tools for early career coaching, creating an interactive online experience to educate young women on the pay gap and enable informed decision making when selecting a career path;

3. Help inform negotiations by providing feedback, tips, and critiques that guide users through the process of negotiating starting salary, pay rate, job level, or requesting a promotion or raise, as well as educate users about their legal rights;

4. Promote online mentoring by expanding a person's access to broader communities and mentorship opportunities and providing a means to connect with others for career guidance.

On April 17, 2012, Secretary of Labor Hilda Solis announced the four winners of the Equal Pay App Challenge grand prize. The winning submissions, as described on the Equal Pay App Challenge website, are as follows.[17]

-   *Aequitas*: a mobile personal career management solution that empowers users with current wage data, interview, résumé, and negotiation tools. It also provides wage and Equal Pay Act information and connects to equal pay–related social networks and discussions.

-   *Close the Wage Gap*: a website designed to educate users about the gender wage gap and arm them with information and negotiation tools to eliminate it. By merging data from multiple sources and tapping into the developers' own negotiation know-how, the website provides innovative ways to help users take steps toward closing the wage gap.

-   *Gender Gap App*: designed to boost public awareness of the salary differences between men and women who are doing the same jobs. Data behind the app are taken directly from the U.S. Department of Labor.

---

[17]"Equal Pay App Challenge: Final Results & Prize Winners," U.S. Department of Labor, www.dol.gov/equalpay/apps-winners.htm.

- *Demand Equal Pay for Women*: an application that makes it easy for everyone to see how the pay gap affects nearly every woman in every industry. The app allows users to compare what they make with the national averages at the industry and occupational level, so users know how hard they need to push during salary negotiations.

The DOL's Women's Bureau launched its own version of an equal pay application in its website. The Equal Pay Toolkit includes a White House Equal Pay Day Fact Sheet, a statement from Hilda Solis on Equal Pay Day, the Women's Bureau Regional Data Fact Sheet Highlighting Women's Earnings, and charts demonstrating the cumulative impact of the pay gap on women's lifetime earnings.

These are just two of the many examples of the public education and outreach efforts undertaken to inform people about the pay gap and equal pay laws. Other agencies, such as the EEOC and the DOJ, are reviewing their educational tools and materials for employees and the general public and may develop new resources for training individuals on their rights under equal pay laws and how to identify potential compensation discrimination.

Agency Employee Education

Members of the task force are also revisiting the information available to their employees and other agencies responsible for enforcing equal pay laws. For example, the EEOC is reviewing its staff training materials to improve training for enforcement staff on how to use wage data to identify and assess wage disparity cases, how to investigate wage discrimination charges, and the differences in analysis between an Equal Pay Act claim and a Title VII wage claim.

The EEOC, DOJ, and OFCCP are engaging in joint staff training and cross-training. The EEOC has created a new compensation discrimination training program, which was designed in consultation with OFCCP, the DOJ, and the Wage and Hour Division to address opportunities for improving efficiency and effectiveness through interagency collaboration in enforcement activities. As of March 2012, the EEOC had trained approximately 2,000 enforcement personnel from the EEOC, OFCCP, the Wage and Hour Division, and state and local civil rights agencies.

OFCCP is undertaking substantial efforts to enhance its training and education of its field staff and managers. As noted in the "Equal Pay Task Force Accomplishments":

> In addition to participating in EEOC's compensation discrimination training, OFCCP is developing improved and expanded protocols for its field staff to address a broader range of compensation issues and to

identify and address discrimination in pay. OFCCP is devoting substantial resources to developing and implementing national and regional training for its managers and compliance officers on investigating and addressing equal pay issues.[18]

Member agencies of the task force are taking steps to improve training of their own employees, as well as cross-train employees of other member agencies. These cross-training efforts also link back into the task force's goal of increased interagency cooperation.

Employer Education and Outreach

The overall education and outreach campaign also includes resources for employers. For example, the EEOC, DOL, and DOJ are assessing their educational tools and materials for employers. They are evaluating the development of guidance on how to examine pay disparities in the workplace with respect to equal pay for equal work and occupational segregation by gender.

The Women's Bureau hosted a series of meetings with employers, federal contractors, and advocates to highlight available resources and educational materials. The bureau conducted four regional events focusing on equal pay issues and co-sponsored an additional thirty-four events in collaboration with the EEOC and OFCCP.

The EEOC is focusing a significant amount of resources on employer training and education. In 2011, the commission's Training Institute hosted a series of technical assistance seminars on equal pay. These seminars were designed to help employers learn how to comply with federal equal employment opportunity laws regarding compensation.

In its *Strategic Plan for Fiscal Years 2012–2016*, the EEOC announced plans for several new programs aimed specifically at areas of the employer community that are historically underserved, such as small businesses and new businesses.[19] This focus is motivated at least in part by the agency's belief that discrimination can be prevented through education and outreach. As stated by EEOC Commissioner Chai Feldblum:

> *Most employers that I meet want to comply with the law. The thing is, they're also just trying to make a business happen. They have a lot of other things on their minds.... I'm going from the premise that employers would like to comply with the law. I'm also going from the premise that some things about the law are very simple and straightforward, and employers*

---

[18]"Equal Pay Task Force Accomplishments," p. 5.
[19]*Strategic Plan for Fiscal Years 2012–2016*, U.S. Equal Employment Opportunity Commission, February 22, 2012, www.eeoc.gov/eeoc/plan/strategic_plan_12to16.cfm.

> *don't actually need a lot of technical assistance.... But other aspects of the law are more complex, and therefore it is our job as an agency to make sure that employers understand what the law actually requires, so they can then make sure that their supervisors and their managers are applying the law correctly.*[20]

The ability to partner with the EEOC on compliance efforts will be a significant benefit to employers, particularly those in areas of the business community that are historically underserved.

Implications for Employers

The implications for employers of the focus on education and outreach are dual. First, more resources and information are now available for employers than have been in the past. The wider availability of technical guidance and compliance assistance will be beneficial as employers navigate the more complex areas of equal employment law.

Second, employers should understand that their employees—and the general public—are more sensitive to equal pay issues as a result of recent education and outreach efforts. In some respects, these efforts have been disproportionately directed at employees and the general public. Many messages used in the public education and outreach campaigns cite discrimination as the cause of any differences in compensation among employees. Employees may not understand that there are legitimate nondiscriminatory factors that account for differences between their compensation and that of their counterparts and jump to the conclusion that any difference is unfair and discriminatory.

To address this concern, it is important that compensation policies are transparent and that employers clearly communicate compensation policies to employees. Compensation decisions should be based on a set of consistent and well-articulated factors. It should be clear to anyone reviewing the policy what factors and metrics are used in the compensation decision making process. It is important that the policies and decision making processes are communicated to employees in a concise and easily understandable manner. Employees should understand how their compensation is determined and what is expected of them to achieve the next merit increase or incentive payment.

---

[20]"EEOC Commissioner Feldblum Talks to The Proactive Employer," *The Proactive Employer*, March 16, 2012, www.blogtalkradio.com/theproactiveemployer/2012/03/16/chai-feldblum-discusses-the-eeoc-strategic-plan.

Eleven-Cent Wage Differential among Federal Employees

According to a White House report regarding the accomplishments of the task force, "members have made notable progress in efforts to ensure equal pay in the federal workforce."[21] Specifically:

- A joint memo from the EEOC and OPM was released to federal employees, Chief Human Capital Officers, and EEO directors pledging the agencies' commitment to rigorous enforcement of equal pay laws for federal employees;

- Under the leadership of Commissioner Feldblum, the EEOC is working closely with the OPM, GAO, and experts on pay equity to determine what additional data may be required to better understand the eleven cent wage differential among federal employees;

- The OPM is continuing to evaluate the role of Federal Women Program Managers and women in the Senior Executive Service (SES). The OPM is working with partner agencies on a pilot project to increase diversity of applicants for certain SES positions.

The federal government is continuing to take steps toward improving its role as a model employer and eliminate the reported eleven cent per hour wage differential among federal employees.

Understanding the Full Scope of the Wage Gap

The task force believes that part of the difficulty in identifying and combating compensation discrimination is the government's inability to understand the full scope of the wage gap. This limited understanding, according to the task force, is attributable to insufficient information and data:

> *Private sector employers are not required to systematically report gender-identified wage data to the federal government. This lack of data makes identifying wage discrimination difficult and undercuts enforcement efforts. We must identify ways to collect wage data from employers that are useful to enforcement agencies but do not create unnecessary burdens on employers.*

---

[21]"Equal Pay Task Force Accomplishments," p. 8.

The task force believes that having access to more compensation data from employers will improve its understanding of the wage gap and allow regulatory agencies to better target enforcement efforts. To have access to these data, the task force recommended that the EEOC evaluate their data collection needs and capabilities and make modifications to existing EEO reports. The task force also recommended the reinstatement of the EO Survey or similar instrument. This recommendation has taken on the form of the OFCCP's proposed compensation data collection tool.

EEOC Data and EEO Reports

The EEOC collects workforce data from all public and private employers with more than 100 employees. Currently, this information is collected through four separate EEO reports:

- *EEO-1 Report,* also known as the Employer Information Report, covers all private sector employers with 100 or more employees and reports the composition of their workforces by gender and race/ethnicity category;

- *EEO-3 Report,* also known as the Local Union Report, covers all local unions and reports the composition of their workforces by gender and race/ethnicity category;

- *EEO-4 Report,* also known as the State and Local Government Report, covers all state and local governments with 100 or more employees and reports the composition of their workforces by gender and race/ethnicity category, as well as compensation information;

- *EEO-5 Report,* also known as the Elementary-Secondary Staff Information Report, covers all public elementary and secondary school districts with 100 or more employees and reports the composition of their workforces by gender and race/ethnicity category.

After reviewing the EEO reports in their current form, the EEOC has concluded that there is no federal data source that has employer-specific wage data by demographic characteristics for private sector employees. Of the four EEO reports, only EEO-4, covering state and local governments, collects any wage-related information.

To remedy this, the EEOC is in the process of commissioning an outside study to determine what data it should collect to most effectively enhance its wage discrimination law enforcement efforts. OFCCP and EEOC are working collaboratively on evaluating data collection needs, capabilities, and tools to avoid duplicative efforts.

Reinstatement of EO Survey or Similar Instrument

With respect to the federal contracting community, the task force has recommended the reinstatement of the OFCCP Equal Opportunity Survey or a similar instrument. This recommendation encompasses not only the compensation data and information federal contractors would be required to provide to OFCCP; it also extends to the analysis methodology OFCCP may use in the examination of that compensation data for systemic discrimination.

Original EO Survey

Federal contractors falling under the auspices of the OFCCP may remember the original Equal Opportunity Survey that was implemented in 2000. The survey required contractors to provide information on their affirmative action programs and summary data on personnel activity and compensation.

The original survey had three main goals:

1. Increase compliance with equal opportunity requirements by improving contractor self-awareness and encouraging self-evaluation;

2. Improve the deployment of scarce federal government resources to those contractors who were most likely to be out of compliance;

3. Increase agency efficiency by building on the tiered-review process already accomplished by OFCCP's regulatory reform efforts, resulting in better resource allocations.

The original Equal Opportunity Survey was discontinued in 2006 after an independent consulting group determined that it was not a valid tool and did not predict systemic discrimination. OFCCP then published *The Interpretive Standards for Systemic Compensation Discrimination*, its final document regarding federal contractors' examination of compensation practices with respect to gender, race, and ethnicity.[22]

---

[22]"The Interpretive Standards for Systemic Compensation Discrimination," 71 *Federal Register* 35124, June 16, 2006.

Interpretive Standards for Systemic Compensation Discrimination

The *Standards* outlined the methodology for OFCCP's evaluation of contractors' compensation practices during compliance reviews.[23] The *Standards* were intended to provide, for the first time, a definitive interpretation of the 1978 Sex Discrimination Guidelines, codified at 41 CFR 60-20, as well as Executive Order 11246 with respect to systemic compensation discrimination.

On August 17, 2010, OFCCP Director Patricia Shiu announced the agency's intent to rescind the *Standards*. According to a *Federal Register* notice published in January 2011, the underlying reason for this was as follows:

> OFCCP is proposing to rescind the Standards which have limited OFCCP's ability to effectively investigate, analyze and identify compensation discrimination. In doing so, OFCCP will continue to adhere to the principles of Title VII of the Civil Rights Act of 1964, as amended, (Title VII) in investigating compensation discrimination and will re-institute flexibility in its use of investigative approaches and tools.[24]

The notice also discussed OFCCP's belief that the methodology outlined in the *Standards*, namely, multiple regression analysis of similarly situated employee groupings, is too "rigid":

> The Standard's mandate to use a multiple regression analysis to identify compensation discrimination is also overly narrow and is not required under Title VII principles. While a multiple regression analysis may be a useful tool in identifying compensation discrimination, other statistical or non-statistical analyses may be better suited, depending on the facts of the case.[25]

The notice goes on to say that if the *Standards* are rescinded, "OFCCP will re-institute the practice of exercising its discretion to develop compensation discrimination investigation procedures in the same manner it develops other investigation procedures."[26]

---

[23] The methodology outlined in the *Standards* centered around two characteristics: (1) the formation of "similarly situated employee groupings" and (2) the use of multiple regression analysis.

[24] "Interpretive Standards for Systemic Compensation Discrimination and Voluntary Guidelines for Self-Evaluation of Compensation Practices under Executive Order 11246; Notice of Proposed Rescission," 76 *Federal Register*, January 3, 2011.

[25] Ibid.

[26] Ibid.

Even though the *Standards* have not formally been rescinded as of the date of this writing, the general consensus among experts is that the rescission will take place. When the *Standards* are officially rescinded, federal contractors will no longer have a roadmap to the kinds of analyses OFCCP will be performing on contractors' compensation data. OFCCP will be free to select analysis tools and methodologies—statistical and nonstatistical, formal and informal—at will. This, coupled with the proposed Wage Data Collection Tool, poses serious concerns for federal contractors regarding the manipulation of increasing amounts of compensation data by OFCCP.

Compensation Data Collection Tool

Based on the task force's belief that insufficient compensation data exist to understand the full scope of the wage gap, OFCCP is proposing a new compensation data collection tool. This tool would provide OFCCP with a greatly expanded database of contractor compensation information.

According to the OFCCP Advanced Notice of Proposed Rulemaking, the purpose of the new compensation data collection tool is as follows:

> To provide insight into potential problems of pay discrimination by contractors that warrant further review or evaluation by OFCCP or contractor self-audit. Accordingly, it is envisioned primarily as a screening tool, although it may have research value. The tool would allow OFCCP to effectively and efficiently identify supply and service contractors whose compensation data indicated further investigation is necessary to ensure compliance with the non-discrimination requirements of the Executive Order and would provide contractors with a self-assessment tool that may be used periodically to evaluate the effects of their employee compensation decisions. The data collected through this tool may be used to identify contractors for compensation focused reviews as well as full compliance reviews.[27]

In the Advanced Notice of Proposed Rulemaking OFCCP sought comments from stakeholders and the business community on fifteen aspects of the compensation data collection tool:

1. What data or information should be collected to assess whether further investigation into the contractor's compensation decisions and policies is necessary?

2. By what set of job categories should the data referred to in question 1 be collected?

---

[27]"Non-Discrimination in Compensation; Compensation Data Collection Tool," 76 *Federal Register* 154, August 10, 2011.

3. What elements of compensation should be collected?

4. Is there a set of questions that would capture information that would be helpful in understanding a contractor's compensation system, such as policies relating to promotion decisions, bonuses, shift pay, setting of initial pay?

5. What type of compensation trend analyses would be appropriate to conduct on an industry-wide basis?

6. What specific categories of data would be most useful for identifying contractors in specific industries for industry-focused compensation reviews?

7. What specific categories of data would be most useful for conducting compensation analyses across a contractor's various establishments?

8. What practical concerns might contractors have regarding responding to the compensation data request, and how do contractors currently record and maintain compensation data?

9. What specific categories of data would be most useful to contractors interested in conducting self-assessments of their compensation decisions?

10. What were the strengths and weaknesses of the compensation section of the 2000 EO Survey?

11. What factors should OFCCP take into consideration if contractors are required to submit data electronically?

12. What are the benefits and drawbacks of requiring businesses that are bidding on future federal contracts to submit compensation data as part of the request for proposal process?

13. Should OFCCP decide to expand the scope of the compensation data collection tool beyond supply and service contractors to include construction contractors, what factors or issues particularly relevant to such contractors should be kept in mind?

14. Are there other constructive suggestions for the design, content, analysis, and implementation of a compensation data collection tool?

15. OFCCP encourages small entities to provide data on how they may be affected by the requirement to provide the compensation data requested by the new data collection tool.

OFCCP is contemplating collecting the following data, some of which would be at a very granular level:

- Number of employees in each gender and race/ethnicity category

- Average starting or initial compensation (including paid leave, health and retirement benefits, etc.)

- Average pay rate

- Average bonus payments

- Minimum and maximum salary

- Standard deviation or variance of salary

- Average compensation by job series

- Average employee tenure

- Total W-2 earnings

- Base salaries

- Hourly wage rates

- Holiday pay

- Shift differentials

- Commissions and bonus payments

- Paid leave

- Health benefits

- Retirement benefits

- Other elements of compensation

Employers may be required to produce these data separately for each job category. Possible candidates for job categories include two- or three-digit Standard Industrial Classification (SIC) Codes, salary bands within EEO-1 categories, and individual job titles. It is also possible that employers would be required to produce employee-level data for all types of compensation and benefits.

Additionally, employers may be required to produce their policies and procedures for initial pay setting, shift pay, bonus decisions, promotion decisions, and any other decisions affecting compensation and benefits.

According to OFCCP Director Patricia Shiu, the agency received more than 7,000 comments in response to the Advanced Notice of Proposed Rulemaking. She pointed out that many of the comments received "were not particularly constructive or helpful. . . . Many of them did not answer the questions we asked."[28] She acknowledged that the proposed data collection tool requires "a great deal of analysis."[29] The tool is still in the clearance phase. OFCCP continues to work on its development, so it is not yet clear whether the tool will be adopted and, if so, what its final form will be.

The Solution Is Not More of the Same Data

OFCCP should be commended for its efforts at creating equal opportunity workplaces. Undoubtedly, compensation discrimination does exist, and OFCCP can—and should—play a role in ending discrimination. On its face, the compensation data collection tool appears to be one way to accomplish this.

However, a close review of the Advanced Notice of Proposed Rulemaking leads to the conclusion that the OFCCP's desire to collect compensation data is motivated by an inaccurate understanding of the question at hand:

> *Women still earn only 77 cents for each dollar earned by a man. . . . Potentially non-discriminatory factors can explain some of these differences. Even so, after controlling for differences in skills and job characteristics, women still earn less than men. Some scholars find that these differences can be explained, to some extent, by differences in education and prior labor market experience. Others identify job segregation as an important cause of the pay gap. Ultimately, the research literature still finds that an unexplainable gap exists even after accounting for potential explanations. Moreover, research literature finds that the narrowing of the pay gap has slowed since the 1980s. To the extent that these factors, such as type of job or amount of continuous labor market experience, are also influenced by discrimination, the "unexplained" difference may understate the true effect of discrimination.*

---

[28]"Good Jobs for Everyone with OFCCP Director Pat Shiu," *The Proactive Employer*, June 21, 2012, www.blogtalkradio.com/theproactiveemployer/2012/06/21/good-jobs-for-everyone-wit-ofccp-director-pat-shiu.
[29]Ibid.

The argument is predicated on the assumption of discrimination. Although OFCCP acknowledges the vast body of research that indicates occupation, industry, labor market experience, and other factors explain a large portion of the gender pay gap, this research is dismissed.[30] Yet the data points that would be collected by the compensation data collection tool are the same kinds of data points that have been examined in this body of research.

There is no doubt that the compensation data collection tool would provide OFCCP with an enormous volume of data, which could be used to detect patterns of discrimination. However, the tool would collect the same kinds of compensation data that have been collected and analyzed for years. Using this "traditional" compensation data, we still are unable to successfully predict and prevent discrimination.

To successfully predict and prevent discrimination, a different approach is required. An understanding of how compensation expectations are formed (and how they differ by gender), willingness to engage in compensation negotiations, and the reasons underlying personal choices made by men and women are necessary to advance our understanding of the gender pay gap. Continuing to study greater volumes of the same kinds of data we have been studying for years is not likely to provide deeper insight into the causes of and potential solutions to the pay gap.

Implications for Employers

The task force strongly believes that the inability to understand the full scope of the wage gap is attributable to insufficient information and data. As a result of this belief, the EEOC and OFCCP are considering measures to dramatically enhance the depth and breadth of employer compensation data collected.

In terms of implications for employers, there are numerous open questions with respect to the collection of compensation data. The EEOC is studying its compensation data needs and evaluating how that information should be collected. It is unclear when and in what form the data collection tool will be approved and adopted. It is likely, however, that employers will be required to produce expanded compensation data to the EEOC and/or OFCCP in the near future. Employers should begin reviewing their document retention policies and data collection procedures to ensure that they are capturing comprehensive compensation and benefits information for all employees.

---

[30]Explanations of the gender pay gap, such as occupation, industry, labor market experience, and so forth, are explored in Chapter 9.

Existing Laws Provide Inadequate Tools

The task force believes that existing laws governing compensation discrimination, including the Equal Pay Act of 1963, do not provide federal officials with adequate tools to combat compensation discrimination.[31] Loopholes exist in the act that provide employers with "unjustified defenses to their discriminatory conduct."[32]

The task force made the following recommendation to remedy this problem:

> Although the Equal Pay Act of 1963 was an important historical milestone, it has not been updated since then, despite nearly half a century of legal and economic developments. The Paycheck Fairness Act would significantly enhance the Equal Pay Act. Among other things, the new law would allow women to receive the same remedies for sex-based pay discrimination as those available under some other laws to individuals subjected to race or national origin discrimination. The Act would bar retaliation against workers who disclose their wages, and would strengthen protections against wage discrimination by clarifying the scope of affirmative defenses. The Administration will continue working with lawmakers on this legislation and supporting its enactment.[33]

Task force members are hailing the Paycheck Fairness Act as a piece of legislation that has the potential to end compensation discrimination permanently.

The Paycheck Fairness Act

The Paycheck Fairness Act would augment the Equal Pay Act, allowing for an expanded definition of what constitutes pay discrimination and providing additional remedies for victims of pay discrimination.

The Equal Pay Act of 1963 specifically addresses defenses employers may use with respect to differences in compensation by gender:

> No employer having employees subject to any provisions of this section shall discriminate, within any establishment in which such employees are employed, between employees on the basis of sex by paying wages to employees in such establishments at a rate less than the rate at which he pays wages to employees of the opposite sex in such establishments

---

[31]National Equal Pay Enforcement Task Force, White House, www.whitehouse.gov/ sites/default/files/rss_viewer/equal_pay_task_force.pdf.
[32]Ibid.
[33]Ibid.

for equal work on jobs the performance of which requires equal skill, effort, and responsibility, and which are performed under similar working conditions, except where such payment is made pursuant to (i) a seniority system, (ii) a merit system, (iii) a system which measures earnings by quantity or quality of production, or (iv) **a differential based on any other factor other than sex.** *(emphasis added)*

The Paycheck Fairness Act would change the "any factor other than sex" defense. Employers would be required to show that the pay differential is caused by (1) a bona fide factor other than sex, (2) that the factor is related to job performance, and (3) the factor is consistent with business necessity.

From a practical standpoint, common sense tells us that men and women who are similarly situated (i.e., performance of equal work under similar working conditions on jobs requiring the same skill, effort, and level of responsibility) should be paid the same, and compensation decisions should in fact be based on legitimate factors consistent with business necessity.

Practical Implications of the Paycheck Fairness Act

When we look closely at the Paycheck Fairness Act, however, we see that it has some unusual implications for the way employers compensate their employees. For example, consider the following three scenarios:

A. John and Jane have identical characteristics (education, work experience, etc.) and differ only by gender. ABC Company makes offers of employment to John and Jane on the same day, for identical positions, at the same starting salary of $45,000. Jane accepts the offer, but John negotiates the salary and ends up with a starting salary of $50,000.

B. Sam and Sally have the same education, work experience, and so on, and are both hired by WidgetCo on the same day for identical positions. The company sets both Sam's and Sally's starting salary at $2,500 more than they were earning at their previous jobs. Sam was earning $37,500 at his previous job, and Sally was earning $36,000. Their starting salaries at WidgetCo are $40,000 and $38,500, respectively.

C. Brad and Bridget both work for Alpha Inc.; have the same job title, same level of responsibility, and so on; and are earning $100,000 a year. Brad asks for a 5% raise, and Bridget does not. Brad gets the raise and ends up earning more than Bridget.

In these three examples, the differences in pay are attributable to factors other than gender. In the first example, the difference is attributable to John's negotiation and Jane's failure to negotiate. In the second example, the difference is attributable to differences in salary histories with previous employers. In the third example, the difference is due to Brad asking for a raise and Bridget's failure to ask for a raise. The employers' decisions are based on factors other than gender. Under the current equal pay laws, these scenarios are perfectly fine and the employers' decisions would not be considered discriminatory.

Under the Paycheck Fairness Act, however, the outcome would be very different. An employer would have to demonstrate that its pay practices are divorced from any discrimination in its workplace or at the employee's prior workplace, that the pay practice is job-related, and that the practice is consistent with business necessity.

In Scenario A, under the Paycheck Fairness Act, ABC Company would be required to increase Jane's starting salary to $50,000, the same as John's negotiated starting salary. The fact that Jane's starting salary is lower than her male counterpart's due to her failure to negotiate is not job-related. Most likely, this decision would be found not to be dictated by business necessity. Because ABC was willing to pay John $5,000 more than initially offered, the company should be willing to pay Jane the same amount for the same job. Under the Paycheck Fairness Act, ABC would have to adjust for Jane's failure to negotiate and offer her the same $50,000 as if she had negotiated like John did.

▨ **Note** The Paycheck Fairness Act would require employers to adjust for differences in employees' or candidates' negotiation skills and willingness to engage in compensation negotiations.

In Scenario B, under the Paycheck Fairness Act, WidgetCo would be required to set Sam's and Sally's starting salaries at the same dollar amount of $40,000. The fact that Sally was earning less than Sam in her previous position, whether due to discrimination, market forces, and so on, is not related to her job at WidgetCo. As in the previous example, the pay decisions are most likely not dictated by business necessity. Assuming that Sally's lower previous salary was due to discrimination by her former employer, WidgetCo would be required to adjust for the prior employer's discrimination and increase her starting salary to that of Sam's.

▨ **Note** The Paycheck Fairness Act would limit employers' flexibility in addressing differences in employee and candidate salary histories and would require employers to remedy past discrimination by employees' and candidates' former employers.

In Scenario C, under the Paycheck Fairness Act, Alpha Inc. would be required to give Bridget a 5% raise. The fact that her salary is now lower than Brad's because she failed to ask for a raise is not job-related. As in the previous examples, the pay decisions are most likely not dictated by business necessity. Under the Paycheck Fairness Act, Alpha would have to increase Bridget's pay by 5% as if she had asked for a raise like Brad did, even though she did not do so.

Note The Paycheck Fairness Act would limit employers' flexibility in addressing differences in employee salary demands and require employers to adjust for these differences in salary demands.

These are just three examples of how the Paycheck Fairness Act would substantially alter the way U.S. businesses are permitted to compensate their employees. The act would limit the flexibility of employers in addressing different salary histories, different salary demands, and so on. Businesses would have to make adjustments for any gender differences in negotiating skills, as well as willingness to engage in negotiations. They would also be required to right the wrongs of employees' previous employers if those previous employers engaged in discriminatory pay-setting practices.

The Paycheck Fairness Act also has implications for compensation discrimination litigation. Specifically, it would make it easier for plaintiffs to bring class-action lawsuits.[34] Under the Equal Pay Act, plaintiffs must "opt in" to a class action by providing written consent. If an individual fails to provide written consent, he or she has not opted in and is not part of the class of plaintiffs.[35] Under the Paycheck Fairness Act, individuals would automatically be included in the class and would have to opt out if they did not want to be a party to the litigation.[36] Under the Paycheck Fairness Act, employees would not need to affirmatively join a case to be included in the class action. Because of this, it would be easier for plaintiffs to bring class-action lawsuits on behalf of very large groups of employees.

---

[34] A class-action lawsuit is a form of lawsuit in which a large group of people collectively bring a claim to court and/or in which a group of defendants is being sued.

[35] The Equal Pay Act is governed by the procedural rules of the Fair Labor Standards Act, which requires opt-in.

[36] The Paycheck Fairness Act would permit "opt-out" class actions under Rule 23 of the Federal Rules of Civil Procedure.

Furthermore, damages and penalties for employers who are found guilty of discriminatory compensation decisions would be altered. The Equal Pay Act provides for equitable relief, such as back pay awards. Under the Paycheck Fairness Act, unlimited compensatory and punitive damages would be permitted.[37]

Supporters of the Paycheck Fairness Act have argued that this "commonsense" piece of legislation has the power to end the gender pay gap—and gender discrimination—once and for all.

Unfortunately, the Paycheck Fairness Act is destined to fail in terms of delivering on this promise. As noted by one critic:

> [The Paycheck Fairness Act] isn't as commonsensical as it might seem. It overlooks mountains of research showing that discrimination plays little role in the pay disparities between men and women, and it threatens to impose onerous requirements on employers to correct gaps over which they have little control.[38]

As with OFCCP's proposed compensation data collection tool, the argument in support of the Paycheck Fairness Act is predicated on the assumption of discrimination, despite the vast body of research indicating a variety of legitimate, nondiscriminatory factors explaining a substantial portion of the gender pay gap.

Implications for Employers

It remains to be seen whether the Paycheck Fairness Act will be signed in to law. It has been introduced—and defeated—in Congress several times. There appears to be continued support for the Paycheck Fairness Act, and members of Congress have promised to reintroduce it in the current session.

Organizations should review their compensation policies and practices to determine which, if any, would be affected by the Paycheck Fairness Act. Companies should begin making some contingency plans under the assumption that the act will be signed in to law. The Paycheck Fairness Act has sweeping implications for all businesses, and proactive employers will begin preparing for those implications now.

---

[37]Compensatory damages are awarded to compensate plaintiffs for loss or harm suffered. Punitive damages differ in that they are not awarded to compensate plaintiffs. They are awarded to punish the defendant(s) for outrageous conduct and discourage the defendant(s) from engaging in similar behavior in the future.

[38]Christina Hoff Sommers, "Fair Pay Isn't Always Equal Pay," New York Times, September 21, 2010.

Causes of the Gender Pay Gap

Right now, women are a growing number of breadwinners in the household. But they're still earning just 77 cents for every dollar a man does—even less if you're an African American or Latina woman. Overall, a woman with a college degree doing the same work as a man will earn hundreds of thousands of dollars less over the course of her career. So closing this pay gap—ending discrimination—is about far more than simple fairness. When more women are bringing home the bacon, but bringing home less of it than men who are doing the same work, that weakens families, it weakens communities, it's tough on our kids, it weakens our entire economy.

—President Barack Obama, April 6, 2012

The movement of women into the labor force has been referred to by some as the greatest social transformation of our time. Figure 9-1 presents the gender composition of the civilian labor force from 1960 to 2010. In 1960, approximately one out of three workers in the civilian labor force was female. By 2000, 47%—nearly half—was female.

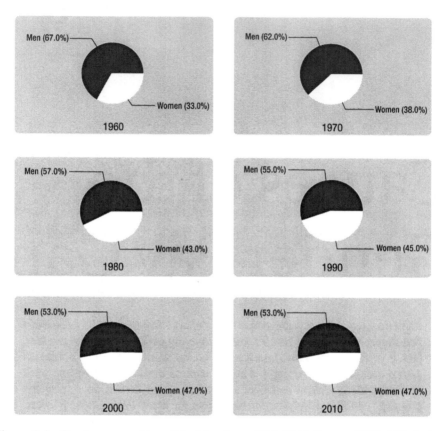

Figure 9-1. Gender composition of the labor force, 1960–2010 (Source: "Table 588: Civilian Population—Employment Status by Sex, Race and Ethnicity," *2012 Statistical Abstract of the United States, U.S. Department of Census*)

This percentage has held steady: as of August 2012, approximately 47% of the labor force was female.[1]

More opportunities for women exist now than ever before, and the presence of women in a wide range of workplaces is common. Yet one issue that's still being discussed is the gender pay gap.

The most commonly cited statistic in the current gender pay gap discussion is the "77 cents" statistic: women earn 77 cents for every $1 earned by their male counterparts.

---

[1]Bureau of Labor Statistics, "Table A-1, Employment Status of the Civilian Population by Sex and Age" (www.bls.gov/news.release/empsit.t01.htm).

This statistic is presented very frequently. It has been cited by White House Senior Adviser Valerie Jarrett, Acting EEOC Chairman Stuart Ishimaru, Secretary of Labor Hilda Solis, and various scholars, academics, consultants, and practitioners. The 77 cents statistic has been adduced as supporting evidence in discussions ranging from abstract theoretical musings on the role of women in society to concrete policy proposals such as the Paycheck Fairness Act.

The current administration has given gender pay equity a high priority. An interagency task force has been created, and one of their main objectives is to better understand the full significance of the gender wage gap.

All of the current administration's work, however, is being driven by the 77 cents statistic and the assumption that the 23 cents per hour differential is attributable to gender discrimination. The 77 cents statistic does not accurately depict the real gender pay gap. It references the raw gender pay disparity and does not consider the impact of legitimate nondiscriminatory factors.

When one examines the gender wage gap accounting for legitimate nondiscriminatory factors such as occupational choice, industry, work experience, hours worked, the cash/benefits trade-off, and so on, the pay gap significantly narrows. In fact, there may be no gender pay gap at all.

The 77 Cents Statistic

In September 2010, the U.S. Census Bureau released its report on income, poverty, and health insurance coverage.[2] In that report, they indicate that the 2008 and 2009 ratio of female-to-male earnings of full-time, year-round workers fifteen years and older was 77%.[3] This ratio is consistent with the findings of other research.[4]

The first thing that many people think of when they hear this statistic is that women earn 77 cents for every dollar earned by men because of discrimination. In actuality, the statistic tells us nothing about gender discrimination. One cannot automatically assume that an observed differential in the earnings of men and women is attributable to gender discrimination. More important,

---

[2]Carmen DeNavas-Wait, Bernadette D. Proctor, and Jessica C. Smith, *Income, Poverty and Health Insurance Coverage in the United States: 2009*, U.S. Census Bureau, Current Population Reports, 60-238 (Washington, DC: U.S. Government Printing Office, 2010).

[3]A full-time, year-round worker is a person who worked thirty-five hours or more per week (full-time) and fifty or more weeks during the previous calendar year (year-round).

[4]Heather Boushey and Ann O'Leary, eds., *The Shriver Report: A Woman's Nation Changes Everything* (Washington, DC: Maria Shriver and the Center for American Progress, 2009), www.americanprogress.org/issues/women/report/2009/10/16/6789/the-shriver-report/; Francine Blau and Lawrence Kahn, "The Gender Pay Gap: Have Women Gone as Far as They Can?" *Academy of Management Perspectives* (February 2007).

77 percent is the raw earnings difference, and it fails to consider a variety of factors that create legitimate differences between the earnings of men and women.

A Closer Look

As noted by Francine Blau and Lawrence Kahn, "some of the raw wage gap is due to differences in the measured characteristics of men and women."[5] In fact, Blau and Kahn found that approximately 59% of the raw wage gap could be explained by factors such as occupational category, industry, work experience, race, and union status.

As shown in Figure 9-2, 27.4% of the raw wage gap is explained by occupational category. Industry category accounts for 21.9%, and labor force experience accounts for 10.5% of the raw wage gap. Union status and race account for 3.5% and 2.4% of the raw wage gap, respectively.

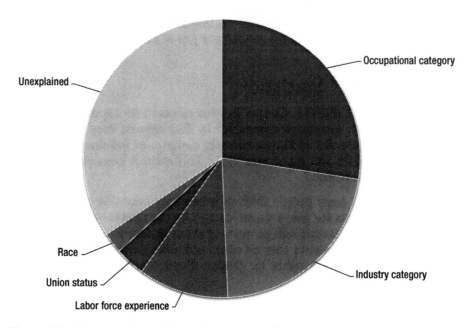

Figure 9-2. Decomposition of the gender wage gap (Source: data from Francine Blau and Lawrence Kahn, "The Gender Pay Gap: Have Women Gone as Far as They Can?" *Academy of Management Perspectives* [February 2007])

---

[5]Francine Blau and Lawrence Kahn, "The Gender Pay Gap," *Economists' Voices* (June 2007).

Blau and Kahn also found that accounting for education reduces the raw wage gap by 6.7%.[6] This is consistent with research by the U.S. Department of Labor, which found that women were more likely than men to graduate from high school, more likely to attend college,[7] and more likely to earn bachelor's, graduate, and professional degrees.[8]

After controlling for occupational category, industry category, labor force experience, union status, and race, a different picture of the gender wage gap emerges: women earn 91 cents for every $1 earned by their male counterparts. But this 9-cent differential is not automatically attributable to gender discrimination. It's likely that most—if not all—of this differential can be explained by looking at the choices individuals make.

In 2009, the Department of Labor commissioned a study on the gender wage gap.[9] In the foreword to this report, Deputy Assistant Secretary for Federal Contract Compliance Charles James stated:

> *This study leads to the unambiguous conclusion that the differences in compensation between men and women are the result of a multitude of factors and that the raw wage gap should not be used as the basis to justify corrective action. Indeed, there may be nothing to correct. The differences in raw wages may be almost entirely the result of individual choices being made by both male and female workers.* (emphasis added)

Some of the choices that may contribute to the gender pay gap include differences in career interruptions, willingness to negotiate, compensation expectations, hours worked, and the cash-versus-benefits trade-off.

---

[6]Women's educational attainment has a positive effect on the gender wage gap. An editorial by Christina Hoff-Summers (*New York Times*, September 21, 2010) cited a study indicating that young, childless, single urban women earn 8% more than their male counterparts. This is largely attributable to the fact that more of the women in this demographic category earn college degrees compared to their male counterparts.

[7]Bureau of Labor Statistics, "America's Youth at 22: School Enrollment, Training and Employment Transitions Between Ages 21 and 22 Summary," Economic News Release, January 28, 2010, www.bls.gov/news.release/nlsyth.nr0.htm.

[8]U.S. Census Bureau, "Educational Attainment in the United States: 2009," April 20, 2010, www.census.gov/prod/2012pubs/p20-566.pdf.

[9]CONSAD Research Corporation, "An Analysis of the Reasons for the Disparity in Wages Between Men and Women," prepared for the U.S. Department of Labor, Employment Standards Administration, January 2009.

Occupational Differences

Historically, men and women have worked in different occupations. This phenomenon has been referred to by researchers as occupational selection, occupational sorting, and occupational segregation. Although differences in the occupational choices of men and women have narrowed over the past thirty years, the differences persist. Using data from the Bureau of Labor Statistics, we can take a closer look at the gender pay gap by occupational category.[10]

Figures 9-3A through 9-3G show three pieces of information for each of the twenty-two major occupational categories from BLS Report 1031:

- The relative size of the occupational category, in terms of total number of workers. This is represented by the size of the circle.

- Female workers as a percentage of all workers in the occupational category. This is shown along the vertical axis.

- The ratio of female-to-male median weekly earnings. This is shown along the horizontal axis.

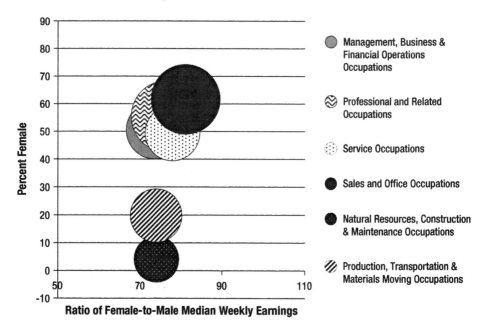

Figure 9-3A. Earnings and employment by broad occupational category

[10]Bureau of Labor Statistics, "Highlights of Women's Earnings in 2010," Report 1031, July 2011, www.bls.gov/cps/cpswom2010.pdf.

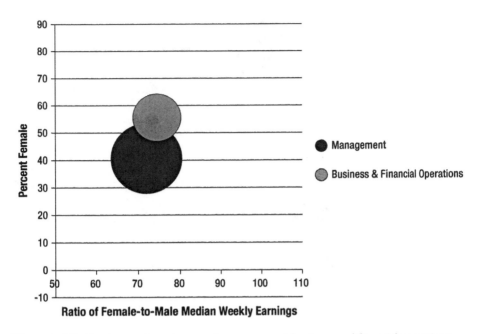

Figure 9-3B. Earnings and employment in management, business, and financial operations occupations

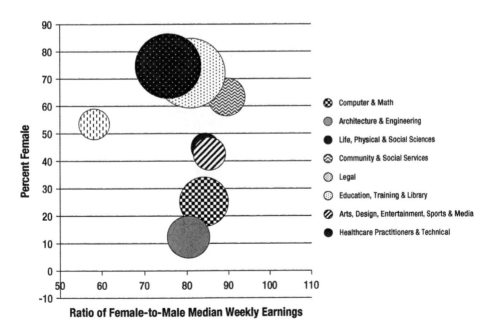

Figure 9-3C. Earnings and employment in professional and related occupations

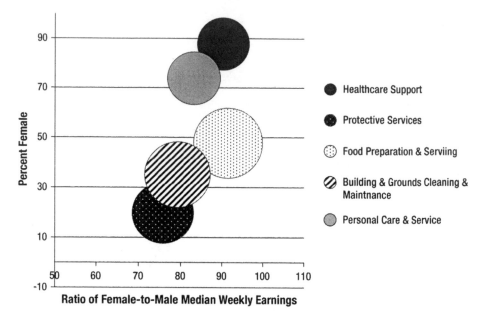

Figure 9-3D. Earnings and employment in service occupations

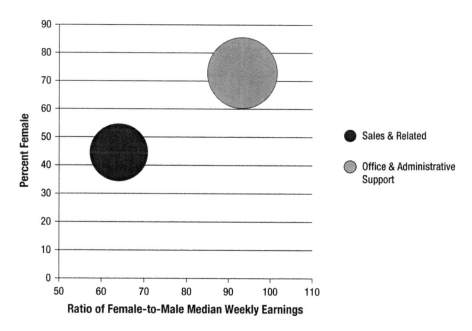

Figure 9-3E. Earnings and employment in sales and office occupations

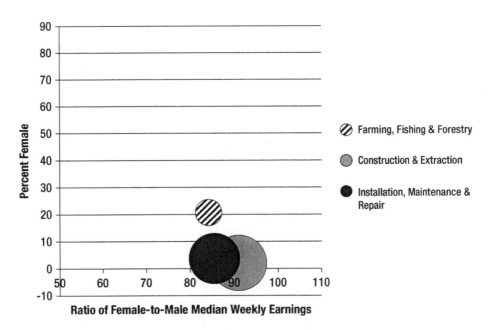

Figure 9-3F. Earnings and employment in natural resources, construction, and maintenance occupations

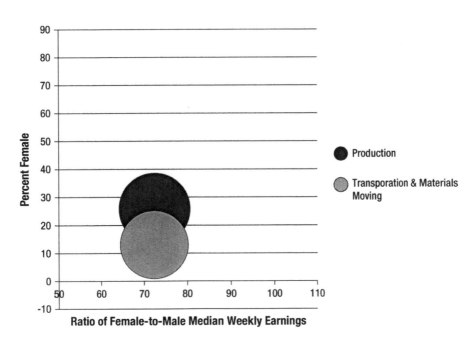

Figure 9-3G. Earnings and employment in production, transportation, and materials moving occupations

There are some key observations from Figures 9-3A through 9-3G:

- Office and administrative support occupations employ the most individuals (14% of the total workforce aged sixteen and older).

- Farming, forestry, and fishing occupations employ the fewest individuals (0.7%).

- Health care support occupations have the largest percentage of women (88%).

- Construction and extraction occupations have the smallest percentage of women (2%).

- Office and administrative support occupations have the largest ratio of female-to-male median weekly earnings (ratio = 93%).

- Legal occupations have the largest difference between female and male weekly earnings (ratio = 58%).

In all occupational categories, the ratio of female-to-male median weekly earnings is less than one, meaning that the typical female in the given occupation earns less than her male counterpart in the same occupation.

The gender pay gap can be elucidated at a more granular level by looking at the various positions within a given occupational category. For example, within the legal category, which has the smallest ratio of female-to-male earnings (58% as shown in Figure 9-3C), there are four subcategories: (a) lawyers; (b) judges, magistrates, and other judicial workers; (c) paralegals and legal assistants; and (d) miscellaneous legal support workers. The gender composition of these four subcategories is shown in Figure 9-4.

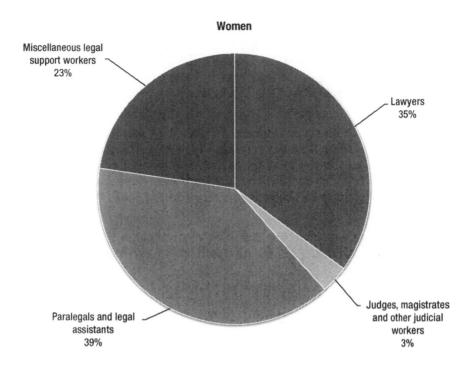

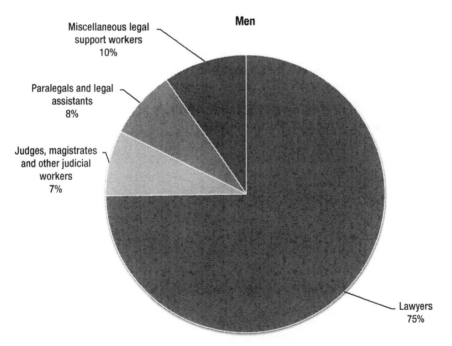

Figure 9-4. Distribution of men and women within legal occupations. (Source: Data from Bureau of Labor Statistics, *Highlights of Women's Earnings in 2010*, Report 1031, July 2011)

An interesting pattern emerges when we look at the gender distribution within the four subcategories. Three out of every four men working in the legal category are lawyers (75%). On the other hand, nearly two out of every three women working in the legal category are paralegals, legal assistants, or legal support workers (62%). Only 35% of women working in the legal category are lawyers.

It should come as no surprise that the earnings of paralegals and legal assistants are typically less than the earnings of lawyers. This example sheds light on why differences in the earnings of men and women still exist even when controlling for broader occupation category. If we were able to refine occupation sufficiently, it may be the case that more of the gender pay gap could be explained.

Unfortunately, as we refine our definition of occupation further, less and less data are available, making gender comparisons of earning more difficult and less reliable.

Industry Differences

Industry also plays a role in the gender pay gap. Figures 9-5A through 9-5D shows three pieces of information for each of the thirteen broad industry categories:[11]

- The relative size of the occupational category, in terms of total number of workers. This is represented by the size of the circle.

- Female workers as a percentage of all workers in the occupational category. This is shown along the vertical axis.

- The ratio of female-to-male median weekly earnings. This is shown along the horizontal axis.

---

[11]Bureau of Labor Statistics, *Women in the Labor Force: A Databook*, Report 1034, December 2011, www.bls.gov/cps/wlf-databook-2011.pdf.

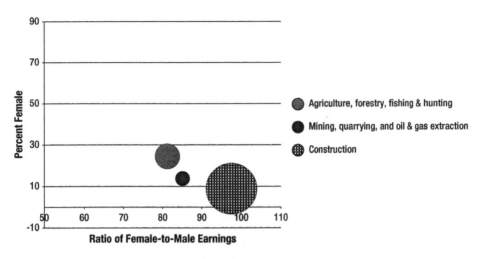

Figure 9-5A. Earnings and employment by broad industry category

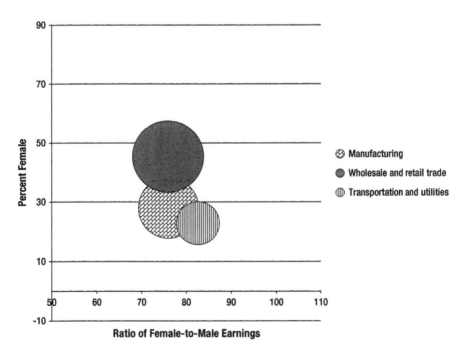

Figure 9-5B. Earnings and employment in manufacturing, wholesale and retail trade, and transportation and utilities industries

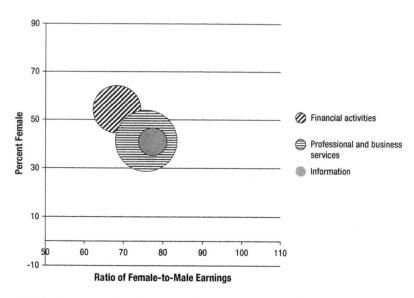

Figure 9-5C. Earnings and employment in financial activities, professional and business services, and information industries

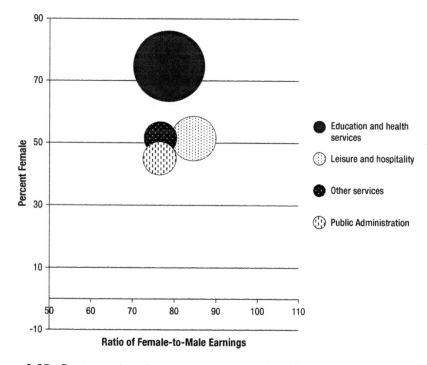

Figure 9-5D. Earnings and employment in education and health services, leisure and hospitality, other services, and public administration industries

In all categories, the ratio of female-to-male median weekly earnings is less than one, meaning that the typical female in the given occupation earns less than her male counterpart in the same occupation.

As with occupation, the distribution of women within each of these industry categories at least partly explains the overall ratios of female-to-male earnings of less than one.

Judith Fields and Edward Wolff examined the size of the gender wage gap by industry.[12] They found that in some industries the wage gap was positive, and in others the wage gap was negative. Another interesting finding is that industries that pay relatively high wages to men generally also pay relatively high wages to women. According to Fields and Wolff, industry can account for as much as 22% of the gender wage gap. Furthermore, the observed differences in the distributions of men and women among industries can account for an additional 19% of the raw wage gap. Fields and Wolff found that in total, industry can account for as much as 37% of the gender wage gap.

Prior Work Experience

Although there is consensus surrounding the observation that accounting for prior work experience reduces the size of the gender wage gap, research has shown that the way work experience is measured affects the amount of this reduction.

Not surprisingly, it has been empirically demonstrated that the actual amount of a person's work experience accounts for a much larger portion of the gender wage gap than does potential work experience.[13] Potential work experience is often measured as the person's age minus years of schooling, minus age when first attending school (usually assumed to be five or six).

Frequently, potential work experience is used as a proxy for actual work experience. Cases in which this proxy is commonly used include situations in which actual work experience is unknown or unavailable, available only in a form that is not conducive to formal analysis (e.g., hard-copy documentation), or situations in which creating a data set for actual work experience is prohibitive in terms of time and/or expense.

---

[12]Judith Fields and Edward Wolff, "Interindustry Wage Differentials and the Gender Wage Gap," *Industrial and Labor Relations Review*, 49 (October 1995), 105–20.
[13]P. E. Gabriel, "The Effects of Differences in Year-Round, Full-Time Labor Market Experience on Gender Wage Levels in the United States," *International Review of Applied Economics*, 19 (July 2005), 369–77.

The problems with using potential work experience as a proxy for actual work experience are twofold. First, potential work experience may not reflect relevant actual work experience. If an individual changes from one occupation to another, and the skill sets and human capital requirements are different for those occupations, potential work experience is likely to overstate actual relevant work experience.

Second, and perhaps more important to the current discussion, using potential work experience in a compensation model can introduce an artificial gender bias. This artificial gender bias stems from the fact that women typically experience greater periods of absence from the labor force than men because of childbearing and child rearing. This can distort the true picture of compensation equity.

Consider the following example. A thirty-five-year-old male employee and a thirty-five-year-old female employee hold the same job and have identical educational backgrounds. Both entered the labor force at age twenty-two, right after completing bachelor's degrees. Assume that the male employee has thirteen years of prior relevant experience, and the female employee has eight years of relevant prior experience because she left the labor force after giving birth and did not return until her child began elementary school. Assume further that the male earns $2,500 per year more than the female employee, and we know with certainty that this $2,500 difference is attributable to the five-year difference in experience and nothing else.

Using potential work experience does not, and in fact cannot, account for the situation just described. Our calculation of potential work experience would indicate that both individuals have thirteen years of experience. If we compare the compensation of the male employee and the female employee and control for gender and potential work experience, the model will indicate that the $2,500 difference in earnings is attributable to gender. More specifically, one might infer that the difference is attributable to gender discrimination, when in fact the difference is attributable to differences in actual work experience.

Hours Worked

Contributing to the gender pay gap are differences in the number of hours usually worked during the week by men and women, shown in Figure 9-6.[14]

---

[14]Bureau of Labor Statistics, "Highlights of Women's Earnings in 2010."

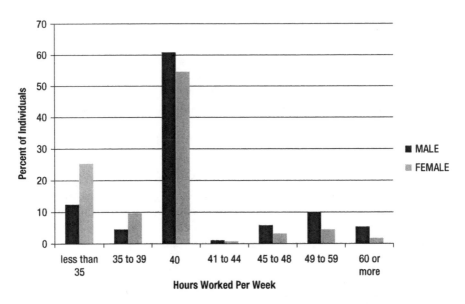

Figure 9-6. Usual hours worked per week by gender

Not surprisingly, the majority of male and female employees usually work forty hours per week: 61% of men and 55% of women.

An interesting pattern emerges when we look at those employees who usually work more than forty hours per week: they are predominantly male. According to data from the Bureau of Labor Statistics, one in five men (20%) and only one in ten women (10%) usually work more than forty hours per week.

It logically follows that if men are generally working more hours—specifically more overtime hours—their earnings will be greater than the earnings of women.

This raises an interesting point about the way we measure the gender pay gap. The majority of empirical studies examines earnings, rather than pay rates. This could be distorting the real picture of gender pay equity. If men are choosing to work more overtime hours, as indicated in Figure 9-6, then even if male and female employees have the same base pay rate, the male employee's earnings will be greater than the female employee's earnings, simply because of overtime pay.[15]

---

[15]This discussion assumes that overtime is granted to male and female employees equally, and the only difference in overtime actually worked is attributable to individual choice.

Career Interruptions

As mentioned previously, work experience explains a substantial amount of the gender pay gap. Empirical research has found that the continuity of work experience also plays an important role in earnings. Judy Goldberg Dey and Catherine Hill found that career interruptions, such as taking a leave for child-birth or raising children, are associated with reduced earnings.[16] They also found that these career interruptions were more prevalent among mothers than among fathers.[17]

The results of a study by Audrey Light and Manuelita Ureta indicate that after a career interruption of at least one year, the earnings of men decline approximately 25% on returning to work.[18] The decline in earnings among women is approximately 23%. Interestingly, after a career interruption of at least one year, women's earnings recover faster than men's earnings.

Light and Ureta also found that the timing of career interruptions is important. Based on their statistical analysis, they estimate that the differences in the frequency, duration, and scheduling of periods of nonemployment account for as much as 12% of the raw gender wage gap.

Negotiation

Research indicates that there is a substantial difference by gender in the willingness to engage in negotiations. Linda Babcock and Sara Laschever examined compensation negotiations by students graduating from professional schools.[19] Women were significantly less likely than men to engage in negotiations to improve on the initial compensation offer. Only 7% of the female students attempted negotiation, compared to 57% of the male students. Babcock and Laschever also found that women are twice as likely as men to feel "a great deal of apprehension" about negotiating.

---

[16]For a discussion of the relationship between motherhood and women's earnings, see D. J. Anderson, M. Binder and K. Krause, "The Motherhood Wage Penalty Revisited: Experience, Heterogeneity, Work Effort, and Work-Schedule Flexibility," *Industrial and Labor Relations Review*, 56 (2003), 273–94.

[17]J. G. Dey and C. Hill, *Behind the Pay Gap* (Washington, DC: American Association of University Women Educational Foundation, 2007).

[18]A. Light and M. Ureta, "Early-Career Work Experience and Gender Wage Differentials," *Journal of Labor Economics*, 13 (1995), 121–54.

[19]L. Babcock and S. Laschever, *Women Don't Ask* (Princeton, NJ: Princeton University Press, 2003).

As noted by Hannah Bowles, Linda Babcock, and Lei Lai, women's reluctance to initiate negotiations, as compared with men, may be an "important and underexplored explanation" for the gender pay gap.[20]

Negotiating styles also differ between men and women. Studies of simulated salary negotiations by Cynthia Stevens and colleagues and Vicki Kaman and Charmine Hartel indicate that on average, men negotiate more aggressively than women.[21]

This difference in style is likely a contributing factor to the differences in negotiation outcomes by gender. Barry Gerhart and Sara Rynes examined the negotiation behaviors and salary outcomes of graduating MBA students. They found that monetary returns to negotiation, in terms of starting salary, were lower for the female students than for their male counterparts.[22]

Compensation Expectations

Intertwined with negotiation is compensation expectation. As noted by Mary Hogue and colleagues, pay expectations play a role in the gender pay gap.[23] Considerable empirical support exists for the notion that women set lower compensation goals than men.

Differences in compensation expectations likely make up a contributing factor to women's lower willingness to engage in negotiation, as well as lower compensation as a result of negotiation.

Several studies of college students indicate that female students have lower compensation expectations than do male students. One study showed that women's estimates of "fair pay" for their first job averaged 4% less than men's estimates; the estimate of fair career-peak pay by women was 23% lower than

---

[20]Hannah Bowles, Linda Babcock and Lei Lai, "It Depends Who Is Asking and Who You Ask: Social Incentives for Sex Differences in the Propensity to Initiate Negotiation," http://cbdr.cmu.edu/papers/pdfs/cdr_099.pdf.

[21]Cynthia K Stevens, Anna Bavetta, and Marilyn Gist, "Gender Differences in the Acquisition of Salary Negotiation Skills: The Role of Goals, Self-Efficacy and Perceived Control," *Journal of Applied Psychology*, 78, no. 5 (1993), 723–35; Vicki Kaman and Charmine Hartel, "Gender Differences in Anticipated Pay Negotiation Strategies and Outcomes," *Journal of Business and Psychology*, 9 (1994), 183–97.

[22]Barry Gerhart and Sara Rynes, "Determinants and Consequences of Salary Negotiations by Male and Female MBA Graduates," *Journal of Applied Psychology*, 76, no. 2 (1989), 252–62.

[23]M. Hogue, C. L. Z. DuBois, and L. Fox-Cardamone, "Gender Differences in Pay Expectations: The Roles of Job Intention and Self-View," *Psychology of Women Quarterly*, 34 (2010), 215–27.

men's estimates.[24] Another survey of undergraduate business students found that women's salary expectations were between 3% and 32% lower than the expectations of men for the same positions.[25]

Melissa Williams and colleagues conducted a study in which participants were given pairs of male and female first names and asked to estimate their salaries. Women, as well as men, tended to estimate significantly higher salaries for the male names than for the female names.[26]

William Sauser and C. Michael York found that despite the fact that women typically earn less than men in similar positions, women's satisfaction with their pay tends to be equal to or greater than that of men.[27]

Cash versus Benefits Trade-off

Benefits account for nearly 30% of total compensation, yet have been largely ignored in studies of the gender pay gap.[28] Part of the reason benefits are disregarded stems from the fact that pay and benefits are interrelated. Fringe benefits are provided more frequently to employees with relatively high levels of skill, job commitment, work experience, and job tenure.[29] Employees with these characteristics also tend to receive higher levels of wages and salaries. This positive correlation makes empirical analysis difficult, and statistical analysis methods and data sets must be developed to account for—and circumvent—this correlation.

Eric Solberg and Teresa Laughlin conducted a study that accounted for this positive correlation.[30] They estimated the size of the gender wage gap using only wages as the measure of earnings. They then reestimated the size of the gap using an index of total compensation that included not only wages

---

[24]Linda Jackson, Philip Hardner, Linda Sullivan, "Explaining Gender Differences in Self-Pay Expectations: Social Comparison Standards and Perceptions of Fair Pay," *Journal of Applied Psychology*, 77 (Oct. 1992), 651-663.

[25]Beth Ann Martin, "Gender Differences in Salary Expectations When Current Salary Information Is Provided," *Psychology of Women Quarterly*, 13 (1989), 87–96.

[26]Melissa Williams, Elizabeth Levy Paluck, and Julia Spencer-Rogers, "The Masculinity of Money: Automatic Stereotypes Predict Gender Differences in Estimated Salaries," *Psychology of Women Quarterly*, 34 (2010), 7–20.

[27]William Sauser and C. Michael York, "Sex Differences in Job Satisfaction: A Re-Examination," *Personnel Psychology*, 31 (1978), 537–47.

[28]Bureau of Labor Statistics, "Employer Costs for Employee Compensation—June 2010," www.bls.gov/news.release/pdf/ecec.pdf.

[29]CONSAD, "An Analysis of the Reasons for the Disparity in Wages Between Men and Women."

[30]E. Solberg and T. Laughlin, "The Gender Pay Gap, Fringe Benefits, and Occupational Crowding." *Industrial and Labor Relations Review*, 48 (1995), 692–708.

but nine types of fringe benefits.[31] Solberg and Laughlin concluded that "any measure of earnings that excludes fringe benefits may produce misleading results as to the existence, magnitude, consequence, and source of market discrimination."[32]

The Role of Discrimination

Legitimate factors such as occupation, industry, and prior work experience account for approximately 54% of the gender wage gap, reducing the raw difference of 33 cents per hour to an adjusted difference of 9 cents per hour.[33] When personal choices, career interruption patterns, willingness to engage in compensation negotiation, compensation expectations, hours worked, and the cash versus benefits trade-off are considered, this 9-cents-per hour difference is reduced even more.[34]

This is not to say, however, that gender pay discrimination does not take place. Unfortunately, discrimination is a workplace reality, and cases of gender pay discrimination do occur. As discussed in previous chapters, discrimination may be unintentional (disparate impact), or it may be intentional (disparate treatment).

Gender pay discrimination may play a role in explaining the wage gap, but it certainly does not explain the totality of the gap. In fact, even if the gap is not fully explained by the legitimate factors and personal choices researchers have identified to date, one cannot simply infer that any remaining differential is attributable to gender discrimination. It is *possible* that the remaining differential is attributable to gender discrimination. But it is also possible that other factors not yet identified and/or incorporated into quantitative models of gender pay equity explain the remaining difference.

---

[31]The nine categories of benefits included in the analysis are retirement benefits, life insurance benefits, medical benefits, dental benefits, training and education benefits, profit sharing, maternity/paternity benefits, flexible work hours, and employer-subsidized child care.

[32]Solberg and Laughlin, "The Gender Pay Gap, Fringe Benefits, and Occupational Crowding," 706.

[33]Blau and Kahn, "The Gender Pay Gap: Have Women Gone as Far as They Can?"

[34]The amount of reduction after considering these factors varies by researcher, groups of employees studied, and how the explanatory factors are defined and calculated. There is consensus across this research that these factors do explain a portion of the raw gender wage gap.

Litigation Avoidance and Proactive Self-Analysis

Self-analysis of internal pay equity is a valuable tool in the employer's risk management toolbox. Unfortunately, few organizations make use of this strategy. In light of the changing landscape of pay equity enforcement, coupled with dramatic increases in employment litigation and regulatory investigation, employers can no longer afford to ignore this important tool.

Importance of Litigation Avoidance

Employment practices liability claims are one of the most commonly faced risks by companies. According to Chubb's *2010 Private Company Risk Survey*, more than 20% of the employers they surveyed had experienced an employment-related lawsuit in the past five years.[1] The median award in employment practices lawsuits in 2011 was $325,000, an increase of approximately 88%

---

[1] Chubb Group of Insurance Companies, *2010 Private Company Risk Survey,* www.chubb. com/businesses/csi/chubb12192.pdf.

from the previous year.[2] If the employer is found guilty of discrimination, the average amount of punitive damages awarded is $2.7 million.[3]

These amounts do not include legal fees; 46% of companies surveyed by Chubb reported legal costs associated with employment litigation ranging from $20,000 to $750,000.

In addition to private litigation, regulatory litigation is also increasing. According to Gerald Maatman, "government enforcement litigation has reached 'white hot' levels."[4] The Equal Employment Opportunity Commission has received more than 10,000 charges of wage discrimination since January 2010, of which about 40% alleged wage discrimination based on sex.[5]

▨ **Note**   Since January 2010, the EEOC has obtained more than $62.5 million in monetary relief through administrative enforcement for victims of sex-based wage discrimination, obtained changes to workplace practices that benefit over a quarter of a million workers, and filed five cases including sex-based wage discrimination claims.

The Office of Federal Contract Compliance Programs (OFCCP) has rapidly increased the proportion of its work dedicated to addressing pay discrimination. The OFCCP has evaluated the pay practices of more than 10,000 businesses that employ over 4.3 million workers since January 2010.[6] During this same time period, the OFCCP closed more than fifty compliance evaluations with financial settlements remedying compensation discrimination on the basis of gender and race. In doing so, the agency recovered $1.4 million in back pay and salary adjustments for more than 500 workers. In 2011, 20% of the OFCCP's financial settlements resolved matters relating to compensation claims, a substantial increase over previous years.[7]

Employment practices litigation poses serious risks for organizations of all sizes in all sectors of the economy. No company is immune. The damage from employment litigation can be severe. Chubb's *2010 Private Company Risk Survey* reported that "36% of the executives responded that an [employment practices liability] lawsuit would cause the most financial damage to their company."

---

[2]*Jury Award Trends and Statistics* (Westlaw, 2012–2013).
[3]"The Cost of Conflict in the Workplace," Conflict Solutions Center, available at www.cscsb.org/mediation/cost_of_conflict.html.
[4]Gerald Maatman, "Annual Workplace Class Action Litigation Report: 2012 Edition," Seyfarth Shaw, LLP, 2012, p. 1.
[5]"Equal Pay Task Force Accomplishments," White House, April 2012, p. 3, available at www.whitehouse.gov/sites/default/files/equal_pay_task_force.pdf.
[6]Ibid., p. 4.
[7]Ibid.

The nonfinancial costs of employment litigation are more difficult to express in terms of dollars but are just as significant:

> *The non-economic costs of employment litigation that can be independently taxing and not as measurable include current employee-witnesses spending significant time talking with the employer's attorney(s), giving depositions or attending court proceedings in connection with the litigation instead of spending time conducting the business of the employer. In addition, the employer is required to gather and produce every document potentially relating to the plaintiff's employment with the employer, including electronically stored documents (which can be an expensive and onerous burden for which the company may not be prepared). Finally, in some cases (particularly involving EEOC lawsuits), employment practices changes may actually be compelled through a consent decree.*[8]

Given the significant financial and noneconomic costs associated with lawsuits and investigations, litigation avoidance should be a top priority for any organization. With respect to compensation-related litigation, one of the most effective strategies for prevention is a proactive compensation self-analysis.

Business Case for Proactive Self-Analysis

In Chapter 1, the business case for internal pay equity was presented. Socioeconomic arguments as well as strategic arguments and competitive advantages were discussed. Many of the same arguments apply to the business case for self-analysis. Self-analysis provides employers with the opportunity to identify and correct potential problem areas, thereby improving internal pay equity. This, in turn, allows them to leverage the competitive advantages associated with internal pay equity, as well as mitigate the risk of litigation.

As previously noted, many organizations fail to take advantage of a proactive compensation self-analysis. The explanations for this failure range from the mundane to the psychologically elaborate. Some of the more common reasons include:

> **Denial:** *"The whole issue is blown out of proportion. Internal pay equity is not as big a deal as our attorneys or the media make it. It's not going to happen to us."* Companies ignore the possibility of compensation litigation happening to them and pretend that if they don't acknowledge it, it isn't real.

---

[8]David Nenni, "The Costs of Employment Litigation and the Benefits of Litigation Prevention and Employment Audits," *National Law Review*, May 10, 2011.

Making excuses: *"I know we should do it, but we just don't have the time/money/personnel/buy-in from senior management right now. It's on our agenda, and we're going to get to it as soon as we can."* The importance of this preventive measure is given lip service without any real commitment of resources to accomplish the task.

False sense of safety based on past events: *"We've never had a problem before, so we won't have a problem in the future."* Events that have not occurred in the recent past may be subjectively judged as having a lower probability of occurrence due to the availability heuristic.[9]

Overconfidence: *"We don't need to do that because I know we're doing things equitably."* This response is more commonly associated with people who have compensation decision-making authority. This response may come from a true sense of overconfidence: an overestimation of their knowledge, an underestimation of the risks, and an exaggerated sense of ability to control events. In other cases, this response will be produced by a perceived criticism of the person's ability to carry out the duties and responsibilities of his job.

Dismissal of analysis utility: *"We aren't going to learn anything new about our compensation policies and practices by slicing and dicing the same data different ways."* Companies downplay the importance of these analyses and discount the information that they provide.

Fear: *"What if we find problems? I could lose my job if we find problems! I'd rather not know."* The fear of finding potential inequities can be so paralyzing, companies forgo the proactive analysis, thereby eliminating any possibility of correcting potential problems prior to the commencement of litigation or regulatory investigation.

Most of these explanations are unfounded and incorrect. The truth of the matter is that internal pay equity is a priority issue for regulatory agencies, lawmakers, the plaintiff's bar, and your employees. The possibility of compensation-related litigation or investigation is very real, and organizations need to take proactive steps to minimize this risk. The fact that an organization has never faced compensation-related litigation or investigation in the past does not immunize it from future scrutiny. Without taking a serious look at compensation policies and practices using quantitative

---

[9]The availability heuristic is a mental shortcut that occurs when people make judgments about the probability of events based on how easily they can think of examples.

tools, companies cannot be sure that problems don't exist. A self-analysis provides the organization with an opportunity to identify any potential problem areas and take corrective action, where appropriate, before the situation escalates to litigation or regulatory investigation.

With respect to the cost of performing a compensation self-review, it is true that such an analysis can be expensive in terms of time and money. However, if problems exist and are not detected, litigating and remedying those problems will be even more expensive.

To illustrate this point, consider the following example.

> *AstraZeneca, one of the largest pharmaceutical companies in the world, will pay $250,000 to 124 women who were subjected to pay discrimination while working at the corporation's Philadelphia Business Center in Wayne, Pa. The action resolves a lawsuit filed by the U.S. Department of Labor in May 2010 alleging that the company discriminated against female sales specialists by paying them salaries that were, on average, $1,700 less than their male counterparts. . . .*

> *Under a consent decree and order filed with the department's Office of Administrative Law Judges, in addition to making financial restitution, the company has agreed to work with OFCCP to conduct a statistical analysis of the base pay of 415 individuals employed full time as "primary care" and "specialty care" level III pharmaceutical sales specialists in Alabama, Delaware, Indiana, Kentucky, Maryland, New Jersey, New York, North Carolina, Pennsylvania, South Carolina, Tennessee, Virginia, West Virginia and the District of Columbia. If the analysis concludes that female employees continue to be underpaid, the company will adjust salaries accordingly.*[10]

As noted in OFCCP's June 2011 *Events and News*: "If AstraZeneca fails to comply with the consent decree, it may be subject to sanctions, including cancellation of its current federal contract, valued at more than $2 billion, and debarment from acquiring future ones."

In thinking about the AstraZeneca timeline, the entire sequence of events could have been different had the company conducted a proactive self-analysis of compensation. In some respects, the timeline is backward. AstraZeneca is conducting a statistical analysis of compensation *after* an OFCCP investigation, in addition to paying $250,000 in settlement.

Had the company conducted a statistical analysis of compensation prior to the involvement of OFCCP, they would have been provided with an opportunity to identify any potential problem areas and take corrective action where appropriate.

---

[10]"Pharmaceutical Giant AstraZeneca Agrees to Pay $250,000 to Settle Sex Discrimination Lawsuit Brought by US Department of Labor," OFCCP News Release, Release Number 11-0829-PHI, June 6, 2011.

As noted previously, there are a variety of reasons companies fail to perform a self-analysis of compensation, and in many cases the financial cost comes in to play: "We simply can't afford to do it right now." The AstraZeneca situation suggests an interesting counterargument. As a result of the settlement decree, the company is required to perform a statistical analysis of the base pay rates of sales specialists in thirteen states and the District of Columbia. If this analysis reveals any disparities, they will be required to take remedial action and make appropriate adjustments. The cost of performing the analysis and making necessary adjustments is in addition to the $250,000 paid in settlement. AstraZeneca did not realize any cost savings by failing to engage in a statistical analysis of compensation; under the consent decree they are *required* to perform this analysis.

Had AstraZeneca performed this statistical analysis prior to OFCCP involvement, they likely would have spent the same amount on the analysis as they now have to spend, but could have avoided the additional $250,000 settlement payout. In the long run, performing a self-analysis of compensation would have *saved* AstraZeneca time and money.

In light of this example, one can see how the question of "Can we afford to do a compensation self-analysis right now?" easily becomes "Can we afford to NOT do a compensation self-analysis right now?" There is no question that a compensation self-analysis has nontrivial economic and noneconomic costs. But like many other preventive measures, proactively spending the resources on a self-analysis can—and often does—result in lower resource expenditures on legal fees and fines in the future. Legal fees and fines are a drain on the organization; those resources are better used for growing the organization and its employees.

Required Data and Documentation

Once the decision has been made to conduct a compensation self-analysis, a thorough review of the organization's compensation data and documentation should be undertaken. There are a variety of laws governing what compensation and benefits-related information companies must maintain; these laws also specify the period of time for which this information must be retained. Table 10-1 summarizes the types of information required by the Internal Revenue Service (IRS), the Department of Labor (DOL), the Fair Labor Standards Act (FLSA), and the Family and Medical Leave Act (FMLA).[11]

---

[11]Other regulatory agencies and employment laws have data and document retention requirements as well. Examples include EEOC, Title VII, the Age Discrimination in Employment Act, the Americans with Disabilities Act, the Immigration Reform and Control Act, Executive Order 11246, Vietnam Era Veterans' Readjustment Assistance Act, and Section 503 of the Rehabilitation Act. Some of these requirements involve compensation and benefits-related information, but they are largely concerned with hiring, promotion, termination, disability accommodation, workforce utilization, and so on.

Table 10-1. Required Documentation and Retention Schedules

	Required retention (years)			
	IRS	DOL	FLSA	FMLA
Demographic/employment information				
Name, address, SSN, occupation, dates of employment	4	3	3	3
Gender		3	3	
Date of birth (if under age 19)		3	3	
Certificates of age (if under age 19)		3		
Compensation				
Hours worked each workday and each workweek		3	3	3
Beginning dates of each employee's workweek		3	3	3
Regular rate of pay for overtime weeks		3	3	3
Straight time earnings (including straight time portion of overtime earnings)		3	3	3
Overtime earnings		3	3	3
Total wages paid for each pay period including additions and deductions		3	3	3
Total compensation paid to each employee during calendar year	4			
Dates and amounts of compensation paid each pay period	4	3	3	3
Pay period covered by each pay date	4		3	
Employee tip reports	4			
Fair market value of in-kind wages	4			
Wage rate tables and piece rate schedules		2		
Work time schedules establishing hours and days of employment		2		
Benefits				
Summary plan descriptions and relevant policy documentation	4			
Dates and amounts of annuity and pension payments	4			
Fringe benefits records	4			
Dates and amounts of wage continuation payments due to illness or injury	4			
Documentation regarding employee benefits and/or employer policies and practices regarding paid and unpaid leave				3

(continued)

Table 10-1. (*continued*)

	Required retention (years)			
	IRS	DOL	FLSA	FMLA
Tax documentation				
W-4 employee withholding	4			
Compensation subject to federal withholdings	4			
Explanation of differences in total compensation and taxable compensation	4			
Dates and amounts of tax deposits	4			
Dates and amounts of adjustments or settlements of taxes	4			
State unemployment contributions made	4			
Compensation subject to FUTA and all info shown on Form 940	4			
Employee copies of W2 statements returned as undeliverable	4			
Policies, certificates, etc.				
Plans, trusts, contracts, and collective bargaining agreements			3	
Written agreements or memoranda summarizing terms of oral agreements			3	
Certificates of notice listed or named in FLSA regulations			3	
Sales and purchase records reflecting total dollar volume of sales and total volume of goods purchased or received			3	
Written training agreements			3	
Leave information				
Dates FMLA leave is taken				3
Hours of FMLA leave taken (if leave is taken in increments of less than one full day)				3
Copies of written notices of leave from the employee to the employer				3
Copies of written notices given to employees as required under FMLA				3

Because the compensation and benefits-related information listed in Table 10-1 is legally required, it is routinely maintained by employers as part of normal business operations. In addition to this information, there are supplementary data sets and documentation that employers should be maintaining but typically do not. This information is referred to as "compensation decision documentation." As noted by Philip Miles:

> When you, as an employer, decide your employees' wages, salaries, pay increases . . . how do you arrive at a specific figure? I'm talking about performance reviews—what metrics were used? Signed copies of the completed review, signed copies of the criteria at the start of the review period. Often companies will conduct or purchase industry statistics to ensure that they're paying people in the expected range for their industry. . . . Employers are not 'dart-boarding' compensation decisions. Record where these figures are coming from.[12]

Compensation decision documentation, such as industry surveys, external benchmarks, the criteria used to evaluate employees (as well as any validation studies of those criteria) and complete copies of performance evaluations signed by the evaluator and the employee should be retained. Additionally, employee-specific data relating to criteria used in the compensation decision-making process, such as educational attainment, certifications and licenses, continuing education activities, prior employment history, and so forth, should be retained. Finally, any data or documentation relating to special circumstances of particular employees (e.g., red circling) should be retained.

This information will facilitate a quantitative self-review of compensation, and also allow an assessment of whether the organization's compensation policies and practices are being followed.

The Compensation Self-Analysis

Conducting a self-analysis of compensation can seem like an overwhelming task. Breaking the self-evaluation into distinct phases can make the process more manageable. The following subsections describe the compensation self-analysis in terms of ten discrete phases, as shown in Figure 10-1. Some of these phases (e.g., the construction of similarly situated employee groupings) were discussed at length in previous chapters. In these cases, only summaries of the key points will be provided.

---

[12]"Ledbetter and Compensation Document Creation and Retention with Philip Miles," *The Proactive Employer,* April 10, 2010, www.thomasecon.com/tpe/shows/119-apr-2-2010-ledbetter-and-compensation-document-retention.html.

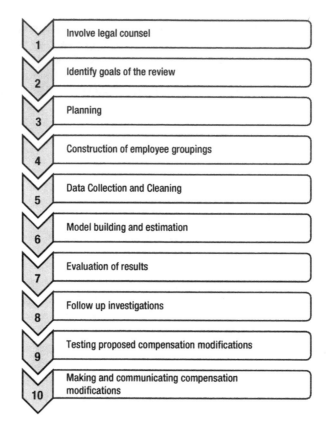

1. Involve legal counsel
2. Identify goals of the review
3. Planning
4. Construction of employee groupings
5. Data Collection and Cleaning
6. Model building and estimation
7. Evaluation of results
8. Follow up investigations
9. Testing proposed compensation modifications
10. Making and communicating compensation modifications

Figure 10-1. Stages of the compensation self-analysis

1. Involve Legal Counsel

Any proactive or potentially self-critical study should be done under the auspices of legal counsel. It is imperative that legal counsel be involved in the compensation review. In-house counsel—and ideally outside counsel as well—should be involved from the very beginning. Attorneys who are familiar with compensation reviews and the laws governing internal pay equity should be brought on board as early in the process as possible.

The participation of legal counsel throughout the compensation review process will, in most cases, allow the organization to take advantage of attorney–client privilege and attorney work product protections. This can help maintain the confidentiality and nondiscoverability of the analyses.[13] Ideally, all

---

[13]Privilege issues are very complex and beyond the scope of this discussion. Readers are encouraged to contact legal counsel with any questions regarding attorney–client privilege, self-critical analysis, or discoverability issues.

correspondence, communication, data exchanges, and analysis results—especially if outside consultants are involved—should be handled through legal counsel.

2. Establish Goals

Having a clear understanding of what the organization hopes to accomplish by conducting a compensation review is essential. If the goals are clearly articulated, the process of tailoring the analysis to achieve those goals is greatly simplified.

Commonly identified goals of a compensation review include:

- Assessment of an organization's exposure to compensation discrimination litigation;

- Assessment of an organization's exposure to regulatory investigation;

- Assessment of internal pay equity of all employees, irrespective of protected class status;

- Integration of new employees as a result of a merger, acquisition, or other corporate transaction;

- Assessment of the correct execution of the organization's compensation policies and practices;

- Monitoring compensation as part of an organization's integrated risk management strategy.

Having a clear understanding of what the organization hopes to accomplish is critical to successfully designing and completing an analysis that provides the relevant conclusions and inferences.

3. Planning

During the planning phase, the groups of employees to be studied and the specific compensation metrics to be examined are defined. At this stage it is also important to determine which internal personnel will be involved and how outside counsel and consultants will be used.

Areas of the Organization to Be Studied

The first issue to be addressed during the planning stage is what area(s) of the organization will be studied. Depending on the goals of the compensation review, the analysis may be limited to a particular set of job titles, specific departments, locations within a specific geographic region, employees reporting to a given supervisor, and so on. Having a well-defined study population will facilitate all of the other decisions made during the planning stage, including what aspects of compensation will be examined, who will be involved in the compensation review process, and what data are required.

The choice of study population will be guided by the underlying goals of the analysis. If the goal is to evaluate a new sales compensation plan that was recently implemented, the study population may be limited to the sales force. If there have been formal or informal complaints of pay inequities among a group of employees reporting to a particular supervisor, the study population may consist of that supervisor's direct reports. If the goal is to construct an ongoing monitoring program for risk management purposes, the entire work-force may be chosen as the study population.

Types of Compensation to Be Studied

As noted in Chapter 4, virtually any type of compensation paid to an employee can be examined with a statistical review. The choice of compensation metric will be governed by the study population.

Because different groups of employees are likely to receive different types of compensation, it is important to identify which types are appropriate for which groups. The choice of compensation metrics may differ across employee groupings; this is perfectly acceptable as long as the metrics are consistent *within* each employee grouping.

Internal and External Involvement

When planning a compensation review, it is important to determine who will be involved in the review process. A decision should be made as early as possible about the external and internal personnel who will be involved in the project. Making this decision early in the planning process has several distinct advantages.

As previously noted, it is preferable to involve outside legal counsel in the review process. It may also be useful to involve outside consultants to per-form the statistical analysis. Aside from potentially offering an additional layer of privilege and confidentiality, a qualified outside consultant will have the required expertise, experience, and statistical tools to perform the analysis and assist in interpreting the analysis results.

One of the biggest concerns regarding compensation reviews is confidential-ity within the organization. Limiting the involvement of internal personnel can address this concern directly. Only those individuals with instrumental knowl-edge of compensation plans and those who will be directly involved in data collection and production should be involved. In most cases, these individuals will be senior human resources, payroll, and information systems employees.

4. Construction of Similarly Situated Employee Groupings

Considerable time was spent in Chapter 4 discussing the construction of similarly situated employee groupings. It is worth reiterating, however, that the grouping of employees for analysis must be performed with the utmost care. Errors in groupings can render the results generated from a compensation review meaningless.

Furthermore, the similarly situated employee groupings constructed by the employer serve as a memorialization of the organization's view of its employees and the functions they serve. In the event of litigation or regulatory investigation, employers may be constrained to the definitions of similarly situated employee groupings previously used in internal analyses.

5. The Data

The compensation review hinges on data. After defining the groups of similarly situated employees, the determinants of compensation within each grouping should be identified. As previously noted, it may be the case that the determinants of compensation differ by employee grouping. It is important to have a thorough understanding of which determinants of compensation apply to which groups of employees and to build these determinants into the compensation review as appropriate.

The goal of collecting and assembling data for the compensation self-analysis is to construct a complete and comprehensive employee-level data set that captures all relevant information for each employee in the study population.[14] The relevant information will be defined by the determinants of compensation for each similarly situated employee grouping. It is not enough to simply extract each employee's identification number and compensation amount; information regarding all of the determinants of compensation, as well as any other relevant information, must be collected.

In most cases, the data phase (identification, collection, assembly, cleaning, and verification) consumes more time than any other phase of the self-review. Organizations will be well served to spend the time necessary to construct a complete and comprehensive data set before moving forward in the self-review process. Gaps in the data or errors in the way the data set was constructed (e.g., missing explanatory factors, missing job codes, and so forth) will greatly increase the time required and financial expense of completing the compensation self-review.

---

[14]Note that the study population may include multiple similarly situated employee groupings.

6. Model Building and Estimation

Choosing an appropriate model specification for the compensation self-analysis will be based on the goals of the analysis, the type(s) of compensation metrics being examined, the determinants of compensation, and other factors unique to the organization. There is no "one-size-fits-all" specification for compensation models.

Multiple regression analysis is the preferred statistical technique for identifying the presence or absence of compensation discrimination. Various specifications for multiple regression models (i.e., the classical model, the separate equations model, the interactive model, and the overall equity model) were presented in Chapter 5.

In cases where multiple regression analysis is inappropriate (e.g., the number of individuals in the similarly situated employee grouping is too small to permit multiple regression analysis), there are a variety of statistical and nonstatistical techniques available.

The model specification chosen will dictate how the estimation process proceeds.[15] The choice of model specification will also dictate which compensation questions can be answered. For example, choosing a separate equations structure in which the similarly situated employee grouping is stratified on the basis of gender can, by definition, provide no information regarding the presence or absence of discrimination on the basis of race and ethnicity.[16] The inferences drawn from and questions addressed by the analysis will depend partly on how the model is specified.

7. Evaluation of Results

As discussed in Chapter 3, there are five key aspects to consider in the evaluation of the results from a multiple regression analysis: the magnitude (and direction) of the estimated coefficients, the statistical significance of the estimated coefficients, the practical significance of the estimated coefficients, the size of the sample being analyzed, and the overall explanatory power of the model.

When interpreting regression results, it is essential to keep two points in mind. First, the results *cannot* be interpreted in a causal manner. A statistically

---

[15]For example, the choice of the classical model structure will naturally lead to multiple regression analysis. The choice of a means test will lead to the performance of a *t*-test.

[16]It is not uncommon in practice to choose a class of model structure, such as separate equations, and estimate multiple specifications of the model for the same similarly situated employee grouping. For example, the first specification may be separate equations stratified by gender, the second specification may be separate equations stratified by race, and so on.

significant relationship between compensation and protected group status does not mean that protected group status causes compensation differences. Second, the nature of statistics themselves should be kept in mind when interpreting results. The results express the *likelihood* of certain outcomes, not whether certain outcomes will or will not occur. Even though an event may be very rare—such as getting ten heads in ten flips of a coin—and its associated likelihood is small, that likelihood is not zero.

8. Follow-Up Investigations

Analysis follow-up is a crucial step in the self-review process. Without proper follow-up, the opportunity to learn from the analysis—and the opportunity to correct potential problem areas—is lost.

As noted in Chapter 7, there are various methods of follow-up at both the systemic and individual employee levels. The choice of follow-up will be dictated by the results of the analysis. If follow-up investigations reveal a deficiency in the compensation model, such as the omission of a determinant of compensation or failure to account for red-circling, this deficiency should be addressed, and the model should be reestimated to assess whether the potential inequities originally observed are still present.

If no deficiencies in the compensation model are found, and no legitimate explanation for potential inequities are identified, it may be necessary to make modifications to compensation.

9. Testing Proposed Modifications to Compensation

Depending on what is learned during the follow-up investigations, modifications to compensation may be warranted. It is strongly recommended that before modifications are made, they are fully discussed with legal counsel and empirically tested.[17] What may appear to be a minor change can have wide-sweeping implications for the compensation structure of the entire organization. It is essential to understand the ramifications of the proposed modifications prior to implementation.

---

[17]Typically, empirical testing of the proposed modifications is reestimation of the compensation model(s) substituting proposed compensation, rather than actual compensation, as the pay metric. For example, if compensation modifications are proposed for ten individuals within a similarly situated employee grouping of sixty employees, the model would be reestimated using proposed compensation amounts for the ten people for whom modifications are recommended and actual compensation amounts for the remaining fifty individuals in the similarly situated employee grouping.

10. Making and Communicating Modifications to Compensation

As noted in Chapter 7, legal counsel should also be involved in planning how the compensation adjustments will be communicated to employees. The preferred communication approach will vary depending on the number of employees receiving adjustments, the magnitude of the necessary adjustments, and whether the employer has been (or is currently) involved in compensation-related litigation or regulatory investigation, among other factors.

Generally speaking, communication with employees about pay equity adjustments should emphasize that the organization is committed to a fair and non-discriminatory workplace. In an effort to provide a fair workplace, a review of compensation practices was performed, and that review uncovered potential inequities. The adjustments are being made to address those potential problem areas and to ensure that everyone—irrespective of protected group status—is paid fairly and equitably.

Conclusion

The compensation self-analysis is a valuable tool that can assist employers in managing the risk of compensation-related litigation and regulatory investigation. It can facilitate a deeper understanding of the organization's compensation policies and practices and provide an empirical test of whether those policies and practices are being followed.

The Basics of Statistical Inference

Statistics is a branch of mathematics that focuses on the collection, presentation, and analysis of quantitative information. Generally speaking, there are two kinds of statistics: descriptive and inferential. Descriptive statistics summarize information; examples include averages, medians, minimums and maximums, percentages, charts, and graphs. Descriptive statistics are used to describe what is going on in the data.

Inferential statistics is concerned with drawing conclusions from data. An example that most people are familiar with is an opinion poll. The researcher selects a subgroup of people from the general population as his sample. He questions the sample members on how they feel about a particular issue. Then, based on the responses he collects from the sample, he makes a statistical inference regarding how the population as a whole feels about the issue.

Inferential statistics can also be used to make judgments about how likely it is that something will—or will not—occur. The simplest example of this is flipping a coin.

The Coin Flip Game

To see how inferential statistics works, let's play a game. Let's flip a coin ten times. For every head that comes up, you pay me $1. For every tail that comes up, I pay you $1.

To make things more interesting, I go behind a screen and flip the coin ten times. I come back out from behind the screen, tell you that I got ten heads in ten flips, and ask you to pay me $10.

The question that you have to answer is whether you were cheated.

What evidence do you have? You might have direct evidence. For example, if there was a security camera recording me flipping the coin behind the screen, you could review the video footage. If the video revealed that I only got six heads out of ten flips, you would have direct evidence that I cheated you.

You could also inspect the coin. If you discovered that it was a two-headed coin, or that it was weighted toward heads, this would also be direct evidence that you were cheated.

But what if no direct evidence exists? What if there is no video footage, and you cannot physically inspect the coin? What evidence would you have to decide whether you were or were not cheated? How will you decide whether to pay me or accuse me of cheating?

Probability

You could use indirect evidence to decide if you were cheated. You know that the likelihood of getting one head in one flip of a fair coin is 50%. Based on that likelihood, you would expect that out of ten flips, heads would come up 50% of the time. You would therefore expect five heads:

$$10 \text{ flips} \times 50\% \text{ chance of heads} = 5 \text{ expected heads}$$

My reported result of ten heads in ten flips is five more than you would have expected. We have a surplus of five heads:

$$10 \text{ actual} - 5 \text{ expected} = \text{surplus of } 5 \text{ heads}$$

Is this surplus of five heads big enough for you to feel comfortable with accusing me of cheating?

If we flip a coin ten times, more often than not we will not see exactly five heads. We might get four heads or six heads. The question you have to answer is whether ten heads out of ten flips is unlikely enough that you feel comfortable of accusing me of cheating.

To answer this question, we can use probability. *Probability* is a way of expressing how likely it is that something will occur. Table A-1 shows the probabilities associated with our coin-flipping game.

Table A-1. Coin Flip Probabilities

# of Flips	Probability	Standard Deviation
10	0.001	3.10
9	0.010	2.30
8	0.044	1.60
7	0.117	0.95
6	0.205	0.32
5	0.246	Expected result

Starting at the bottom of this table, our expected result is five heads out of ten flips. The likelihood—or probability—of getting six heads out of ten flips is about 20% (0.205), or about one in five. The probability of getting seven heads out of ten flips is about 12% (0.117). The probability of getting eight heads out of ten flips is about 4% (0.044). The probability of getting nine heads out of ten flips is 1% (0.010). The probability of getting ten heads out of ten flips is 0.1% (0.001), or about one in a thousand.

Rather than reporting how likely it is that something will occur in percentages and odds, social scientists often use something called *standard deviation*. Standard deviation is another way of expressing how likely it is that something would occur, or how far away from the expected outcome the actual result is. The greater the number of standard deviations, the further away from the expected result the actual outcome is, and the less likely we are to actually observe that outcome as a result of pure chance.

The probabilities in our coin flip game are drawn from the binomial distribution. These probabilities can be graphically represented as shown in Figure A-1.

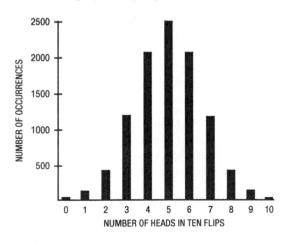

Figure A-1. Number of heads in ten flips

As we move further away from our expected result of five heads (which is in the middle of the distribution) to six heads, seven heads, and so on (or to four heads, three heads, and so on), the likelihood of getting that number of heads as a result of chance gets smaller and smaller. What does this tell you about the likelihood that you were cheated in our coin flip game?

It is important to note that just because the actual outcome of ten heads is different than the expected outcome of five heads, you cannot be 100% certain that you were cheated. Deviations from expected results can occur due to random chance.

It is possible that I did not cheat. In fact, we would expect to see ten heads in ten flips once every thousand games. In the probability graph, the number of times we expect to get ten heads (or, in the alternate, zero heads) is not zero.

The central issue is whether ten heads in ten flips is a "sufficiently rare" outcome where the likely explanation is not random chance.

Statistical Significance

How rare is "sufficiently" rare? Where do we draw the line?

The general rule of thumb used by social scientists is that if the actual outcome is likely to occur less than 5% of the time, which is approximately equal to two units of standard deviation, it is considered to be sufficiently rare. If an outcome is sufficiently rare, it is said to be statistically significant.

This rule of thumb has also been adopted by courts. In *Hazelwood School District v. United States*,[1] the U.S. Supreme Court held that "a disparity of at least two or three standard deviations" is statistically significant.

Where does this leave us in terms of our coin flipping game? Are you going to pay me $10 or accuse me of cheating? Based on probability, the likelihood of getting ten heads in ten flips is one out of a thousand, or 3.10 units of standard deviation. This satisfies the rule of thumb used by social scientists and satisfies the threshold of two or three units established by the court in *Hazelwood*. The difference between my reported ten heads and the expected five heads is statistically significant. Thus, you would infer that I cheated you.

There is one important point to keep in mind about probability and statistical significance. Even if the difference between the actual and expected outcomes is adverse (that is, more heads than expected, fewer members of a protected group hired, higher salaries for men than for women), no adverse inference should be drawn unless the difference is statistically significant.

---

[1] *Hazelwood School District v. United States*, 433 U.S. 299 (1977).

For example, if I reported getting eight heads out of ten flips, you would not infer (based on probability) that I cheated you. Although eight heads in ten flips is three more heads than expected, it is not a statistically significant difference. The standard deviation of that difference is 1.60 units. Because it does not meet that two or three unit threshold, you would conclude that it was not sufficiently rare enough to accuse me of cheating.

From a statistical perspective, a difference that is not statistically significant is not different from zero. No adverse inference should be drawn unless the difference is statistically significant.

Sample Size

Statistical significance is a function of the size of the observed disparity—such as the difference between the actual and expected number of heads in a coin flipping game. But it is also a function of the number of things being studied.

Let's go back to our game, but instead of flipping the coin ten times, we are going to flip it just once. I go behind the screen, flip the coin, and tell you that it came up heads.

Do you think you were cheated? Probably not, because on that one flip there was a fifty-fifty chance of getting heads. You do not really have enough information based on one flip of a coin to know whether you were cheated.

Now let's flip the coin ten times, like in the original game. I go behind the screen, flip the coin ten times, and report that I got eight heads in ten flips. Do you think you were cheated?

We know from our probability table that eight heads out of ten flips is expected to occur about 4% of the time. The difference between eight actual heads and five expected heads is 1.60 units of standard deviation. Even though I got more heads than expected, the difference is not statistically significant. Therefore, you would not accuse me of cheating.

Let's play the game again, only this time we will flip the coin 100 times. I go behind the screen, flip the coin 100 times, and report that I got 80 heads. Do you think you were cheated?

As shown in Table A-2, the difference between the actual eighty heads and expected fifty heads is equal to 6.09 units of standard deviation. This result is statistically significant, and you would therefore infer that you were cheated.

Table A-2. Probabilities for 10-Flip and 100-Flip Games

	Standard Deviation	
% Heads	10 Flips	100 Flips
90	2.30	8.52
80	1.60	6.09
70	0.95	3.95
60	0.31	1.90
50	Expected result	

In the ten-flip game, I got heads 80% of the time (eight heads out of ten flips). In the 100-flip game, I also got heads 80% of the time (80 heads out of 100 flips). Why is it that the same percentage of heads is not statistically significant in the 10-flip game (1.60 units of standard deviation) but *is* significant in the 100-flip game (6.09 units of standard deviation)?

The answer has to do with the amount of information we have. Having 100 flips' worth of information about the game tells us more than the information we get from a 10-flip game. Similarly, we have more information from a ten-flip game than we do from a one-flip game.

There is a complex statistical calculation at play here, which is not discussed. The takeaway is that the more information we have—the more things we are studying—the more powerful the statistical test becomes. The more powerful a statistical test, the more "certain" one can be about the likelihood that an observed disparity is or is not the likely outcome of chance.

As the sample size gets larger, smaller differences between the actual and expected outcomes become statistically significant. If we were to flip the coin an infinite number of times and heads occurred just once more than expected, that difference of one head would be statistically significant. Larger sample sizes mean more information, and more information means it is more likely that an observed difference will be statistically significant.

Practical Significance

When evaluating a difference between the actual and expected outcomes, statistical significance is used to determine if the outcome is sufficiently rare and unlikely to be the result of pure chance. There is an additional question that needs to be addressed in some circumstances: Is the observed difference big enough to be important from a practical perspective?

For example, assume that within a particular grouping of employees, a statistical analysis reveals that women's annual earnings are lower than that of men.

Further assume that the difference in male and female annual earnings is $20 per year. Is the difference of $20 a year big enough to matter?

What if the difference was $2,000 a year, and the average annual earnings was $20,000 a year? Is a difference of $2,000 a year big enough to matter? What if the average annual earnings were $200,000—is the difference of $2,000 a year big enough to matter?

If an observed difference is big enough to matter, it is said to have *practical significance*. Unlike statistical significance, there is no generally accepted rule of thumb for practical significance. It is a question of judgment. One person might argue that a $20 difference in annual earnings between men and women is big enough to matter, but someone else may think it's too small to be consequential.

Practical significance is subjective and depends on the perspectives of the individual reviewer. However, it does play an important role in examining internal pay equity from a risk management perspective.

Index

Other Apress Business Titles You Will Find Useful

CPSIA information can be obtained at www.ICGtesting.com
Printed in the USA
LVOW08s1017011213

363395LV00002B/355/P